Skills, Creativity and Innovation in the Digital Platform Era

Skills, Creativity and Innovation in the Digital Platform Era: Analyzing the New Reality of Professions and Entrepreneurship brings together two important areas: the separate research topics of professions, platforms, and entrepreneurship, and the various dimensions of what platformization means to work and to professions in contemporary societies. One of the most noteworthy global aspects in current societies is the intensifying presence of technology, to the extent that we can talk about the omnipotence of technologies, a kind of technological imperative that prevails in societies. This new type of technological imperative emerges in the working lives of practicing professionals from medical doctors to lawyers and from teachers to preachers. Platforms have become a powerful actor as enablers and reorganizers of work, creating new types of inequalities but also expanding the market relations for new professions such as social influencers. How do platforms govern and shape work and lead to new questions concerning organizing of work and professions? These are few of the key questions Poutanen and Kovalainen explore in this profound and insightful book.

Seppo Poutanen is Senior Research Fellow and Docent of sociology at the University of Turku's School of Economics, Finland. He is trained both in philosophy and sociology, and his areas of expertise include metaethics, social epistemology, social theory, sociology of science and technology, gender studies, methodology of social sciences, and economic sociology. He has also worked as faculty fellow at Harvard University, Stanford University, and London School of Economics and Political Science.

Anne Kovalainen is an economic sociologist by training and Professor at the University of Turku's School of Economics, Finland. She is a member of the Finnish Academy of Science and Letters and the Finnish Society of Sciences and Letters. She has also worked as faculty fellow at Harvard University, Stanford University, and London School of Economics and Political Science.

Routledge Studies in Entrepreneurship

This series extends the meaning and scope of entrepreneurship by capturing new research and enquiry on economic, social, cultural and personal value creation. Entrepreneurship as value creation represents the endeavours of innovative people and organisations in creative environments that open up opportunities for developing new products, new services, new firms and new forms of policy making in different environments seeking sustainable economic growth and social development. In setting this objective the series includes books which cover a diverse range of conceptual, empirical and scholarly topics that both inform the field and push the boundaries of entrepreneurship.

Entrepreneurship in Indonesia
From Artisan and Tourism to Technology-based Business Growth
Edited by Vanessa Ratten

Driving Entrepreneurship in Southeast Asia
Edited by Vanessa Ratten

Entrepreneurship and the Creation of Organization
Daniel Hjorth and Robin Holt

Entrepreneurship in Creative Crafts
Edited by Vanessa Ratten

Dark Sides of the Startup Nation
Winners and Losers of Technological Innovation and Entrepreneurship in Israel
Sibylle Heilbrunn

Skills, Creativity and Innovation in the Digital Platform Era
Analyzing the New Reality of Professions and Entrepreneurship
Seppo Poutanen and Anne Kovalainen

For more information about this series please visit: www.routledge.com/Routledge-Studies-in-Entrepreneurship/book-series/RSE

Skills, Creativity and Innovation in the Digital Platform Era

Analyzing the New Reality of Professions and Entrepreneurship

Seppo Poutanen and Anne Kovalainen

Routledge
Taylor & Francis Group
NEW YORK AND LONDON

First published 2023
by Routledge
605 Third Avenue, New York, NY 10158

and by Routledge
4 Park Square, Milton Park, Abingdon, Oxon, OX14 4RN

Routledge is an imprint of the Taylor & Francis Group, an informa business

Library of Congress Cataloging-in-Publication Data
Names: Kovalainen, Anne, author. | Poutanen, Seppo, author.
Title: Skills, creativity and innovation in the digital platform era : analyzing the new reality of professions and entrepreneurship / Anne Kovalainen and Seppo Poutanen.
Description: Abingdon, Oxon ; New York, NY : Routledge, 2023. | Series: Routledge studies in entrepreneurship | Includes bibliographical references and index.
Identifiers: LCCN 2022056524 | ISBN 9780815360704 (hardback) | ISBN 9781032491981 (paperback) | ISBN 9781351038546 (ebook)
Subjects: LCSH: Labor supply—Effect of technological innovations on. | Professions. | Entrepreneurship. | Work. | Technological innovations—Economic aspects.
Classification: LCC HD6331 .K7135 2023 | DDC 331.12—dc23/eng/20230104
LC record available at https://lccn.loc.gov/2022056524

ISBN: 978-0-8153-6070-4 (hbk)
ISBN: 978-1-032-49198-1 (pbk)
ISBN: 978-1-351-03854-6 (ebk)

DOI: 10.4324/9781351038546

Typeset in Bembo
by Apex CoVantage, LLC

Contents

Preface

Several interdisciplinary questions on professions, expertise, and new powerful forms in economy have risen to the forefront in recent years in social sciences and humanities, neighboring disciplines such as business studies included. Professions and professional expert work as part of the traditional, constitutive societal powers, entrepreneurship as a new emerging power in societies and economies, and finally, digitalization and digital platforms possessing an inevitable transformative force globally have all been researched and addressed, but almost always entirely separately, as the disciplinary boundaries still govern the intellectual endeavors. The present book is intended as an intellectual contribution to disentangle and tie these three major topics together.

One of the most noteworthy global aspects in current societies is indeed the intensifying presence of technology, to the extent that we can talk about the omnipotence of technologies, a kind of technological imperative that prevails in society. This omnipotence, a new type of technological imperative emerges in the working lives of practicing professionals from medical doctors to lawyers and from teachers to preachers. Technological development through algorithmic decision-making and machine learning has introduced permeable processes through which technology has entered most professions and professional work, even if the 'core' of the professional identity would not have technology as part of it. Much as in our everyday life, where technologies govern and shape our consumption of goods and services, the societal and economic fabric is technologically impregnated.

Digital platforms have quickly become the key enablers of not only scaling up businesses but also creating new activities in societies, and managing practically all spheres of human life. Conditions and prospects for doing work are changing with the new technologies, and equally so for entrepreneurs and professionals. Platforms as enablers inevitably lead to new questions concerning organizing of work. How do technologies transform expertise within professions? Do algorithms require new types of professions, and if so, is this development visible already, are few of the key questions we explore in the book.

The idea for this book originated partly during a happy 6-month visit at the Weatherhead Center for International Affairs at Harvard University. The discussions and seminars at the Center inspired the development of this book. We thank our colleagues at Harvard University, and also at MIT and Northeastern University for continuing collegiality and the friendly and intellectually inspiring discussions, meetings, and seminars.

A number of research discussions at conferences and visits in intellectually stimulating environments have given us the benefit of receiving comments to develop some of the arguments presented in this book further. During the pandemic different virtual visits and online discussions with colleagues and friends abroad were important intellectual stimulus.

For the financial support we are grateful to the Academy of Finland Strategic Research Council (grant number 303667), and to Rector Jukka Kola for the University of Turku Grant.

We have been fortunate to work with very committed and talented people at Routledge. We introduced our book idea to the senior editor David Varley at Routledge's New York office. David and the editorial board enthusiastically found our thoughts very inspiring, and for that we thank David and the whole editorial board, as well as Business and Management editor Brianna Ascher and her editorial assistant Jessica Rech who have been very supportive and efficient throughout the process.

Seppo Poutanen and Anne Kovalainen

1 The changing relationship between technology and professions

Why is research on professions and technologies still so limited?

Technological development through algorithmic decision-making and machine learning has introduced permeable processes through which technology has entered most professions and professional work in its wider meaning, even when technology is not part of the 'core' of the given professional identity. Technological features and apps are examples of adaptable technology that may ease some workaday tasks; however, these may also predetermine the ways in which the expert work is organized, without the expert's conscious knowledge. These technological changes call for constant learning and training in the given professions. Technology creates ecosystems around professions. As a result, a plethora of new industries and jobs have been emerging to meet the new demands of professional work, including training people to use and service the new technologies and transforming professional knowledge into apps and other mechanizations. These are some features of the technological ecosystems that relate to the transformation of professions and expertise. Without falling into technological determinism, we suggest that technologies do have social and material consequences for work, professional qualifications, and also the ways expertise, professions, and occupations are positioned in society.

Another aspect of the evolving relationship between professions and technology is the changing landscape in which professionals operate. Organizations are not static, not even the civil organizations employing professionals such as medical doctors, lawyers, and teachers that previously framed analyses of professions. Management organizational structures and strict definitions of positional tasks and responsibilities are the foremost methods by which work is controlled. These forms of control are increasingly replacing the collegiality of occupational professionalism (Evetts, 2016). This is partially due to the increase in externally imposed rules that govern work, which leave little or no maneuvering space for professionals' expertise. To a considerable extent, professional expertise finds its realization through entrepreneurship and self-employment. The growth of self-employment,

DOI: 10.4324/9781351038546-1

own-account working, and entrepreneurship has introduced new markets into the core of professionalism: how has the historical legacy of professions, expertise, and professionalism fared under the pressure of shifting from an earnings-based logic to a logic of capitalizing one's own skills and capabilities to the fullest?

It is indeed argued that keeping pace with technological changes requires constant training and re-calibrating of one's own skills, creativity, and innovation abilities to meet market demand (Duffy and Pooley, 2019), be it technologically wired additions or the latest technology-related services. This aspect of the changing relationships between technology and professions, understood as expertise, is a largely unexplored area.

In addition to altering the content of professions, technological developments and changes also challenge the process of renewing previous literature's classification of certain groups of legitimate white-collar occupations as *professions*; such classifications being based on levels of professional knowledge and training needed and governed by sets of ethical and often legal codes of conduct. The temporal aspect is important as well, as the longer an occupation has been existing, the more likely it is to be recognized as a profession. What is the relationship between professions and technology? To address and excavate these relationships in depth, a brief dive into the development of the research on professions is needed. In this way, we can open up the rationale for why research on professions has not fully taken technology onboard and vice-versa.

Given this backdrop of the pervasiveness of technology within professions, it is timely to dissect the reasons behind the long-running divergence of research on professions and occupations and research on technology. We ask why have they been represented as separate and distinct fields of inquiry with few or no issues in common for so long, irrespective of the disciplinary field in question? Even as we observe these gaps in the literature, the connections are being carved out by scholars and stakeholders, not the least due to globalization processes and changing organizational contexts for professions.

In this book, we take a wide approach to considering the relationships between professions as changing and evolving fields and technology, and the discussions will reflect these broad interests. In exploring the research on professions and professionals, it is necessary to define the terminology used. We also consider Watson's (2002) assertion that concepts in profession studies are often too homogeneous. The aspects of expertise, for example, within professions are enmeshed with technology, but little addressed in research on professions.

In the following, we address some of the background related to development of research on professions. We then move to an overview of new perspectives on professions and professionalism that are up for study, and analyze ways in which technology becomes part of professions. Next, we address technology's influences on a broader scale at the profession, occupation, expertise, and market levels.

A brief history of perspectives on professions

One of the key pillars in societies is the continuity of work built on expertise and skills and integrally contained by professions and occupations, as well as by the stability of the jobs of professionals, experts, and workers alike. Research on the crucial role that expert positions and professions have in building society has done its part to build the sociological canon on societal development and progress through Marx and Weber and also through Durkheim and Parsons (Parsons, 1939; Kuhlmann, 2006; Evetts, 2002). Weber's texts on professions and bureaucracy and on the economy and society, Marx's work on the formation of social classes and stratification, Durkheim's analyses of moral communities, and Parsons' recognition of the relationship between professions and social order have formed the key theoretical foundations in research on professions (Poutanen and Kovalainen, 2016). This firm foundation eventually did serve to shift researchers' gaze toward the level of society and the public good and away from actual work processes within the professions studied.

The academic field of profession studies did not originally draw a strict line between professions and occupations. However, in the 1960s, research on professions became a research field of its own, and researchers justified the shift by separating professions from occupations. The separation was further emphasized in the institutions the professions or occupations were connected with (Abbott, 1988, 1993). In addition, many societal gatekeeping institutions, such as professional associations, fostered the maintenance of professions' high status (Parsons, 1939; Barley and Tolbert, 1991). Historically, professions have been associated with the public good and public services (Haber, 1993), requiring normative orientation toward professions (Barber, 1963). Abbott was the first to introduce a more general theory of professions in 1988. According to him, the power of a profession resides both in its jurisdiction and in the constant renegotiations of boundaries between professions (Abbott, 1988, 1999). With this notion, researchers' interests shifted from building up theory on professions as legally defined and formally empowered entities to developing material on the sets of practices undertaken by a given group of people who organize themselves to 'constitute and control a market for their expertise' (Larson, 1977, xvi).

While 'profession' as a research term refers to a distinct category or group, 'professionalization' refers to a process of developing and maintaining the perceived or existing status of that category. In contrast to these, 'professionalism' refers not to group or perceived status but to a process whereby occupational values are combined with possible meanings of expertise (Evetts, 2013; Coupland, 2016). The actual changing content of professional work and tasks is not often the focus of analysis in research; rather, status differences and power hierarchies among professionals have been the principle targets of contemporary scholars (Barley and Tolbert, 1991). Professions can earn their income as salaried employees, as self-employed, or as entrepreneurs. The patterns of income-earning modes and possibilities for experts vary, and for most, the expert position in larger organizations has been the most available one.

Interest in professional and expert talk and the meanings given to such talk has grown in importance in the research, and this has shifted interest from analyses of professions to analyses of professional and expert discourses for maintaining and renewing experts' and professions' legitimation processes. Researchers following this line of argumentation emphasize that professions do not hold fixed and distinct identities, but rather, as Coupland (2016) states, are recrafted, challenged, and reshaped in interactions and everyday practices. However, most professions retain a relatively stable identity as regards their expertise and skills, although these are considered relative rather than absolute, as expertise can be developed.

Traditionally, researchers have made a distinction between profession and occupation through analysis of three main factors: stability of expertise, the position of the expertise in relation to markets and the public sector (or in relation to private vs. public good), and autonomy in the implementation of professional/expert qualifications (or, independence from the prevailing markets or bureaucracy). It has long been assumed that occupations, but not professions, are created by and through the markets, but does it hold true, is an essential question. Professions, in contrast, were for a long time assumed to be an essential part of society-building and progress, both societal elements not connected to markets; however, this classical distinction no longer applies, as professions are tied up with and permeated by the market. It has also been expected that it is primarily the occupations and not the professions that are based on the consumption of goods and services. Moreover, it has been argued for some time that a profession is a prestigious occupation, such as medical doctor, that is founded on theoretical and practical knowledge and extensive training in a particular field (Riska, 2001). Accumulation and safeguarding of specialized knowledge and the restriction of practice by the profession's central body were assumed to ensure the quality and ethical conduct of member professionals (Larson, 1977; Riska, 2007). Societal forces such as markets were nonexistent in this logic. We can justifiably ask whether these categorizations hold their ground even today.

Several factors have contributed to research on professions. Chief among them are the increasing interest in analyses of processes within professions; the major changes in the social science theory (e.g., the shift toward emphasis on agency) and practice, and the malleability of professional boundaries and organizations. These factors indicate that both historical and Foucaultian analyses have grown in importance (Ball, 2010). Foucault's influence in studies of economic phenomena is vast, but the historians studying professions, such as scholars of the medical and legal professions, began studying the constructions of professions and the processes of professionalization rather late compared to other social science fields. This led to a growing critique of 'attribute studies' on professions and professionalization with solely functionalist aims. The growth of historical and Foucaultian analyses adds new dimensions and presents another shift in the researcher's gaze, this one toward the construction and processual features of professions and professionalization.

Occupations have traditionally been classified as professions, semi-professions, and nonprofessions (Barley and Tolbert, 1991). The categorization makes sense as a way of illuminating the differences and stabilities in the status hierarchies of expertise and the roles that cultural factors, such as education, play in the formation of such status hierarchies. These types of demarcating classifications typically count who belongs to a specific category of profession and who does not. The differentiations between professions in these classifications stem from the classical canon of research on professions and occupations in social sciences and build on an implicit assumption that positions in society are relatively stable. The rank-ordering of occupations based on occupational prestige, has been relatively consistent across societies (Treiman, 2003). Be that as it may, rank-ordering, measured along with the problematic concept of 'prestige', does not speak to changes in occupations and the emergence of new occupational groups, nor do rank-orderings translate into the changing skills and competencies that are needed and elevated in contemporary societies.

The stability of the basic occupational hierarchy in societies is considered a product of the simple skill distinctions between occupations (Jesuthasan and Boudreau, 2022); however, variations in the hierarchies are increasingly emerging and being negotiated in localized spaces such as organizations, workplaces, and specific social contexts such as migrant professionals with varying skills entering the field. Income and job permanency are indeed the most common organizational resources affecting such hierarchies. Further, resources such as overall access to on-the-job training, mentorship, and qualification-dependent status are playing growing roles in job prestige. Research has shown that occupations are regarded as social resources that actors attempt to monopolize, and that localized social contexts and intersectionalities of gender, class, and race, for example, are important in defining the status of individuals within occupations (Vallas, 2006). Researchers have recently challenged the national rank-ordering of occupations and have demonstrated empirically that workplace hierarchies are more influential on individuals' positions at work and their work situations than national rank-orderings (Avent-Holt et al., 2020), as workplaces are the actual local spaces that individuals live and work.

Robust classifications such as professions, semi-professions, and nonprofessions soon lead to complex questions of independence in the practice of a profession, definitions of expertise and skills, and the recognition of expertise in society at large. While educational attainment and autonomy in many jobs do increase over time, the criteria for these classifications can wear thin. This type of research paradigm assumes that professionalization of occupations follows from the relative stability of society and the economy. While the classification categories for occupations remain relatively stable statistically, new classification categories also emerge over time. Furthermore, according to recent studies, due to the contextual nature of occupations, occupation alone is a rather imprecise indicator of an individual's earnings and of any nonpecuniary rewards for individual jobs (Sakamoto and Wang, 2020). This has led to requirements that researchers should 'trade in' the old perspective of stratification studies that focus on the comparability of occupations for a new perspective focusing on firms and jobs. Despite the problems of measuring continuity in firms and jobs, this perspective may lead to a more complex and fuller picture of earning potential in and differences between contemporary occupations.

Some researchers, among them Abbott (1993) hold the view that *professionalization* is in fact part of a societal level theory on how occupations and occupational groups transform into professions in society and how professions develop over time through evolving expertise and skills. This transformation from occupation to profession takes place through a set of structural changes within the occupational group, such as licensing practices, associations and guilds, and codes of ethics. The social entities that are emergent in the processes of constructing social boundaries are important in Abbott's work, where he argues that multiple professions seek to establish control over a certain expertise area (Abbott, 1993).

New perspectives on professions and technology

In contrast to classic sociological research, still quite popular in studies on professions and professionalization, we take on another view on professions and professionalization, one that addresses both technology and its fostering of entrepreneurialism in contemporary society. The rise of research perspectives that highlight the processual nature of expertise in professions plays an important role in changing our understanding of how professions are constructed and how they change over time (Bailey and Leonardi, 2015). Thus, any form of expertise can become a profession. Accordingly, the 'markets' in a classical sense do not differentiate between occupations, expertise, and professions, nor are the relationships between these singularly dependent on markets. As Barley and Tolbert (1991) noted, professionalism could also be understood as an institutional form, or alternatively as a cultural template for organizing work.

Professionalism can thus be understood not only as formal competence but also, and perhaps more importantly, as a cultural resource. In a similar fashion, professionalization should be understood as a process whereby an occupation becomes legitimated as the principle for organizing particular work (Barley and Tolbert, 1991; Liu, 2017; Sela-Sheffy, 2016). The aspects *of boundary work* and *scripting* of work become increasingly important in the analyses of professions and technologies. Gieryn (1995, 406) defined boundary work as 'rhetorical games of inclusion and exclusion', in order to study the construction of differences between 'us' and 'them' in workplaces and within organizations. The concept of boundary work was first used to study the rhetorical construction of differences between science and nonscience activities (Gieryn, 1995). Since then, boundary work theory has also been applied to analyze the construction of boundaries between professions and nonprofessions.

When Autor and his colleagues developed their automated labor hypotheses in 2003, they assumed that routine jobs would soon disappear. However, what constitutes a routine job and what does not? Autor et al. (2003) argued that 'medical diagnosis' work and 'legal writing' work would be safe from automation and remain nonautomated tasks; however, less than 20 years after such forecasts, both tasks are to some extent performed by machines, even if they cannot be left without human supervision. Clearly, they misestimated the scope, depth, and magnitude of the impending changes, even if only a small proportion of all medical diagnosis and legal writing is done by machines. Still, digital labor is growing in all sectors of Western societies (Scholz, 2012). Technology impregnates expertise and changes professions from inside, and automation is one part of this profound change within professions (Poutanen et al., 2020). This book argues along these lines, emphasizing a broader perspective that enmeshes nature of expertise, creativity, and situated knowledge. Allowing for specificity, situatedness, and socio-materiality in the analyses of expertise and professions lets in a wider perspective on the role of digital technologies.

Bringing boundaries and how they are erected to the fore in research on professions has generated new theoretical insights into social processes in relation to work and professions, namely boundary-work and the territorialization, politicization, relocation, and institutionalization of boundaries. How are we then to understand boundaries in relation to technology development and professions? Lamont and Molnár (2002) note that social boundaries and hybridization processes in societies have grown more permeable, which directly concerns the transformation of jobs and work that accompany the increasing presence of workplace and work-related technology. Nevertheless, some things do remain the same in professions, and professions are rather stable in society, perhaps more so than other types of jobs and occupations. Professions remain the same while simultaneously being transformed internally and content-wise and even as professional content is being taskified to an ever-larger extent. In this way, boundaries between expertise are transcended, even when the profession's title does not change. How does this take place in practice, within professions?

Two examples of how technology irreversibly transforms professions' skills and expertise

The ways in which technology enters professions are many, and the professions' relation to technologies varies widely. Within medical professions, pathology is an excellent example of how a professional title has remained unchanged even as technology has irreversibly and in major ways changed the content of the profession. Legal professions are examples of those professions (juridical, teaching) where technological changes request additional skills and augment professional contents but the profession can also be maneuvered without these skills. The specter of technologies' immersion in established professions varies between these extremes.

Pathology as a profession of technology

The pathologist is both a professional and an expert. Pathology is indeed a profession with long and specific expertise; pathologists gain professional qualifications only after lengthy and structured education and training typically consisting of numerous years of general medical training followed by additional years of clinical training in their specialization. Pathologists perform activities and work tasks that aim to identify, differentiate, and deconstruct illnesses from samples and images as part of their everyday work. Traditionally, pathologists' tools consist of various types of microscopes and digitized X-rays and images; however, the scope of tools available to contemporary pathologists had widened to include DNA-techniques such as next-generation sequencing and digital imaging such as magnetic resonance imaging and positron emission tomography that require collaboration with other specialists, namely radiologists. Technological advancements have also transformed occupations specializing in medical imaging and technical engineering and lifted them to the core of the professions in question.

Like all medical professions, pathologists undergo extensive, intensive, highly specialized education and training for the 'field' and in practice. After general medical training, the extensive period of specialization requires numerous hours of working with bodies – including those of the deceased – and the cells, tissues, and organs that reveal bodily illnesses, practicing and developing the analytic skills of the profession. Most of the work days are spent at the microscope. How though to train pathologists in medical skills that go beyond or outside the professions of traditional clinical medicine? How is the pathologist to develop the eye and the ability to recognize and dissect abnormalities, markers for all diseases? How does the pathologist learn to present multiple explanations and hint at alternative diagnoses? It is here that technology and its practical applications live very close to the core skills of pathologists. Specialization impacts pathology as a profession in multiple ways. The digital environment requires competencies ranging from information management and integrated knowledge systems to knowledge of sophisticated analytics tools and their output.

Pathology exemplifies a high-level profession within medicine where technology and digitalization have recently effected major disruptions and transformations in the ways the work is done and progress in the work is achieved. With digitalization, technical expertise has become a part of the

profession. For example, in the US, the professional pathology community initially showed resistance to the implementation of digital pathology in their routine work practices. This resistance to the digitalization of the profession was not due to problems with the technology being implemented, but rather, according to the professional medical guild, to pathologists' lack of experience with the digital pathology technologies in play. Widespread acceptance of the whole-slide imaging system to be used in primary diagnosis began with the US Food and Drug Administration's (FDA) formal approval of the technology in 2017 (Yaeger et al., 2019).

After this, the automated technology rather quickly gained acceptance as part of the task repertoire of the profession, aiding pathologists in differentiation and diagnostics. FDA and professional approval also led to the standardization of digital pathology in everyday pathology practice (Dacic and Hartman, 2018). Soon most pathologists adopted digital pathology as part of their work practice; digital pathology refers to the use of cloud computing, AI, and machine learning to find patterns and deviations in massive data sets. Scanning and analyses of massive data sets are beyond humans' time capabilities but are fully available in the new computational landscape.

The importance of AI and machine learning has vastly increased within medicine, particularly in the field of pathology research. The AI systems can learn to make the differentiations needed for accurate diagnoses, and can detect cancer, for instance, in prostate needle biopsy samples, at an accuracy level 'comparable to that of international experts in prostate pathology' (Ström et al., 2020, 222). Applications of AI in radiology, for example, of course allow other types of differentiations, and recently have focused on image interpretation tasks such as classifications and segmentations, which is much needed. According to scholars, the prostate cancer example is a good 'case study' in medicine in terms of demonstrating the potential benefits of machine learning, because so many technological platforms are involved in its diagnosis and treatment (Goldenberg et al., 2019; Parwani, 2019). Concurrently, it testifies to the transformation within the medical profession. At present, collaboration between pathologists, other medical professionals (such as urologists in the case of prostate cancer), data scientists, computer researchers, and engineers is required to ensure that AI-based decision-support applications are properly trained and are properly operated within the profession. Surgeons using AI and machine learning in robot surgery are just another example of the ways in which technology becomes immersed in professions. The hybrid activities the AI brings into health care practices make the experts work together in novel ways and lead not to replacing expertise but to bringing out new forms of expertise that require reskilling of previous competences.

Machine learning is currently used and in use in many ways in almost all professions: by aforementioned pathologists to predict, for example, genetic variations and genetic phenotypes of various cancer types, to dissect and decrease false-positive responses, and to improve the differentiation in answering the various typical pathology questions. Machine learning is helpful in any analysis setting that benefits from the detection of patterns in complex data (Dreyer and Geis, 2017). Reading and interpreting the results of machine learning analyses is one new skill required in the professions of pathology and radiology, following from AI-replacement, that is, tasks that are completely taken over by AI. The impact and 'infiltration' of machine learning and AI to aid in the diagnostic process in pathology is difficult to measure. The gradual acceptance of technology as part of general professional knowledge led to its relatively rapid acceptance in healthcare and by the public during the 2000s, though the direct effects of this are challenging to gauge.

The potential applications of technology in pathology and other medical professions are vast, from automating existing forms of screening and creating new ones, to the use of big data in answering population-level health questions, to discovering new risk factors, among others. All these examples relate to the availability of good, unbiased data, its explainability, and the enhancement of causal reasoning regarding it. Ultimately, it relates to the medical professions, and how successfully these professions adapt to and adopt new technology, such as the techniques and elements of machine learning and its possibilities. The new tasks that are brought by the technologies into professions such as pathology generate new questions to be solved within such professions. The new tools and technologies such as digital pathology and AI are altering the field of pathology. The computer-assisted methods used in the analyses of the histopathological slides help the diagnosis made by the pathologist and with that analysis, to improve accuracy of the work of an expert (Parwani, 2019). To this end, further education and training for professionals is needed. Still, several ethical concerns remain with the co-called black box algorithms (Durán and Jongsma, 2021).

Legal professions enter new age of technology

The legal profession is one of the backbones in the birth and reproduction of the state institutional structure. In that role, the profession faces the need to adjust to those technological imperatives that are developing in society. In their central societal role, legal professions are an excellent example of how technology gradually enters professional practices without changing the title of the profession.

In the legal professions, the idea of a profession where professional status is not changing but the skill set required is changing becomes highly visible. Solicitors and lawyers have maintained their professional rank status, but the tasks within the professions, and even more importantly the legal landscape and its tools, are changing. Technological changes are the major rationale behind changes in tasks and in the overall legal landscape. Indeed, within legal professions, technology can manage some of the highly time-consuming but highly necessary tasks, such as case analyses. It can be argued that technology can increase productivity in professions by performing some of the tasks of professionals, freeing up working time for use on other tasks. This may entail learning to use new apps, programs, and platforms.

Machine learning can be directly helpful in professional legal work, especially in decision-making, by retrieving, assembling, and reviewing large numbers of legal documents. Algorithms can offer advice, for example, based on analyses of large data sets and can assist attorneys in structuring large numbers of cases within big data masses and in reducing court congestion by preparing and structuring data. Pattern recognition algorithms may find correlations between cases in a large data set that would otherwise likely remain undetected. Software tools also affect various aspects of lawyers' work, including tasks that have traditionally relied on judgment by human experts, such as predicting court outcomes. Machine learning algorithms can reduce the complexity in large legal materials and may lead to more accurate predictions and even higher accuracy (Alarie et al., 2018; Willson, 2017; Dietvorst et al., 2015). But algorithms may also reproduce biases and add experiences of injustice (Aloisi and De Stefano, 2022; Delfanti, 2019; Ajunwa, 2018).

Susskind (2021, 40) refers to the problem of the uniqueness of expertise in professional work, stating that much of the work done by white-collar professionals is actually not very 'sophisticated' but rather comprises 'routine' tasks that can often be automated. Indeed, professionalism is not only about professional knowledge and expertise but also about the 'processual enactment of professionalism' (Coupland, 2016, 99), suggesting that to be accepted in a profession, one must learn to play the part. New technologies will undoubtedly lead to a 'productivity gap' in the legal profession, because learning to take advantage of the new technology requires retraining and updating of skills. With the growth of technology, professional work cannot remain unchanged but becomes 'decomposed or disaggregated' (Susskind and Susskind, 2015, 122), meaning that in practice the professional content will be broken down into tasks. Many of these tasks will be changed by technology, and some of them will be allocated to other people or to machines, and a greater focus on networking as tasks of the profession will ensue. Susskind and Susskind (2015, 71), among others, predict that these 'advanced systems' may replace traditional lawyers and that professional legal work will be delegated to 'less costly workers' as the computerization of due diligence work and automatization of documentation has become a standard practice within the field. This also applies to the practices of tax law and auditing; in these legal professions, computer-assisted audit techniques have evolved mainly through private corporations' own R&D work (Serpeninova et al., 2020).

All professions are knowledge-based, and certainly, knowledge is at the core of legal professions. Technology can deliver part of that knowledge more systematically than through purely human action. This will ultimately lead to a point where technology not only analyzes data and condenses masses of data in reportable form but also produces 'a voice that symbolically renders . . . processes so that they become visible, knowable and shareable in a new way' (Zuboff, 2019, 9). For legal practitioners, this could mean applying tools and apps in document production and in general breaking down legal work into more basic tasks and outsourcing the most routine and repetitive tasks, often through platforms.

AI does not ensure neutrality, despite its capability for analyzing large datasets. On the contrary, major biases may be ingrained in AI algorithms. For example, AI has been shown to be biased in its predictions and in racial matters and other sensitive areas (Ajunwa, 2020; Ajunwa and Greene, 2019). It is generally acknowledged that AI-generated correlation, even if found within a large pool of legal data, is not yet a sufficient claim for a legal decision. Nonetheless, the arrival of technology in the fields of professions, such as the example of law shows, is an irreversible process. The rather quickly spreading impact of technology on professional fields is much due to platforms and their network effects. The case of online dispute resolution platforms, used in many countries and by many companies for mediating online shopping-related disputes between buyers and sellers, illustrates how quickly efficient and functional AI solutions can become absorbed into the everyday practices of legal professionals. The effects of technology, such as these functional AI systems show, seep into the work tasks of professions, and become integrally part of the profession.

Task-level changes and professional hybridity

What then will happen to professions like radiology, pathology, or law when advanced machine learning technologies and knowledge related to such technologies become ingrained in and part of such professions? It is clear that pathology, radiology, and law will be drastically transformed as professions and in practice as digital applications and machine learning algorithms increasingly become the tools of such professions. Notably, for the pathologist, the radiologist, and the solicitor, professional title and qualifications for entry remain rather unchanged, while the educational processes, knowledge space, environment, modes of practice, and tasks and tools, the overall content of the professions, are being irreversibly transformed by the technologies and the knowledge being implemented within them. Some of the most notable changes in radiology, for example, have taken place when applying AI to workflow and protocols, in addition to AI diagnostic tools used already by professionals (Langlotz, 2019; Dreyer and Geis, 2017). While the professions themselves and the status afforded them remain stable, massive changes are taking place in the tasks within and around such professions and in the ecosystems that support and feed data into their professional knowledge spheres. What roles will these professions play in the future? Will machine learning models become constant companions or assistants to practitioners of medicine, law, and other high-status, stable professions, or will AI and machine learning become embedded in the practices of such professions in such a way as they are no longer separable from professional identities?

Exploring these questions takes us to the task-based changes taking place within professions and to the concept of hybridity in professions. A profession's tasks, as touched upon earlier, are often considered the divisible parts of a profession, and as such, automatable or supportable by technological solutions. However, as suggested earlier, applications of digitalization, AI, and machine learning are increasing the number of tasks comprising a given profession's body of tasks; new tasks and professional dimensions are being added that widen the scope of the given professions and the possibilities for its practice.

With this influx of new technologies, questions of which parts or tasks within a given profession are automatable arise. Automatable activities refer to the scalable nature of those activities. In medicine, diagnostic and treatment practices are based on the idea that data interpretation and treatment recommendations are ultimately the purview of humans, even if they are assisted by AI and machine learning in the analysis of massive data. Multiple expert-level tasks, including dose estimations and interpretations of findings, are done by and with the help of automated processes. These processes are not new; computer-aided detection and diagnosis have been used for decades in medicine (Takahashi and Kajikawa, 2017). Breast cancer screening is one of the first areas to apply machine learning, and other medical fields that recognize the diagnostic value of machine learning and the overall scalability of technology are also encouraging pathologists and radiologists to work more closely with one another (Gu et al., 2016).

The hybridity of professions may well take place through this datafication; one profession can become many, with new fields of internal specialization coming into being and multiple professions may be subsumed in a new, hybrid model. The conditions under which various boundaries in society generate differentiations or categorizations between occupations and expertise, are still largely unexplored. The concept of boundaries is useful for analyzing how social actors construct groups (e.g., professions) as similar and different and how this construction shapes such actors' understanding of their responsibilities toward such groups (Lamont and Molnár, 2002).

The ways technologies transform the professions, and invade and change the permanence of professions among practitioners is continuous, as the examples of professions taken up earlier show. Technologies alter the environments and surroundings in which professions are practiced, which and what types of connections professionals have with other experts, how communication is managed, how information is proffered, and how knowledge is stored within professions. By their very nature, technologies such as machine learning develop complex and high-dimensional functions that cannot be easily unpacked or explained, even when they deal with the core knowledge of a profession. As such, technologies are not presently autonomous, new tasks for professionals can include supervising and monitoring the performance of machine learning systems in, for example, drafting legal proposals, rendering medical diagnoses, performing stability calculations, and accounting procedures (Vähämäki et al., 2020).

Adoption of new technologies depends on the level of expertise needed, and these forms range from replacement to maintenance (Schraagen and van Diggelen, 2021). *AI-replacement tasks* are tasks that are completely taken over by the AI, such as legal case search, or deep learning in the visual interpretation of radiology images. *AI-augmentation tasks* are tasks that require closer interwoven collaboration between AI and humans, for example, on the question of the brittleness of images. *AI-maintenance tasks* are new tasks brought forward by the complexity of AI that relate to systemic functioning of the activities, training included.

New constellations of professions, professionalism, and technology-driven changes to practices and operations require new types of analyses. Technology within professions is not just an 'add-on' to skills and capabilities; rather technology is plentiful and will be subsumed into professions and professionalism. Thus, technologies such as AI will most probably never exist in professions without some form of human expertise as an entity in the processes of technology. We will discuss some of these key technologies in the following section. Vital to understanding how technologies change professions is thinking in terms of tasks and expertise, and not in terms of single occupations or professions in isolation. The focus on tasks and expertise generates questions of by what means technology becomes submerged in the tasks that are part of the work of experts in professions and occupations.

Technologies shaping and generating professions and occupations

Macro level views

Technology irrevocably changes both production and services in the sectors in which it is applied, and consequently all the work and its arrangements in these sectors. At the global level, the impact of technology on the employment structure has become more visible by intensified globalization. Added to that, globally, educational expansion has fostered occupational development in developing countries. The trend over the past 50 years has been that educational attainment in vocational colleges and universities has risen and globally increased the share of workers with tertiary education (OECD, 2021).

Technology is not, however, applied in a similar manner across all industries and in all places; rather, the implementation of technology, adjusting it to old technologies in use, is rather more day-by-day activity and thus continually transforming some work practices, invalidating others, and elevating still others. Simultaneously, the larger transformation in the form of platforms and digitalization taking place in society and the economy is paving the way for all things electronic at work, from everyday apps at work to major industrial online activities and new patterns of working. Accordingly, specifying the type of technology is crucial for understanding its effects and their magnitudes. The diffusion of technology is primarily explored at the macro level, and rarely in the context of professions and the future of professions.

The relationship between professions and technology is becoming more blurred with AI's development and spread. The monitoring and assessment of AI and its technical progress and societal impact, has, however, become increasingly important – and continuously more difficult. Researchers focusing on AI and its measurable effects and on productivity contributions of IT explain that AI is being adopted but its effects become visible only slowly because of its nature as a so-called general-purpose technology (GPT). Efforts to measure and isolate the systematic effects of AI are reported for instance in the AI Index Report that tracks the data related to AI (Brynjolfsson et al., 2019; HAI Stanford University, 2022). GPTs refer to pervasive technologies that spread over many sectors and industries and improve their functionalities and forms over time (also see, Arntz et al., 2019; Jovanovic and Rousseau, 2005). A GPT is 'a single technology, recognizable as such over its whole lifetime that initially has much scope for improvement and eventually comes to be widely used, to have many uses, and to have many spillover effects' (Lipsey et al., 2012, 96). For example, bioinformatics can be considered a GPT, because data sequencing, data mapping, and data integration are all elements of GPT that have gained importance in laboratories across all bioscience fields and thus transformed the science field in its entirety, from drug development and vaccinations to energy innovations with plant-based biofuels.

With this wide range of applicability and its use, it is clearly not possible to isolate and measure the influence and efficiency of one technology or application nor to grasp how a given GPT is changing – for example, bio-industries at the macro level and experts' work tasks in laboratories at the micro level. This assumption is valid for all sectors in economies and societies where AI is being implemented, that is, from education to food production. Estimation of the effects of AI in a systematic and robust way across industries is a highly complex undertaking and refers mostly to processual analyses of the assumed, contextualized effects, and this in turn may lead to overfitting and overstatement of progress (Filimowicz, 2022; Mishra et al., 2020; Christin, 2020; Delfanti and Frey, 2020).

As stated earlier, *independence of practice* of the profession is indeed the key element that has defined 'profession' and distinguished it from 'occupation' in traditional sociological classifications. It becomes equally crucial to underline that while we still use 'old' definitions, categories, and descriptions of professions, skills, and jobs to approach the issues, technology disrupts not only the ways to practice the profession but also these very definitions and their content in many ways. Technology disrupts not only work and jobs but also our earlier understandings of jobs, tasks, professions, and occupations. The process through which some jobs become worse than others often relates to technological development (Kalleberg, 2011). Technology changes the societal order of posts and positions, jobs, and their content, and it disrupts our ideas of *who* does these jobs, what the level of autonomy is in the jobs, and what the future of the jobs looks like. In a complex manner, technology also 'creates' new industries, new professions, and new work and advances new tasks and 'occupations' that are more and more based directly on technological advancement–related skills and less and less on existing occupational categories. These jobs are difficult to place into traditional and contemporary occupational categories. Classifying them as entrepreneurs – based on their earning possibilities – would put together the very differing possibilities for entrepreneurial activities within professions and occupations.

While the disappearance of numerous occupations (mostly due to automation and robotization) is predicted to accompany technological advancements, many jobs remain, at least in title, but have nonetheless changed due to changing practices. According to estimates from several Asian countries where certain fields are undergoing drastic technological changes and where the population pyramid is very different compared to Europe or the US, new jobs are primarily in information and communication technology and carry data-related job titles (Khatiwada, 2020; European Commission, 2021; Dossani and Kenney, 2009). It is important to realize that the technology – employment relationship is highly contingent; the adoption of technology in a specific sector or within certain professions influences employment levels. This connection is not always straightforward nor is it only positive (Matthess and Kunkel, 2020).

The macro effects of technology adoption are at national and global levels, and they speak very little to micro-level changes such as the changing content of the tasks and jobs, changing job descriptions, and practitioners' job-related bargaining powers. In general, emerging jobs and occupations within technological sectors that are defined as occupational groups come with new job titles and higher wages. Currently, workers who are male, educated, urbanized, and employed in the service sectors are most likely to succeed in these new jobs (Khatiwada and Veloso, 2019). However, while technology has resulted in new jobs for these men, it has resulted in job loss for others. For example, De Vries et al. (2020) imply that in some advanced nations robots have replaced men in some manual labor–based jobs. As is suggested from the first example, it is well known that the adoption of technology in a sector can have positive effects on employment. Automation does not necessarily lead to a disappearance of work even in the affected industry. When industries automate, it has been found in research that their employment levels often rise rather than fall (Bessen, 2020; Derndorfer and Kranzinger, 2021). The picture changes when global dimensions are taken into account. In less developed economies the effects of technology are often positively related only to skilled-labor and product innovations (Ugur and Mitra, 2017; Tomaskovic-Devey et al., 2015).

Mismatches between labor supply and demand is obvious for certain types of jobs, as described earlier. How many jobs and occupations will disappear due to technology? The estimations vary greatly depending on the level of analysis. In their 2014 study, Brynjolfsson and McAfee (2014) predicted that rapid digital technology development would lead to major job losses in the US. Shortly thereafter, Acemoglu and Restrepo (2019) analyzed the actual effects of industrial robots on the US labor markets between 1990 and 2007 and found that there was a clear decline in wages and employment, especially for certain types of routine and low-skilled jobs. Technologies thus continue to be skill-biased in the tendency to support training and education (Dietz and Zwick, 2020).

The 'creative destruction' thesis (Frey and Osborne, 2013) posits that automation and robotization will sweep away numerous occupations in the coming years. The research shows that most of the technology-related changes and job losses are gradual and even contradictory, because automation can increase the demand for labor. The overall outcome depends on the relative productivity of the new technology (Bessen, 2020). Thus there is no single answer to questions of technology and job loss and job creation. Answers are multiple, complex, and still to be revealed. A large German study comprising an analysis of 8,000 tasks among 4,000 occupations predicted whether the given tasks are replaceable by computers or computer-controlled machines. This was done by analyzing the existing technological possibilities and task structures (Dengler and Matthes, 2018) and matching them to the existing use of technologies. Why analyze tasks instead of occupations and jobs? Tasks are activities that individuals have to perform in a specific occupation; tasks can change, disappear, and be replaced or removed, while this is not necessarily the case with occupations, and most occupations consist of multiple tasks (Arntz et al., 2017). According to these predictions noted earlier, only certain tasks in an occupation or in a job, rather than entire occupations, can be replaced by technology. Accordingly, gradual change rather than drastic disruption should accompany this type of development.

Dengler and Matthes (2018) argue that most studies overestimate automation possibilities because they do not begin with tasks but with entire occupations. According to them, occupation-level approaches overestimate the disappearance of job probabilities. Almost all occupations include tasks that are not substitutable. Assuming that only certain repetitive and simple tasks were to be substituted, they found that 15% of German employees were at risk of losing their jobs due to automation in the coming years (Dengler and Matthes, 2018). The impact of digital transformation varies across occupations. Almost all occupations include tasks that require skills that only humans can perform. In particular, unskilled and semi-skilled occupations and specialist occupations have high substitution potential, whereas complex specialists and highly complex occupations present comparatively lower substitution potential (Acemoglu and Autor, 2011).

Digital transformation not only renders *tasks* substitutable but also changes markets and brings new products and services to markets. Accordingly, an overall positive effect on employment is possible, even if some tasks disappear from some occupations. Moreover, the overall macro-level outcome is that occupation-level studies do over-estimate automation potentials across the board, which brings us to the micro-level changes being wrought by technology.

Micro-level changes

When looking at the everyday changes at work and the technological development, it is clear that there are very few jobs and tasks that escape some form of technology adoption, either as part of the tasks of the job or as part of the surveillance of work and its outcomes (Ball et al., 2019; Ball and Webster, 2019; Fiser and Hopkins, 2017). Technologies bring with them new requirements and new tasks and jobs that entangle with data. Part of the tasks is taken care of by algorithms and not by humans. Then again, technologies create new tasks and the need for supervision, correction, and additional taskification, which become immersed in new work tasks, jobs, occupations, and even professions.

Internet and social media 'influencer' jobs are the embodiment of the new technology-driven jobs that hover between being tasks, gig jobs, or occupations in the service sector. These types of work often promote consumerism. Influencers on social media platforms such as Instagram and YouTube could be considered an occupation and even a type of career created by niches in consumer markets and actively reproduced by followers who consume the online influencer character. Based on the traditional definitions used in professions research (e.g., Dent et al., 2016) social media influencers cannot be classified as a profession, as professions are operating with recognized expertise and autonomy in society. Professions are 'achievable' mainly through education, are usually connected to professional groups or associations, and have at least some autonomies in the practice of their professions. Building a job based on expertise with products, lifestyle, or service presentations fulfills the criteria of expertise but not necessarily the criteria of autonomous skills or knowledge.

The traditional focus on professions in social science research has emphasized the role of professions in society at large, and especially the relationships of professions to the state. The changing nature and role of professions have brought new insights for research and raised questions about the shifting nature of state-profession relations (Adams and Saks, 2018). There is a need to take into account the more specific socio-historical circumstances in profession development and diversification. What that would entail will be discussed in detail in Chapters 5 and 6.

Can influencer nonetheless be considered a profession, a career, or an occupation? The content and thereby the definition of the work of an influencer surely varies widely. The social media influencer influences others' buying and consumption decisions. The contemporary influencer most often operates through social media platforms and has authority over or has gained the trust of a distinct group of people. However, the content of the job of an influencer has not always been so. 'Influencer' as a career with some dark undertones was first mentioned in the 1996 film classic *Eraser*, directed by Chuck Russell. In the film, a Russian mob character with money and muscles as assets, played by Arnold Schwarzenegger, was introduced as 'some kind of influencer' (Eraser, 1996). Since then, influencer has become an established and recognized social media position, and as we name it, a new platform profession, discussed in detail in Chapter 6.

Contemporary influencer positions may be best classified as jobs or gigs, but in the following chapters, we argue that influencer may include elements of profession. Sometimes technology and the effects it produces are simply 'glued' onto studies on professions that are assumed to be permanent fixtures in society (Susskind and Susskind, 2015). Such studies predict the degree to which a given 'original' profession will change when technology inevitably comes to call and potentially changes not only whether the profession is needed but, more importantly, the content of the profession. With technological determinism, technology is assumed to be arriving, but the vehicle in which it will arrive is rarely specified. For these reasons, these aspects of technologies and how they will enter the workplace scene must be scrutinized. This is so important because the processes by which technologies enter a work sphere are not on – off with specific or set timelines, but rather the changes such effects generate have been and are taking place in continual processes. Often, the introduction of technology into organizations correlates with cost-efficiency measures that push technology into a cameo role due to its cost-saving qualities despite resulting in problematic changes to everyday practices. In this type of discourse, technology plays a specific, pre-determined role (Bailey and Leonardi, 2015). That being said, technologies do change professions incrementally and profoundly, both from within and through technological devices, practices, and processes in workplaces and organizations. Technologies and their implementations are not pre-determined; and while changes to professions' through their contact with technologies are inevitable, such changes do not take place similarly across and between all professions, but also fully new professions are borne.

As the various online tools for practicing professional expertise become easier to access and operate, online platforms continue to create niches for professionals and para-professionals to work remotely, often from home, and often as independent contractors rather than employees. To work with such online platforms, professionals must develop a new relationship with online work.

With the Covid-19 pandemic, many professions were forced to make drastic changes; the pandemic not only changed functions and practices within professions but also yielded requests and mandates to establish new activities, new models for functioning, and new working practices across ecosystems ranging from those found in education institutions to those surrounding within-profession activities. Acceleration spurred by the pandemic will manifest new stabilizing structures that will remain relatively permanent even after the pandemic is a thing of the past. The professional digital communities that operate on open access principles and share new knowledge globally are example of such structures.

Digital professional communities take different shapes, and while they are familiar to global academic communities – as represented for instance in the rapid sharing of Covid-19 sequencing data among scholars – data-sharing platforms and services are not so common for global businesses. Within the legal profession, digital disruption grew during 2020 and led to the establishment of multiple platforms servicing practicing professionals that are distinct from law schools and their faculty and alumni networks. Digital legal exchange (DLEX) is an example of a global digital community with a large data repository that was established and funded by global corporations in technology services. In the profession of practical medicine, professional communities and NGO-type associations and guilds produce such digital platforms and related services. Networked professions have long acted through social media and other digital platforms.

For example, in the legal profession in the US, the occupation of paralegal is considered a 'semi-profession,' somewhere between a legal professional (e.g., legal clerk to a judge, a job that is often filled by an attorney but can also be a law school intern) and a purely secretarial position. Semi-professions or para-professions are often assigned the roles of technical support personnel for professions, especially in terms of knowledge of technical practices. For example, in the case of law, litigation management software has become a part of legal-technological proficiency and thereby often the purview of the paralegal.

In most professions and semi-professions, mastery of technology is about not only mastering programs and apps but also several other features that relate to competencies and their upkeep. Additionally, it is therefore about mastery of the overall professional competency, as technology is already shaping all practices of professions. In law, this is increasingly taking place primarily through the use of AI and big data analytics and through suitable apps (Susskind, 2021). In education, learning apps and online courses have invaded the working time and space of teachers. Indeed, following the increasing use of data analytics, machine learning, and AI in the work, one former work entity that was taken care of by one professional can in fact become several types of smaller entities, tasks that are performed partially by computer, partially by data analyst, and only partially by the professional. The taskification can give a boost to various types of 'new hybrid professionals' to emerge (Armour and Sako, 2020). Another way to describe this development is as a 'decomposition' process by which professional work is decomposed or disaggregated into multiple constituent tasks and allocated to multiple people (Susskind and Susskind, 2015). With these multitudes of tasks across multiple professions, professional work can no longer be regarded as the work of a monolithic profession but is better described as a relatively open network of expert individuals working for the same firm or official public sector, each performing relevant expert tasks.

As mentioned, numerous online tools, such as online portals and online dispute resolution, are available in legal professions, such as online platforms that identify relevant cases, books, book chapters, and journal articles. Moreover, online dispute resolution (ODR) platforms have grown in popularity, and are currently used in the US more than actual lawsuits to resolve disputes and disagreements. Online platforms for legal research contain legal cases and the latest books and articles on a topic; the number of such publications has grown exponentially, especially through platforms (Legg and Bell, 2020). Online dispute resolution has been used to resolve disputes via the Internet, and relatedly, digital apps for this purpose have been in development since the 1990s (Ebner and Zeleznikow, 2016). The use of online dispute resolution apps has grown due to the growth of platforms such as eBay and Airbnb that offer ODR to assist their customers in resolving disputes. In the case of eBay, users can even pay a small fee to access a professional mediator (see eBay, 2021). Moreover, since 2020 and the onset of the COVID-19 pandemic, the development of all online services, including telemedicine and numerous others, has accelerated exponentially (Cohen, 2020).

Technology is gradually becoming part of everyday professional activities, is being immersed into work practices and processes, and is changing professions and occupations from the inside. This immersion of technology into work raises new questions, such as regarding field governance and pockets of expertise. As the process of technology becoming and unfolding in occupations is not predetermined but depends on 'a unique confluence of multiple varying factors' (Bailey and Leonardi, 2015, 178; Barley, 2020), it still has the power to quietly transform one profession into another newer one or to merge professions into hybrid models. Technologies may have universal characteristics, but technological choices made in organizations and among professions and occupations may be highly specific. Moreover, the demand for combinations of skill types is growing (Dietz and Zwick, 2020; World Bank, 2018). The growth in demand is observable not only in the new jobs that are replacing old ones but also in the new types of skills profiles for contemporary jobs. The major questions of this century involve whether and which services will become automated and to what degree.

References

Abbott, A. (1988). *The System of the Professions: An Essay of the Division of Expert Labour.* Chicago: University of Chicago.

Abbott, A. (1993). The Sociology of Work and Occupations. *Annual Review of Sociology*, 19(1), pp. 187–209.

Abbott, A. (1999). Life Cycles in Social Science History. *Social Science History*, 23(4), pp. 481–489.

Acemoglu, D. and Autor, D. (2011). Skills, Tasks and Technologies: Implications for Employment and Earnings. In: C. David and A. Orley, eds., *Handbook of Labor Economics*. Amsterdam: Elsevier, pp. 1043–1171.

Acemoglu, D. and Restrepo, P. (2019). Robots and Jobs: Evidence from US Labor Markets. *Journal of Political Economy*, 128(6). doi:10.1086/705716.

Adams, T.L. and Saks, M. (2018). Neo-Weberianism and Changing State – Profession Relations: The Case of Canadian Health Care. *Sociologia, Problemas E Práticas*, 88, pp. 61–77. doi:10.7458/spp20188814798. Available at: http://journals.openedition.org/spp/5013.

Ajunwa, I. (2018). Algorithms at Work: Productivity Monitoring Applications and Wearable Technology as the New Data-Centric Research Agenda for Employment and Labor Law. *Saint Louis University Law Journal*, 63(1), pp. 21–54.

Ajunwa, I. (2020). Race, Labor, and the Future of Work. *SSRN Electronic Journal*, 18 p. Available at: SSRN, https://ssrn.com/abstract=3670785 or http://dx.doi.org/10.2139/ssrn.3670785.

Ajunwa, I. and Greene, D. (2019). Platforms at Work: Automated Hiring Platforms and Other New Intermediaries in the Organization of the Workplace. In: S. P. Vallas and A. Kovalainen, eds., *Work and Labor in the Digital Age: Research in the Sociology of Work*. Bingley: Emerald Publishing Ltd.

Alarie, B., Niblett, A. and Yoon, A.H. (2018). How Artificial Intelligence Will Affect the Practice of Law. *University of Toronto Law Journal*, 68(supplement 1), pp. 106–124. doi:10.3138/utlj.2017-0052.

Aloisi, A. and De Stefano, V. (2022). *Your Boss Is an Algorithm: Artificial Intelligence, Platform Work and Labour*. Oxford; London; New York; New Delhi; Sydney: Hart Publishing.

Armour, J. and Sako, M. (2020). AI-Enabled Business Models in Legal Services: From Traditional Law Firms to Next-Generation Law Companies? *Journal of Professions and Organization*, 7(1), pp. 27–46. doi:10.1093/jpo/joaa001.

Arntz, M., Gregory, T. and Zierahn, U. (2017). Revisiting the Risk of Automation. *Economics Letters*, 159, pp. 157–160. doi:10.1016/j.econlet.2017.07.001.

Arntz, M., Gregory, T. and Zierahn, U. (2019). *Digitalization and the Future of Work: Macroeconomic Consequences*. Mannheim: Zew – Leibniz Centre For European Economic Research.

Autor, D.H., Levy, F. and Murnane, R.J. (2003). The Skill Content of Recent Technological Change: An Empirical Exploration. *The Quarterly Journal of Economics*, 118(4), pp. 1279–1333. doi:10.1162/003355303322552801.

Avent-Holt, D., Hällsten, M. and Cort, D. (2020). Occupational Status and Organizations: Variation in Occupational Hierarchies Across Swedish Workplaces. *Research in Social Stratification and Mobility*, 70, p. 100423. doi:10.1016/j.rssm.2019.100423.

Bailey, D.E. and Leonardi, P.M. (2015). *Technology Choices: Why Occupations Differ in Their Embrace of New Technology*. Cambridge: The MIT Press.

Ball, K. (2010). Workplace Surveillance: An Overview. *Labor History*, 51(1), pp. 87–106. doi:10.1080/00236561003654776.

Ball, K., Bellanova, R. and Webster, W. (2019). Surveillance and Democracy. In: K. Ball and W. Webster, eds., *Surveillance and Democracy in Europe*. London: Routledge.

Ball, K. and Webster, W.R. (2019). *Surveillance and Democracy in Europe*. Abingdon and New York: Routledge.

Barber, B. (1963). Some Problems in the Sociology of the Professions. *Daedalus*, 92(4), pp. 669–688. Available at: www.jstor.org/stable/20026806 [Accessed: 30 Jul. 2021].

Barley, S.R. (2020). *Work and Technological Change*. Oxford: Oxford University Press.

Barley, S.R. and Tolbert, P.S. (1991). Introduction: At the Intersection of Organizations and Occupations. In: S.R. Barley and P.S. Tolbert, eds., *Research in the Sociology of Organizations, Vol. 8*. Greenwich: JAI Press Inc., pp. 1–13.

Bessen, J. (2020). Automation and Jobs: When Technology Boosts Employment. *Economic Policy*, 34(100), pp. 589–626. doi:10.1093/epolic/eiaa001.

Brynjolfsson, E. and McAfee, A. (2014). *The Second Machine Age: Work, Progress, and Prosperity in a Time of Brilliant Technologies*. New York: W.W. Norton & Company.

Brynjolfsson, E., Rock, D. and Syverson, C. (2019). Artificial Intelligence and the Modern Productivity Paradox: A Clash of Expectations and Statistics. In: A. K. Agrawal, J. Gans and A. Godfarb, eds., *The Economics of Artificial Intelligence: An Agenda*. National Bureau of Economic Research Conference Report. Chicago: University of Chicago Press, pp. 23–60.

Christin, A. (2020). *Metrics at Work*. Princeton; Oxford: Princeton University Press.

Cohen, M. (2020). Covid-19 Is Transforming the Legal Industry: Macro and Micro Evidence. *Forbes*. 15 Sep. [online]. Available at: www.forbes.com/sites/markcohen1/2020/09/15/ [Accessed: 26 Jan. 2021].

Coupland, C. (2016). Discourses of Professional Work. In: A. Wilkinson, D. Hislop and C. Coupland, eds., *Perspectives on Contemporary Professional Work. Challenges and Experiences*. Northampton: Edward Elgar Publishing, pp. 86–122.

Dacic, S. and Hartman, D.J. (2018). The Future Is Now: Pathology Is Going Digital. *IASLC News*. 12 Dec. [online]. Available at: https://www.ilcn.org/the-future-is-now-pathology-is-going-digital/ [Accessed: 1 Feb. 2021].

Delfanti, A. (2019). Machinic Dispossession and Augmented Despotism: Digital Work in an Amazon Warehouse. *New Media & Society*, 23(1), pp. 39–55. doi:10.1177/1461444819891613.

Delfanti, A. and Frey, B. (2020). Humanly Extended Automation or the Future of Work Seen Through Amazon Patents. *Science, Technology, & Human Values*, 46(3). doi:10.1177/0162243920913665.

Dengler, K. and Matthes, B. (2018). The Impacts of Digital Transformation on the Labour Market: Substitution Potentials of Occupations in Germany. *Technological Forecasting and Social Change*, 137(4), pp. 304–316. doi:10.1016/j.techfore.2018.09.024.

Dent, M., Bourgeault, I.L., Denis, J.-L. and Kuhlmann, E. (2016). General Introduction: The Changing World of Professions and Professionalism. In: M. Dent, I.L. Bourgeault, J.-L. Denis and E. Kuhlmann, eds., *Routledge Companion to the Professions and Professionalism*. London; New York: Routledge, pp. 1–10.

Derndorfer, J. and Kranzinger, S. (2021). The Decline of the Middle Class: New Evidence for Europe. *Journal of Economic Issues*, 55(4), pp. 914–938. doi:10.1080/00213624.2021.1982338.

De Vries, G.J., Gentile, E., Miroudot, S. and Wacker, K.M. (2020). The Rise of Robots and the Fall of Routine Jobs. *papers.ssrn.com*. [online]. Available at: https://ssrn.com/abstract=3769886 [Accessed: 24 May 2022].

Dietvorst, B.J., Simmons, J.P. and Massey, C. (2015). Algorithm Aversion: People Erroneously Avoid Algorithms After Seeing Them Err. *Journal of Experimental Psychology: General*, 144(1), pp. 114–126. doi:10.1037/xge0000033 [Accessed: 12 May 2021].

Dietz, D. and Zwick, T. (2020). Training in the Great Recession – Evidence from an Individual Perspective. *Jahrbücher für Nationalökonomie und Statistik*, 240(4), pp. 493–523. doi:10.1515/jbnst-2018-0072.

Dossani, R. and Kenney, M. (2009). Service Provision for the Global Economy: The Evolving Indian Experience. *Review of Policy Research*, 26(1–2), pp. 77–104. doi:10.1111/j.1541-1338.2008.00370.x.

Dreyer, K.J. and Geis, J.R. (2017). When Machines Think: Radiology's Next Frontier. *Radiology*, 285(3), pp. 713–718. doi:10.1148/radiol.2017171183.

Duffy, B.E. and Pooley, J. (2019). Idols of Promotion: The Triumph of Self-Branding in an Age of Precarity. *Journal of Communication*, 69(1). doi:10.1093/joc/jqy063.

Durán, J.M. and Jongsma, K.R. (2021). Who Is Afraid of Black Box Algorithms? On the Epistemological and Ethical Basis of Trust in Medical AI. *Journal of Medical Ethics*, 47, pp. 329–335. doi:10.1136/medethics-2020-106820.

Ebay.com. (2021). *eBay Services: Buying and Selling Tools: Dispute Resolution Overview.* [online]. Available at: https://pages.ebay.com/services/buyandsell/disputeres.html [Accessed: 25 Oct. 2021].

Ebner, N. and Zeleznikow, J. (2016). No Sheriff in Town: Governance for Online Dispute Resolution. *Negotiation Journal*, 32(4), pp. 297–323. doi:10.1111/nejo.12161.

Eraser. (1996). California: Warner Bros. Available at: www.imdb.com/title/tt0116213/.

European Commission. (2021). *Digital Labour Platforms in the EU Mapping and Business Models* (A study prepared by CEPS for the European Commission, Directorate-General for Employment, Social Affairs and Inclusion (DG EMPL)). Luxembourg: Publications Office of the European Union.

Evetts, J. (2002). New Directions in State and International Professional Occupations. *Work, Employment and Society*, 16(2), pp. 339–351.

Evetts, J. (2013). Professionalism: Value and Ideology. *Current Sociology*, 61(5–6), pp. 778–796.

Evetts, J. (2016). Hybrid Organizations and Hybrid Professionalism: Changes, Continuities and Challenges. In: A. Wilkinson, D. Hislop and C. Coupland, eds., *Perspectives on Contemporary Professional Work. Challenges and Experiences*. Cheltenham: Edward Elgar Ltd, pp. 16–33.

Filimowicz, M. (2022). *Democratic Frontiers: Algorithms and Society*. New York: Routledge.

Fiser, H.L. and Hopkins, P.D. (2017). Getting Inside the Employee's Head: Neuroscience, Negligent Employment Liability, and the Push and Pull for New Technology. *Boston University School of Law Journal of Science & Technology Law*, 44(1), pp. 59–61.

Frey, C.B. and Osborne, M.A. (2013). The Future of Employment: How Susceptible Are Jobs to Computerisation? *Technological Forecasting and Social Change*, 114(1), pp. 254–280. doi:10.1016/j.techfore.2016.08.019.

Gieryn, T.F. (1995). Boundaries of Science. In: A.I. Tauber, ed., *Science and the Quest for Reality. Main Trends of the Modern World*. London: Palgrave Macmillan. doi:10.1007/978-1-349-25249-7_12.

Goldenberg, S.L., Nir, G. and Salcudean, S.E. (2019). A New Era: Artificial Intelligence and Machine Learning in Prostate Cancer. *Nature Reviews Urology*, 16(7), pp. 391–403. doi:10.1038/s41585-019-0193-3.

Gu, P., Lee, W.-M., Roubidoux, M.A., Yuan, J., Wang, X. and Carson, P.L. (2016). Automated 3D Ultrasound Image Segmentation to Aid Breast Cancer Image Interpretation. *Ultrasonics*, 65, pp. 51–58. doi:10.1016/j.ultras.2015.10.023.

Haber, S. (1993). History of Professions in America. In: M.K. Clayton, ed., *Encyclopedia of American Social History*. New York: Schribner's Sons, pp. 1573–1587.

HAI Stanford University. (2022). Artificial Intelligence Index. *aiindex.stanford.edu*. [online]. Available at: https://aiindex.stanford.edu/ [Accessed: 28 Apr. 2022].

Jesuthasan, R. and Boudreau, J.W. (2022). *Work Without Jobs: How to Reboot Your Organization's Work Operating System*. Cambridge: The MIT Press.

Jovanovic, P. and Rousseau, B.L. (2005). General Purpose Technologies. In: P. Aghion and S.N. Durlauf, eds., *Handbook of Economic Growth* (Vol. 1, Part B). Elsevier, pp. 1181–1224. doi:10.1016/S1574-0684(05)01018-X.

Kalleberg, A.L. (2011). *Good Jobs, Bad Jobs: The Rise of Polarized and Precarious Employment Systems in the United States, 1970s to 2000s*. New York: Russell Sage Foundation.

Khatiwada, S. (2020). How Technology Affects Jobs: A Smarter Future for Skills, Jobs, and Growth in Asia. *Education in the Asia-Pacific Region: Issues, Concerns and Prospects*, 55, pp. 263–270. doi:10.1007/978-981-15-7018-6_32.

Khatiwada, S. and Veloso, M.K. (2019). New Technology and Emerging Occupations: Evidence from Asia. *papers.ssrn.com*. [online]. Available at: https://ssrn.com/abstract=3590128 [Accessed: 25 May 2022].

Kuhlmann, E. (2006). *Modernizing Health Care: Reinventing Professions, the State and the Public*. Bristol: The Policy Press.

Lamont, M. and Molnár, V. (2002). The Study ofBoundaries in the Social Sciences. *Annual Review of Sociology*, 28(1), pp. 167–195. doi:10.1146/annurev.soc.28.110601.141107.

Langlotz, C.P. (2019). Will Artificial Intelligence Replace Radiologists? *Radiology: Artificial Intelligence*, 1(3), p. e190058. doi:10.1148/ryai.2019190058.

Larson, M. (1977). *The Rise of Professionalism: A Sociological Analysis*. Berkeley: University of California Press.

Legg, M. and Bell, F. (2020). *Artificial Intelligence and the Legal Profession*. New York: Oxford Hart Publishing.

Lipsey, R.G., Carlaw, K. and Bekar, C. (2012). *Economic Transformations: General Purpose Technologies and Long-Term Economic Growth*. Oxford: Oxford University Press.

Liu, S. (2017). Boundaries and Professions. Toward a Processual Theory of Action. *Journal of Professions and Organization*, 5(1), pp. 45–57. doi:10.1093/jpo/jox012.

Matthess, M. and Kunkel, S. (2020). Structural Change and Digitalization in Developing Countries: Conceptually Linking the Two Transformations. *Technology in Society*, 63, p. 101428. doi:10.1016/j.techsoc.2020.101428.

Mishra, S., Clark, J. and Perrault, C.R. (2020). Measurement in AI Policy: Opportunities and Challenges, pp. 1–25. Available at: https://doi.org/10.48550/arXiv.2009.09071 [Accessed 29 Jan. 2021].

OECD. (2021). Training in Enterprises. In: *Getting Skills Right*. Paris: OECD Publishing. doi:10.1787/7d63d210-en.

Parsons, T. (1939). The Professions and Social Structure. *Social Forces*, 17(4), pp. 457–467.

Parwani, A. (2019). Commentary: Automated Diagnosis and Gleason Grading of Prostate Cancer – Are Artificial Intelligence Systems Ready for Prime Time? *Journal of Pathology Informatics*, 10(1), p. 41. doi:10.4103/jpi.jpi_56_19.

Poutanen, S., Kovalainen, A. and Rouvinen, P. (2020). *Digital Work and the Platform Economy: Understanding Tasks, Skills and Capabilities in the New Era*. New York: Routledge; Taylor & Francis Group.

Poutanen, S. and Kovalainen, A. (2016). Professionalism and Entrepreneurialism. In: M. Dent, I.L. Bourgeault, J.-L. Denis, and E. Kuhlmann, eds., *The Routledge Companion to the Professions and Professionalism*. New York: Routledge, pp. 116–128.

Riska, E. (2001). Health Professions and Occupations. In: W. C. Cockerman, ed., *The Blackwell Companion to Medical Sociology*. London; New York: Blackwell, pp. 144–158.

Riska, E. (2007). Health Professions and Occupations. In: G. Ritzer, ed., *The Blackwell Encyclopedia of Sociology*. Hoboken: Blackwell, pp. 1–4.

Sakamoto, A. and Wang, S.X. (2020). The Declining Significance of Occupation in Research on Intergenerational Mobility. *Research in Social Stratification and Mobility*, 70, p. 100521. doi:10.1016/j.rssm.2020.100521.

Scholz, T. (2012). *Digital Labor: The Internet as Playground and Factory*. New York: Routledge.

Schraagen, J.M. and van Diggelen, J. (2021). A Brief History of the Relationship Between Expertise and Artificial Intelligence. In: M.L. Germain and R.S. Grenier, eds., *Expertise at Work*. Cham: Palgrave Macmillan, pp. 149–175. doi:10.1007/978-3-030-64371-3_8.

Sela-Sheffy, R. (2016). Profession, Identity, and Status. In: C.V. Angelelli and B.J. Baer, eds., *Researching Translation and Interpreting*. London; New York: Routledge, pp. 131–145.

Serpeninova, Y., Makarenko, S. and Litvinova, M. (2020). Computer-Assisted Audit Techniques: Classification and Implementation by Auditor. *Public Policy and Accounting*, 1(1), pp. 44–49. doi:10.26642/ppa-2020-1-44-49.

Ström, P., Kartasalo, K., Olsson, H., Solorzano, L., Delahunt, B., Berney, D.M., Bostwick, D.G., Evans, A.J., Grignon, D.J., Humphrey, P.A., Iczkowski, K.A., Kench, J.G., Kristiansen, G., van der Kwast, T.H., Leite, K.R.M., McKenney, J.K., Oxley, J., Pan, C.-C., Samaratunga, H. and Srigley, J.R. (2020). Artificial Intelligence for Diagnosis and Grading of Prostate Cancer in Biopsies: A Population-Based, Diagnostic Study. *The Lancet Oncology*, 21(2), pp. 222–232. doi:10.1016/S1470-2045(19)30738-7.

Susskind, D. (2021). *World Without Work: Technology, Automation and How We Should Respond*. New York: Penguin Books.

Susskind, R.E. and Susskind, D. (2015). *The Future of the Professions: How Technology Will Transform the Work of Human Experts*. Oxford; New York: Oxford University Press.

Takahashi, R. and Kajikawa, Y. (2017). Computer-Aided Diagnosis: A Survey with Bibliometric Analysis. *International Journal of Medical Informatics*, 101, pp. 58–67. doi:10.1016/j.ijmedinf.2017.02.004.

Tomaskovic-Devey, D., Hällsten, M. and Avent-Holt, D. (2015). Where Do Immigrants Fare Worse? Modeling Workplace Wage Gap Variation with Longitudinal Employer-Employee Data. *American Journal of Sociology*, 120(4), pp. 1095–1143. doi:10.1086/679191.

Treiman, D. (2003). *Occupational Prestige in Comparative Perspective*. New York: Academic Press.

Ugur, M. and Mitra, A. (2017). Technology Adoption and Employment in Less Developed Countries: A Mixed-Method Systematic Review. *World Development*, 96(1), pp. 1–18. doi:10.1016/j.worlddev.2017.03.015.

Vähämäki, M., Kuusi, T., Laiho, M. and Kulvik, M. (2020). The Road to Productivity with Automatization: Dialogue Between the Experienced and Measured. In: S. Poutanen, A. Kovalainen and P. Rouvinen, eds., *Digital Work and the Platform Economy: Understanding Tasks, Skills and Capabilities in the New Era*. New York: Routledge, pp. 116–141.

Vallas, S. (2006). Empowerment Redux: Structure, Agency, and the Remaking of Managerial Authority. *American Journal of Sociology*, 111(6), pp. 1677–1717. doi:10.1086/499909.

Watson, T. (2002). Should We Jump Off the Bandwagon, Better to Study Where It Is Going? *International Studies of Management and Organization*, 32(2), pp. 93–105.

Willson, M. (2017). Algorithms (and the) Everyday. *Information, Communication & Society*, 20(1), pp. 137–150. doi:10.1080/1369118x.2016.1200645.

World Bank. (2018). *World Development Report 2019: The Changing Nature of Work*. New York: World Bank. doi:10.1596/978-1-4648-1328-3.

Yaeger, K.A., Martini, M., Yaniv, G., Oermann, E.K. and Costa, A.B. (2019). United States Regulatory Approval of Medical Devices and Software Applications Enhanced by Artificial Intelligence. *Health Policy and Technology*, 8(2), pp. 192–197. doi:10.1016/j.hlpt.2019.05.006.

Zuboff, S. (2019). *The Age of Surveillance Capitalism: The Fight for a Human Future at the New Frontier of Power*. New York: Public Affairs.

2 Algorithms changing the world

Why are algorithms changing everything?

Already today and increasingly in the close future, all corporation playbooks will consist largely of data and its monetization and assetization. At the driver's seat in the data governance and monetization processes – and in almost all economic activities – are not the managers, boards, or CEOs of corporations, but the algorithms and the machine learning systems within the organization. As managerial and operational devices, algorithms are increasingly building the logic for everyday business and economic actions, and for any long-term planning, or major moves or strategic developments, the algorithms hold the key to govern. The algorithms do not function by themselves, nor are they saviors if the business logic within the organization does not otherwise support their use. Perhaps even more importantly, the algorithms did not originally write themselves but they were originally designed and written by humans, with their cultural understandings, presuppositions, and prejudices included.

The increasing importance of algorithms in all business and management functions is reality today as datafication grows. Algorithms and datafication govern large parts of public life, with effects on individual lives, in areas ranging from tax declarations to health registers. Datafication refers to technologies and processes that transform various activities into quantified data, and through the quantification make it possible to track (real-time) and predictive analyses, based on such data (Mejias and Couldry, 2019; Couldry and Mejias, 2018; Cheney-Lippold, 2019). The datafication enables indexing and searching of any text information, for example (Mayer-Schönberger and Cukier, 2013). Metadata means 'data about data', or data that describe other data. Meta-data can be created manually or through automation, and in organizations meta-data helps to organize information or data into manageable entities. The datafication and meta-datafication processes thus convert the symbolic material into digital form and transform the understanding of the material.

Increasingly algorithms use data as a fuel for organizing and governance of organizational activities. Within organizations, management, professionals,

DOI: 10.4324/9781351038546-2

and experts work for and with the data. However, the data often are not perfect, and thus algorithmic management suffers from the lack of human perspective. The decisions of what type of data is valuable and for whom, how to obtain robust data, and how data is refined, for example, are all complex questions and require expertise and skills to handle the data and decisions made on the basis of data. The questions of whether some gathered data are of value or not, or whether the data have monetary value for company functions, for example, require thorough monitoring of the algorithmic markets and monetization of data. In a similar manner, as the company is addressing the value of data, the company, as the employer, may ask if the experts and professionals it employs bring in enough value for the company.

How to define algorithmic management in its simplest form? The depth of algorithmic management depends on the amount and quality of digital data available. In relation to algorithmic human relations management, three main features of algorithmic management stand out. There are several features and of those, three main features consist of: the generation and use of digital data of all activities, the deployment of software algorithms that process all digital data, and finally, the partial or full automation of human-related decision-making (Meijerink et al., 2021).

The global tech corporations and financial technology sector may have been the first ones to let the algorithms slip into the boardrooms, sit by the board table, and even have a decisive role in decision-making. Industries from services to heavy metal industries were quick to follow tech companies. In many countries, the states and public sector organizations are adopting data-based logics in their activities. The public sector uses increasingly data for its decision-making and allocates resources on the basis of user data or predictions based on data. The following examples show the width of the use of algorithms in practice. Road surfacing repair and maintenance activities are increasingly based on the automated gathering of traffic data and statistics from user responses. In many countries, the intake to public higher education institutions is partially based on the data on birth cohorts, and the data on the labor markets are assumed to give the frame of future education needs. Individual consumption choices and purchases get registered to numerous data dungeons, and with that, automated individualized predictions of current and future needs are fed back in the form of ads and offerings. The logics of predicted consumption patterns is governed by algorithmic automated matchmaking and decisions. The platforms make choices based on algorithmic logics that are not transparent or directly observable (Poutanen et al., 2020).

As algorithms have become part of our everyday lives, ranging from private consumption to all forms of public life, working life, and careers, they have come to greatly influence the choices we have available, the choice we make, and the ways we think about and decide about various matters. These 'automated' shaping techniques frame many aspects of life, from consumption to the educational opportunities or skills we think we need in our future working life. The use of digital tools at work and in social life, monitoring of consumption habits and interest areas, and the algorithmic management of all the large amount of data gathered are radically transforming work content and processes, across fields. Moreover, algorithmic tools change performance management yardsticks both on digital labor platforms and in more traditionally organized companies, as well as in the public sector.

One specific aspect of algorithmic management that takes place in the working life of organizations is the taskification of the existing work: division and standardization of work tasks into smaller entities that are manageable and controllable, more automatable, and even more outsourceable. Algorithms are thus not solely forged by platforms, as argued by Casilli and Posada (2019). The entanglement takes place at several levels and in several processes. The processual view states that with the growth of production and service technologies, algorithms offer a new mode of operational logic. Algorithms function integrally in several preexisting technological solutions, and in practice, these solutions are adoptable by any company or corporation reorganizing its production and service functions. Automation, for its part, is defined as the replacement of human labor with robots. Robots are usually defined as programmable machines that are, unlike other pieces of equipment, designed to replicate human actions.

Hence, even if there is an argument about the necessary connection needed particularly between platformization and automation, with the tech giants benefitting from their users' data (Casilli and Posada, 2019), automation through algorithmic activities does not assume platforms as the necessary condition for functions. In any organization, the practices of accounting automation, for example, artificial intelligence (AI), machine learning (ML), and robotic process automation (RPA) will alter the accounting administration over time.

The taskification of certain parts of professional activities, and thus algorithmic autonomy, can be made an integral part of the existing profession, as discussed in the previous chapter with regard to the legal profession and the automatized legal services. Automated services may assumed to become part of almost any profession's digitalization, but in reality, the digitalization does not take place that smoothly. Even if individual tasks can be automated and can be dissected from the perspective of professional expert work (Kovalainen et al., 2020; Susskind and Susskind, 2015), the boundaries between these two processes are blurred. The work tasks on platforms and the taskification level of work are thus not restricted to simple tasks and singled-out actions, but extend from low-skilled work tasks into highly specified and complex ones, such as those of legal professionals (Aloisi, 2015; Kovalainen et al., 2020), as brought up in the previous chapter with regard to the legal profession.

Algorithmic management means a clear shift from human to machine in decision-making more generally. This development is most prevalent with online labor platforms that automate much of the work, including granting or denying workers' access to platforms, as in the case of gig- and task-related platform decision-making in selection, compensation, and gig and work allocation. Similarly, algorithms decide the pricing (of rides, for example) and compensation for the worker. In management science, algorithmic HRM – in a similar manner as all algorithmic tools in the corporate world – is indeed often considered a purposeful and discrete tool that is expected to have a positive impact on overall HRM practices.

AI-based research tools and assisting devices within any profession offer a variety of analytical and predictive capabilities, as well as the scalability of these capabilities, assumed to make any profession more efficient and productive. The role and impact of technologies within professions matter. Some healthcare professions are changing more rapidly, due to fast development in medical imaging and diagnostics, which help to apply precision therapies or reduce diagnostic errors, for example. This concerns especially the work of radiologists (Krittanawong, 2018). AI technologies such as deep learning have transformed all areas of AI-assisted medical professions, such as radiology. AI-based technologies will most likely lead to new types of workflows, with requirements of new types of expertise and skills within these professions.

Do algorithms recalibrate the skills needed in contemporary working life?

As the preceding examples reflect, algorithmic adaptations and algorithmic management increase the need to reorganize work and expertise, if algorithmic management has not performed that reorganization yet. It is therefore apt to ask where the data-driven and algorithm-governed economy place workers and experts concerning their expertise and skills. How does training at work and in educational institutions relate to technological development? What is the space available for professionals to maneuver with their expertise within workplaces and organizations, and finally, how do human activities fit into this automated economy? Or rather, should we perpetually be asking the question of how the automated economy fits into human activities, education modes, and acquiring skills for work?

In the Western economies c. 40%–60% of the formal economy labor force is classified as working in knowledge-intensive jobs, that is, they are working with intangible goods and services, and not in physical manual work. Globally the share of the workforce working in knowledge-intensive jobs in the formal economy is c. 25%, with a wide range of variation between economies (World Bank, 2021), making global comparisons difficult. Working in knowledge-intensive jobs indeed does not globally mean similar type of work nor conditions for labor, but the contrary: both in developed as well as in developing countries, platform knowledge work usually reflects the harsh reality of global competition and short-termism at work. Even in Europe, the temporarily employed have a higher poverty risk than permanent workers, and they have lower wages in comparison to permanent workers (Van Lancker, 2012; Codagnone et al., 2018).

Globally, the increase in the educational qualifications required in knowledge work may create possibilities and also give assets to combat poverty. Digital platforms are often offered as an easy means to enter job markets. However, there is no conclusive evidence supporting the claim that sharing platforms, for example, would have a positive effect on earnings among the most disadvantaged groups (Codagnone et al., 2018). OECD (2019) states that for emerging economies, the new forms of platforms may offer a route to formalization of work, if states put tax and social protection mechanisms in place. Global labor platforms mediating tasks and gigs globally do not necessarily interact with national taxation or social security systems; these activities are not part of the algorithmic management of platform corporations, but reflect more widely the legacy systems of each country in question.

The recent growth of platforms as a production form and a way to organize the services provided in traditional industrial sectors, such as the process and manufacturing industry, has intensified the use of algorithms in corporations. In this development, algorithmic expertise is in competition with human expertise. There is a growing need to specify what type of technological progress and where and what kind of reshaping of work is taking place, and more importantly, what types of skills and competences reign in that transformation.

As stated in the previous chapter, technology will reduce the number of some jobs but will also facilitate the creation of new types of jobs through innovations, and partially based on renewed skills, but increasingly also through work available online in the so-called global gig economy. In relation to these working-life transformations, technology does change the demand for skills, and skills re-adjustment and re-skilling are increasingly taking place outside of compulsory and formal education and formal jobs. The recent analyses show the importance of on-the-job education and reskilling and upskilling of work-related competences taking place at work (OECD, 2019). Furthermore, the Covid-19 pandemic has caused stalling of training at work and workplaces. According to the OECD, the most usual skills provided by enterprises relate to technical, practical, or job-related skills. In addition, several skills relate to fields of health and security as well as with soft skills, IT skills, and foreign languages. These skills and opportunities to upskill differ in their degree of formalization of training. The reskilling and upskilling opportunities are seen as crucial both for individuals and for enterprises (OECD, 2021).

The reskilling and upskilling of work-related skills usually take place at work or systematically relate to qualifications obtained already in basic education. For those at work and in relatively stable contracts, upskilling does not usually pose any problem, but the question of access to needed skill 're-doing' is far more complicated for those working in part-time, casual, or short-term contracts. The skills needed for technology management and for algorithmic management may be novel, such as relationship work (Hochschild, 1983) with a new twist toward algorithmic translation skills. Re-skilling, learning new skills for a new position, requires stability in work relations (Davies and Eynon, 2018), as does up-skilling, learning current work tasks more deeply.

Knowledge-intensive economies rely on training, and a wide range of research literature exists on firm-provided training. Since the seminal research book by Becker (1975), researchers have analyzed the variety of conditions under which enterprises provide training for general or firm-specific skills (Acemoglu and Pischke, 1999), in class or in work-related training, etc. (Ford et al., 2018). According to key studies (OECD, 2021), enterprises can basically adopt two strategies besides training to address their skill needs: they can either directly hire individuals with specific competences, or they can outsource the activity for which there is a skill gap. In the following, both of these strategies will be addressed in relation to automation, algorithms, and platforms.

Despite the importance of firm-level training in the automated algorithm environment, the training needs are not balanced. The evidence on the effect of employee voice on training provision is scant, but there is evidence that, despite the problems of actually measuring informal learning, learning has proven to be more important than other forms of learning in terms of intensity of learning (Fialho et al., 2019). What is informal learning at workplace? Training opportunities are defined as formal, that is, institutionalized, when the enterprise or an external provider are responsible for setting the learning methods, the schedule, the admission requirements, and the location where learning will take place. If these learning conditions are not fulfilled, then the learning activities are considered informal (OECD, 2021; Eurostat, 2016). For professionals, learning takes place in many formats. In a study analyzing the ways cardiologists adapted to using technologies adopted and recommended by their organization administrators (Menchik, 2020), it became apparent that the physicians made decisions based on the habits and routines they developed over their training, and their subsequent division of labor with colleagues, but not based on the recommendation by the organization administration.

The future of learning related to mastering skills that relate to governance of the automated algorithmic skills of technology does not look too rosy when looking at the national-level data, where employer–employee match data are analyzed. Dietz and Zwick (2020) use a German-linked employer–employee panel dataset to determine the connections between crisis situations and employee training in companies, and find a direct negative effect of the crisis on individual training activities. Furthermore, the German data show that the recession had a stronger effect on employees in unskilled jobs than on employees in skilled jobs (Dietz and Zwick, 2020), supporting the idea of the value of core employees versus peripheral employees in companies' strategies. For those in expert positions, the findings of several studies suggest that lifelong learning will increasingly be part of a successful organization's strategic goals (Li, 2022; Doherty and Stephens, 2021). According to these studies, both individuals and companies need to commit to reskilling and upskilling and make career development an essential phase for the future workforce. More generally, the relationships among higher education, labor markets, and industries should be strengthened, in order to respond to societal demands of reskilling, upskilling, and lifelong learning.

Several research institutes have estimated the intensification of reskilling needs for new technologies, ranging from cloud computing to AI, machine learning, blockchains, and robots. There is a large variation in the estimates given. The World Economic Forum estimates that, by 2025, globally c. 50% of all employees will need reskilling due to adoption of new technology (Schwab and Zahidi, 2020). Other estimates are more modest, and given the time span, perhaps more realistic (e.g., World Bank, 2019). Indeed, despite the fact that new technologies are forecasted to drive most of the future growth across industries, as well as the demand for new job roles and skill sets, there are several caveats ahead, not least with the effects of technologies. It is assumed that algorithms are still mostly used in addressing information and data processing, administrative tasks included, and less used in actual decision-making.

As a learning device, AI uses an algorithm to build an experience from large amounts of correct answers (Bravo, 2015). If the algorithm cannot give a suitable moral code or behavioral pattern as part of the correct answer, it fails to enhance organizational performance. Algorithms reposition command and authority, and in that process assume less human engagement than earlier. It is thus only reasonable to state that indeed it is the algorithms that are in charge when they give orders to workers and experts, albeit the algorithms were originally written by humans. The overall trend is that the algorithms rewrite the organizational playbook and increasingly function without human interference.

When algorithms govern, who is in charge?

In general, platforms are introducing a paradigm shift in the use of human expertise. This paradigm shift ranges from conventional human resource processes related to how the demand for expertise and the supply of expertise are matched, to governance models where algorithms surveil, supervise, and report human activities. The relationship between algorithms and human knowledge work is complex, however. Low-paid algorithmic work is growing, as will be discussed later in this chapter. But, even if algorithmic decision making and running of businesses through and with the help of data is growing, algorithms have not yet completely replaced humans. The following case shows the problems faced by algorithmic decision-making protocols when sufficient human leadership is not involved.

The United Airlines' 're-accommodation of a passenger' case in 2017 is famously an incident that at first seemed to be an unfortunate one-time case of bad customer service gone awfully wrong. The case of forceful removal of a customer from a plane that was overbooked is a landmark case of how algorithms can take over. A passenger in this case had a ticket and a seat and was already sitting on the plane. He did not want to miss the flight due to work-related obligations waiting for him in the city of arrival. Despite already having a ticket and a seat, he was forcefully removed by security from the plane due to overbooking.

The case was highly documented in social media and in newspapers, and with a closer look is not only a case of bad service culture gone horrifically wrong. The mishap epitomized a deeper problem of the power of data and algorithmic governance, which reigned over rules and procedures at United at that time (e.g., Walsh, 2019). Airline companies' standard procedure of overbooking flights and vacating seats led in this case to the violent removal of a customer from his seat, in order to vacate the seat for the crew needed to fly to the destination. The power of algorithmic rules and regulations, and the rigid following of the conduct code dictated by the algorithmic decision making eventually led to the unfortunate case where a passenger was injured, ultimately due to the harsh steps taken by security following the conduct code. Human contextual judgment of the situation and overruling the code in that specific case was obviously fully missing or was not encouraged as a possible pattern to follow in the incident.

In the future, incidents of this type are predicted to grow if machine learning does not easily adapt to humane evaluation mechanisms or have access to a real person or an internal person-like moral compass for guidance in actions such as these. Even though there is a greater demand for employees' nonroutine cognitive and sociobehavioral skills, discrepancies of human skills and machine learning may also increase (Shestakofsky, 2017). Some researchers (Rahman, 2019; Rosenblat, 2019) state that algorithms are rewriting the rules of work. It can be asked whether that rewriting concerns all types of work, or whether the experts as professional groups are outside of these rules, not having to obey or follow them, or indeed, even have the power to rewrite the rules themselves.

In the United Airlines case, the employees were simply following the company rulebook, quite literally, and when algorithmic procedure indicates not only the procedure for the workers to follow but also details the way to handle to overbooking situation, it may be impossible for an individual worker not to follow the instructions of the algorithmic manager. At least in the case of weak organizational culture, following the formal rules is the easier choice, instead of 'playing it by ear'.

In ride-hail companies, for example, algorithmic managers write the script for workers, who are not workers but partners. Through the scripts, algorithms direct the ways drivers behave by using responsive incentives and penalties that affect the pay the drivers receive. The scripts are not, however, able to handle surprisingly unpredictable situations. Technology is currently permanently altering the ways we work, our consumption and driving patterns, and our attitudes toward work and how it is organized; but the idea and uptake of technology relies also strongly on the idea of progress. The impact of Uber, Wolt, Upwork, and several other platform companies is truly profound. But is all technology adoption at work about efficiency progress, or is technology adoption connected to the rise of alternative work arrangements and cost savings, as argued by some economists (e.g., Katz and Krueger, 2017)? The answer relates to the ways technology is part of work and immersed into the practices of work and the ways it plays a key part in work processes and in workers' human capital. The digital economy, exemplified through the platforms, intensifies the use of alternative or new work arrangements, and offers new possibilities through globalization of work tasks and their supply/demand.

In the following, a closer look is taken at technology management through digitalization at work among professionals and entrepreneurs. Technology alters not just the forms of employment, but also alters the labor relations: who is the employer, is it the consumer or the app? What is the worker, are they an employee, entrepreneur, or consumer? And how can technology, through algorithms and digital devices, manage the situation? As algorithms as managerial tools do not differentiate between the qualification of workers but rather between different types of tasks, we will give a general account instead of addressing only expert jobs and highly skilled jobs. As technology changes working life profoundly, the old categories may not be placeholders for major rearrangements; rather, they also change within the major general restructuring.

Governance by algorithms: algorithms as managers and supervisors

Governance by algorithms is governance by technology. It is a form of social ordering which incorporates complex computer-based epistemic procedures. These epistemic procedures are scripts for action, prompting certain procedures and activities in sequences, for example. The underlying idea of algorithmic governance is that digital technologies produce and also reproduce social ordering. Any organization works through and with the help of some sort of technology. Whether all technology includes algorithms, and which parts of the technologies are managerial tools, varies widely (Katzenbach and Ulbricht, 2019). Not only technology but also the maturity of an organization matters in the ways governance by algorithms is organized. Start-up businesses may often foster a certain degree of informality in their organizational structures, with no hierarchies or internal institutions. Thus their use of algorithmic management differs from that of large corporations that have adopted algorithmic management as part of their administrative routines.

Algorithms as managers are essentially about technological mechanisms, tools, apps, or other ways of managing work, activities, and organizations. The most usual idea of algorithms and algorithmic systems is that they are items for consumers and users, relating algorithms to individual apps and webpages. Indeed, individuals can decide whether or not use the consumer applications, if they are not required by the state, for example. When the decisions whether or not to use algorithms are incorporated into the managerial processes, their use is no longer an individual choice. The authority to decide if management can surveil with algorithmic systems is usually not available to an employee, for example. In organizations and workplaces, algorithmic systems can have two different 'professional roles': they can be 'algorithmic managers' that manage and govern workplace decisions, and they can be robotic or algorithmic 'coworkers' that work alongside people and help people. And they can have both these roles simultaneously. But what are algorithms exactly, and more importantly, what do they do?

In their broadest sense, algorithms are encoded procedures for solving a problem by transforming input data into the desired output (Gillespie, 2014). Definitions given by dictionaries define an 'algorithm' as a process or set of rules to be followed in calculations or other problem-solving operations by a computer and as a set of steps that are followed in order to solve a mathematical problem or to complete a computer process (Oxford English Dictionary, 2021; Katzenbach and Ulbricht, 2019).

Most often, an algorithm means a computational formula that can autonomously make decisions, based on statistical models or decision rules without explicit human intervention (Sienkiewicz, 2021). However, humans have written the codes for algorithms which are productions of human design. Indeed, algorithm is often thought as an adjective to describe the sociotechnical assemblage where human is integrally part of the activities (Duggan et al., 2020; Yeung, 2017). Thus the algorithmic assemblage includes humans at all activities, ranging from design to the use of data (as well as users).

The seeming lack of human intervention reflects the development of the autonomous decision-making capabilities of algorithms, from AI and machine learning to the shaping of social and economic life (e.g., Kitchin, 2016). The working of algorithms has wide-ranging consequences for the shape and direction of our everyday lives. Indeed, we cannot avoid meeting algorithms these days, as they are part of the general functioning of technology, and therefore, generalizing about the working of algorithms is highly problematic. The algorithm is formulaic, with a set function or role that determines the steps and the processes. It is also relational, in that it needs to communicate with other systems and structures with which it interacts (e.g., Willson, 2017; Rosenblat and Stark, 2015). The relational aspect, the communication between algorithmic formulae and humans, becomes of interest: is it led by humans or by robots (algorithms)? Or rather, is the relational aspect about the development of the process, where the algorithms and humans collaborate? Some recent studies show variation in organizational contexts to elaborate the common practices and divergent strategies in algorithmic governance (Rosenblat and Stark, 2015; Gorwa, 2019). Indeed, we need further research to disentangle how the various organizational agents collaborate in governance and in management.

In corporate use, the space of algorithms as managers has spread quickly and widened from traditional individual HR tasks such as salary bookkeeping or accounting to ordinary tools of general management and specific tools used in innovation-building. In alliance with many researchers within the field, we call the software algorithms that are designed by humans and given several managerial functions within the organization the 'algorithmic management'. Increasingly, software algorithms optimize and allocate work tasks and evaluate work performance everywhere, not just in companies. Algorithmic management allows human management to organize the work of myriads of workers in an optimized manner, without having to 'human-manage'. But what does this mean for everyday organizational practices?

The contexts where the algorithms for managerial activities are used are crucial. It is not realistic to argue that 'algorithms rule everything today' or conversely, that 'algorithms do not deserve the credit given to them'. In practice, part of the use of algorithms in management is about everyday organizational functionality and efficiency: supporting organizational functions, such as making information flows more effective, calculating salaries, being part of account systems in estimating expenses, or predicting demands in a systematic way, based on previous actions. But part of managerial algorithm use is at the core of the business idea, for instance when managing labor mainly or solely through apps, or servicing customers with apps and without human interference. In so doing, the algorithms create power asymmetries, which enable control, which is the key element in management. Moreover, in the process, algorithms support corporate management and act on behalf of it. This type of algorithm management is visible in the on-demand work found or matched via digital platforms. Data-driven algorithms enable automatic management of transactions between thousands of gig workers and service recipients. The possible problems in algorithmic management are in these cases most often technical and they get explained as tech glitches, as shown in the analyses of ride-hailing platforms such as Uber (Gray and Suri, 2019; Rosenblat, 2019; Rosenblat and Stark, 2015).

The extent to which algorithms manage and govern organizations varies substantially. The online labor platform companies build the whole business idea around the algorithms and use algorithms to match the demand and supply of tasks and doers. The same algorithms are used for control of the doers and those shopping for services. Traditional organizations can use algorithms for a variety of more subtle control or surveillance actions within an organization (Zuboff, 2019). When having to wear bracelets, pacers, phones, and other devices that monitor their activities, the workers do the controlling themselves.

The surveillance of work and worker is always present as remarked and suggested by Zuboff, and thus there is no space where 'the self would retreat from the performative demands of social life' (Zuboff, 2019, 471). This dystopian view is of course debatable. The public/private distinction that has been seen as one of the fundamental categories of modern social life is indeed changing. The two spheres were once largely separate, but with the growth of technology and media, there is now a significant blurring of boundaries and continuous interaction instead, in particular with the growth of the importance of social media. As media technology changes the understanding of the private/public division, as described by Bannerman (2018) and Nippert-Eng (2010), it also shapes the understanding of what aspects of social life belong to the field of privacy. Privacy is seen as an important condition for any part of autonomous selfhood and a fundamental value of democracy (Nedelsky, 2013). Is it possible to uphold this understanding of privacy? It seems that in a networked society, privacy must be shored up also by other-than-legal forms of regulation in order to ensure the kind of privacy that is part of individual rights in democracy. The question of surveillance at work and privacy of workers is one practical aspect of these issues.

While surveillance in management is not new as such, technology development and algorithmic sophistication have given it new layers due to the labor platforms and taskification of even expert work. In practice, the aims of surveillance may serve differing goals: for some part of work and workers surveillance is first and foremost about worker efficiency, tracking the use of working time and implementing digital Taylorism. For other aims, surveillance of work tasks and workers may be about spotting the talents in the pool, amid the possibilities and realities of outsourcing corporate functions and managerial positions to labor platforms and specialized freelancer markets, for example.

All corporations are in principle able to do work-slicing within their organizations, as the online labor platforms do to work. The division of jobs into smaller, more numerous tasks calls for having a larger number of people to do those jobs in reserve. Slicing means dividing tasks on an hourly or task-based basis. For many companies, there is no need to add these workers to the permanent payroll or to the core employees of the company. Indeed, this is the way large organizations have already transferred part of the expertise they need to labor and expert platforms, where short-term project work and gigs are allocated by algorithms. One important question naturally is whether individuals with expertise and experience in highly skilled jobs are willing to be managed by algorithms.

A perfect worker? Algorithmic selection, surveillance, and governance of self

For any organization and its top management, the 'lure' of algorithmic management is in its scalability, procedural simplicity, and the accuracy and overall embeddedness of algorithms into everyday life and functioning everywhere, for example, as wearable technology, of which smart watches and smart rings may be the most familiar items. From the playbook of procedures such as the United Airlines case, algorithmic management has progressed into governable data gathered by the employees and governed by the firms. Already prepandemic, digital connections and links had replaced some of the physical connectivity. Both companies and public sector officials and institutions use currently complex data networks in their operations, irrespective of the field, but in some industries, the use of technologies at work is more crucial for actual work performance than in others. Work-related technology advancements range from algorithms to production- and service-related technologies, and include also wearable technologies and software programs, both aiming to govern through the measurement of efficiency and use of time.

The concerns about wearable technologies at work and measuring software on laptops and mobile phones relate to privacy concerns, and potential surveillance data gathered and used beyond the work-related context (Ajunwa, 2018). Labor-intensive forms of surveillance are still common, but surveillance is increasingly built into everyday software or hardware or even added in as a feature after adoption. In other words, data gathered from employees are not produced for the benefit of organizational management, but have come to epitomize those individuals who work in the organization. Data gathering among personnel takes place similar to consumer data gathering. It is up to an organization how to use the data, within the given legislative boundaries.

Wearable technologies epitomize concretely the blurring of public and private. Zuboff (2019) has shown how technologies used in the workplace contribute to developing panopticon surveillance by the employer, based on the technologies of wearable data that offer features for real-time continuous surveillance by the employer. Algorithmic management needs no specific managerial representations or personifications, as the networked governance reins in the worker self. The wearable technology creates a system of surveillance worn on the self and is seldom optional if its use is based on the deliberate aim to control and surveil.

Even though digital surveillance not only is a work-related matter, but also functions at large at the intersection between institutions and private spheres, surveillance in the work context matters. Walsh (2019) discusses overreliance on algorithmic management by using the known example of Amazon, which received patents for a wristband intended to monitor warehouse workers' movements. The wristband patent, named Ultrasonic Bracelet and Receiver for Detecting Position in 2D, aimed at saving time in locating items in complex warehouses (Ajunwa, 2018; Fiser and Hopkins, 2017). Tracking devices such as wristbands represent a pervasive form of digital Taylorism, yet they fit perfectly with algorithmic management, by offering other information on top of surveillance. Work procedures in the Amazon warehouse are aided by algorithmic technologies, and barcode scanners are used to identify items in the warehouse. At Amazon, by patenting the wearable wristband, management intended to use the same technologies for the surveillance of workers that were used for the search and for the organization of the warehouse inventory (Delfanti and Frey, 2021; Ajunwa, 2018).

With the Covid-19 pandemic, many companies have developed surveillance systems to monitor, for example, the needed social distancing between workers in workplaces. The same technologies that were used to monitor workers' performance and positions in the physical location have been redesigned to warn workers when they get too close to each other. These are usually based on technologies such as Bluetooth or ultra-wideband. During the pandemic, the privacy question did turn into a question of social distancing, where technologies used for surveillance were also helping to protect employees; however, in order to create trust, both employees and employers need to understand the principles of how these technologies work and are used, their limitations, and their capabilities.

This increased machine-based control over workers, the decomposition and taskification of work activities, and further automation of managerial functions is close to Taylorism in its continuous striving for efficiency. Delfanti (2019) calls this co-creation of space by humans and algorithms 'humanly extended automation'; this process is intrinsically based on a division of labor between humans and robots in which workers are exchangeable with automated technology and in which humans intervene mostly to make up for robots' shortcomings. This 'collaborative' work of humans and robots is nowadays part of the accounting and administration procedures, where large chunks of data within organization such as personnel information, salaries, salary compensations, annual leaves, etc., are processed (Vähämäki et al., 2020). Introduction of robots as part of process development at work is, however, not without problems and may lead to myriad measures as proxies for productivity and procedures for task performances. Crucial in this human–machine interaction is the logic of building the interaction and the management of the interaction process.

The varieties of human–machine interaction at work range from collaborative work with robots, as described in Chapter 1, to automated salary calculating systems and crowdwork. The latter is an example of directly algorithmically managed work, although there are many ways to make algorithm work as a boss. That is, crowdwork refers to work delivered or managed through a digital service that functions as a matchmaker or intermediary, often consisting of microtasks. Crowdwork describes digital work that is organized and regulated by platforms. According to several case studies among microworkers, it is evident that platforms are not just neutral intermediaries of work assignments, but they structure the digital labor processes and working conditions (Schor and Vallas, 2021; Gerber and Krzywdzinski, 2019). The managerial structures of crowdwork platforms are seemingly neutral, algorithmic infrastructures. According to researchers, the performance control is equally important and is based on a combination of direct control, reputation systems, and community-building (Krzywdzinski and Gerber, 2021; Schor and Vallas, 2021).

To examine how a crowdworker motivation and output are shaped by perceptions of autonomy and meaning in algorithmic management situation, several researchers have established test settings to evaluate the matter. For example, Toyoda et al. (2020) measured the level of worker motivation with MTurk, Amazon Mechanical Turk, and found that workers were more engaged in meaningless tasks when the AI was framed as their supervisor that answers queries, and not only as their controller, although control was, nevertheless, the main task of the AI.

Irrespective of their work status or field of expertise, platform workers are monitored by the platform, enabled by the algorithmic control, and subjected to performance measurement as if they were employed by an organization (Möhlmann et al., 2021). Online labor platforms basically use algorithms to do two tasks, matching and control.

There is, however, a large difference in the ways algorithms are used as managers outside of an organization, as in micro-work tasks, and as automated managers within an organization. Algorithmic management at large can be defined as active collection and use of data from the platform in order to develop learning algorithms for functions traditionally performed by human managers. The algorithm-based management exercised by digital platforms clearly contributes to several asymmetries between the work provider and purchaser that are pervasive in the platform economy.

Indeed, algorithmic management entangles with managerial surveillance and its boundaries, and as Ajunwa et al. (2017, 772) note, the modern 'limitless employee monitoring has rendered worker privacy illusory'. Research within organizations reports mixed results on people's acceptance of algorithmic recommendations or orders. Some research reports indicate that people trust algorithmic decisions more than humans, while some research suggests that people trust their own judgment more (Dietvorst et al., 2015). Several research reports in management and psychology report similar types of discrepancies. The differences in the research findings concerning algorithmic management may stem from the different types of work tasks and assignments tested and differences in the settings. Indeed, algorithmic management has been tested and analyzed in several controlled settings ranging from luggage screening at airports as a task performed by algorithms (Boskemper et al., 2021), to predicting personnel selection for interviews done by algorithms (Williams et al., 2018).

The airport luggage-sorting task may be perceived as a minor mechanical skill that can easily be performed and supervised by algorithms. The latter example, selection of persons for personnel recruitment interviews, is usually perceived as requiring human skills which cannot be performed or supervised by algorithms. Yet, increasingly in tasks that emphasize mainly mechanical skills, people trust algorithmics in equal amount as to humans (e.g., Williams et al., 2018; Irani, 2013, 2019). On the other hand, the more the tasks require human skills, people trust algorithmic decisions less. Indeed, as several researchers point out, algorithms are written and combined by humans, and thus they reflect elements of discrimination in our societies (Irani, 2019; Ajunwa, 2018). Algorithms may iterate and reiterate the elements of discrimination and societal injustice due to not being able to 'understand' which past outcomes might work as reliable indicators. Using robotic process automation (RPA), which substitutes for humans in highly repetitive tasks, may eliminate errors and improve the speed of performing tasks but does not necessarily remove biased assumptions in the performance of tasks (Jesuthasan and Boudreau, 2022; Durán and Jongsma, 2021; Susskind and Susskind, 2015).

Computers and programs 'learn the prejudices' when humans write the codes. The key question is what constitutes unacceptability in terms of algorithmic decision making and surveillance, which should be decided before implementing an algorithm. Often these biases become visible only after complaints, misjudgments, or research reports identifying such issues (Ball et al., 2019; Ajunwa et al., 2017; Manokha, 2020; De Moya and Pallud, 2020). Understanding the use of algorithms in their larger context is equally crucial in light of the variety of their implementation. As Ball (2010, 88) notes, 'The workplace surveillance can take social and technological forms. Personal data gathering, Internet and email monitoring, location tracking, biometrics, and covert surveillance are all areas of development'. What use and practical consequences these forms of surveillance have in workplaces depend on the organizational culture and practices (e.g., Brause and Blank, 2020).

Governance by algorithms in working life refers usually to automated governance taking place on/through labor platforms. It also includes management of labor within companies by algorithms, for example, through automated rating systems (Ball, 2010; Rosenblat, 2019). The implications of algorithmic management and workplace surveillance for workers' income and autonomy, in general, have become highly important questions when the inequalities within labor, and the future of labor relations vis-á-vis algorithmic management are analyzed (Wood et al., 2018; Seaver, 2017). As stated by Katzenbach and Ulbricht (2019) the forms and practices of algorithmic governance are multiple (Choung et al., 2022). Despite the juxtaposition with digital Taylorism, algorithmic governance does not follow one functional path thriving for optimization and efficiency but is rather dependent on contextual aspects when taken into practice.

Available technologies and management culture matter the most, but the current working climate in any public or private organization emphasizes individual measurement rather than that of a group as a whole. Hence, the management usually works on a basis of individual monitoring, where algorithmic governance has already impregnated management practices.

Digital governance and surveillance are seen as normal, taken-for-granted elements in contemporary working life. Employees indeed expect to have their performance rated and reviewed and information gathered as part of good managerial governance practices. Research reports note, however, that if the employee is measured as part of a group, rather than as an individual, monitoring may indeed be less stressful for the individual (Ball, 2010), while direct comparisons within the group may be more stressful than evaluations that focus on individual aspects.

The power of digital data is in its capacity to homogenize and efficiently measure, monitor, and classify those individuals whose data is available. The increasing use of data in management within organizations based on expertise and datafication may, however, also support nonsensitive ways of managing diversities and people. It is evident that organizations learn from the data they gather – not only in terms of capitalizing data but also of evolving their own functions with the help of data. It may be relevant to ask questions regarding who leads the learning and what the places are for organizations in the technological quagmire. How do organizations develop their activities and skills base?

Algorithms and skills

Digital technologies and their social and economic realizations, such as platforms, not only affect employment shifts and organizing of work but also shape the skills needed at work. Contemporary working life assumes constant renewal of workers' skills amidst technological changes. Platforms as a new economic organizing model and algorithms, together with big data, cloud computing, and AI, are changing the contemporary landscape of working life. Technology is a powerful agent that drives working-life changes and establishes and sets the pace for new skill requirements. Uses of advanced data analytics and algorithms bring forward several questions of expertise and skills needed to operate and manage, for example, the analyses of complex and large data sets, which are gathered, analyzed, and applied in many fields of society and economy. The learning-at-work has become increasingly important but simultaneously it has also become a subject of several tensions. An important aspect of the contemporary and future workforce is who has the responsibility and the means to take care of the renewal of skills.

There is evidence (Fernández-Macías and Hurley, 2016) that the skills development with technology is not one-dimensional; instead, contradictory developments take place simultaneously: the use of computers has grown in all occupational groups, but computerization has had an ambivalent effects in terms of routine work and employment. The analysis of data from the European Working Conditions Survey (EWCS) shows that repetitiveness and standardization of work tasks tended to increase rather than decrease within most occupations, despite a clear decline in employment in routine occupations. Macro-level analysis shows that computerization is associated with the increase of standardization in many occupations (Fernández-Macías et al., 2022; McAfee and Brynjolfsson, 2017); the service sector in particular usually shows increasing standardization within economies.

The new platforms of work that grow in importance and create demand for new capabilities and tasks and skilled jobs (McAfee and Brynjolfsson, 2017) inevitably change educational institutions and their learning cultures, as also the wider learning cultures. They also drastically change the ways the experts think of their own expertise and the upgrading of it (Bollmer, 2018; Billett, 2017). For example, platform workers as freelancers and their complex cultural belonging (or not belonging) to some educational realm is one of the major tensions that will be faced by future organizations and their cultures. It can be justifiably asked, how to define, govern, and contour the work culture if the work consists only of online screen work and future refinements of it. Changes in skills requirements have significant effects on both organizations and individuals, bringing and reinforcing techno-cultural and economic tensions and inequalities such as un(der)employment or marginalization, either in the workplace or more generally in labor markets. Also important are the cultural drivers of technological development; technologies for work interact with the culture of working life in their places of origin, requiring either adoption, adaptation, or rejection of possibly incompatible techno-cultural expectations.

For most expert work tasks, the development of AI has overall spurred optimism regarding the future possibilities within the widening of professions, despite the shrinking of some work tasks across occupations and professions. With various kinds of technologies woven into society and its infrastructure, it is important to address the ethical and societal challenges that can arise from the development of these technologies at large. These challenges and their transparency are especially pertinent in relation to innovations and expert work around them. Technologies and technological operations reclaim extensive new areas of human expertise, and social interaction. The innovative new tasks available with the growing complexity of technology do demand upskilling of competencies in most professions. Algorithms, as part of any program, are part of the increased need for upskilling of competencies. As in most jobs, the request for transparency of technology, often called algorithmic accountability, is difficult to fulfill, often simply because algorithms are business secrets. Furthermore, knowledge of the content of an algorithm does not guarantee an understanding of its complex effects (see Neyland, 2019).

The skills requirements at work now and in the future are not fully separable from the institutions that provide those skills, and their cultures. Tensions and inequities arise when skill requirements and provision mismatch. Importantly, present dynamics emphasize that educational systems and workplaces (organizations) need to rethink and transform the ways in which skills and competencies are cultivated, especially given the difficulty of predicting specific future skill requirements. Addressing this requires learning to become part of working life culture, and vice versa, work cultures (including organization cultures) need to adopt learning as an integral part of their culture. Answers relate to technology as an aid, tool, and also as a vehicle for change – including in learning environments, where technological change requires new cultures of learning within and around organizations. The encounters and entanglements of algorithms in everyday life are now familiar, and the grand narrative of algorithms as 'closest working buddies' is reality in many professions already.

References

Acemoglu, D. and Pischke, J. (1999). Beyond Becker: Training in Imperfect Labour Markets. *The Economic Journal*, 109(453), pp. 112–142. doi:10.1111/1468-0297.00405.

Ajunwa, I. (2018). Algorithms at Work: Productivity Monitoring Applications and Wearable Technology as the New Data-Centric Research Agenda for Employment and Labor Law. *Saint Louis University Law Journal*, 63(1), pp. 21–54.

Ajunwa, I., Crawford, K. and Schulz, J. (2017). Limitless Worker Surveillance. *California Law Review*, 105(1), pp. 735–776.

Aloisi, A. (2015). Commoditized Workers the Rising of On-Demand Work, a Case Study Research on a Set of Online Platforms and Apps. *SSRN Electronic Journal*, 37(3). doi:10.2139/ssrn.2637485.

Ball, K., Bellanova, R. and Webster, W. (2019). Surveillance and Democracy. In: K. Ball and W. Webster, eds., *Surveillance and Democracy in Europe*. London: Routledge, pp. 1–15.

Bannerman, S. (2018). Relational Privacy and the Networked Governance of the Self. *Information, Communication & Society*, 22(14), pp. 2187–2202. doi:10.1080/1369118x.2018.1478982.

Becker, G. (1975). *Human Capital: A Theoretical and Empirical Analysis*. Chicago: The University of Chicago Press.

Billett, S. (2017). Subjectivity and Human Resource Development a Quest for Intersubjectivity. In: M. Lee, K. Black, R. Warhurst and S. Corlett, eds., *Identity as a Foundation for Human Resource Development*. New York: Routledge, pp. 47–66.

Bollmer, G. (2018). *Theorizing Digital Cultures*. London: SAGE.

Boskemper, M.M., Bartlett, M.L. and McCarley, J.S. (2021). Measuring the Efficiency of Automation-Aided Performance in a Simulated Baggage Screening Task. *Human Factors: The Journal of the Human Factors and Ergonomics Society*, 64, pp. 945–961. doi:10.1177/0018720820983632.

Brause, S.R. and Blank, G. (2020). Externalized Domestication: Smart Speaker Assistants, Networks and Domestication Theory. *Information, Communication & Society*, 23(5), pp. 751–763. doi:10.1080/1369118x.2020.1713845.

Bravo, E. (2015). Deskilling, Up-Skilling or Reskilling? The Effects of Automation in Information Systems Context. In: *Proceedings of the 21st Americas Conference on Information Systems, AMICS 2015*. Puerto Rico: AMICS, pp. 1–17.

Casilli, A. and Posada, J. (2019). The Platformization of Labor and Society. In: M. Graham and W.H. Dutton, eds., *Society and the Internet. How Networks of Information and Communication Are Changing Our Lives*. Oxford: Oxford University Press, pp. 293–306.

Cheney-Lippold, J. (2019). *We Are Data: Algorithms and the Making of our Digital Selves.* New York: New York University Press.
Choung, H., David, P. and Ross, A. (2022). Trust in AI and Its Role in the Acceptance of AI Technologies. *International Journal of Human – Computer Interaction*, pp. 1–13. doi:10.1080/10447318.2022.2050543.
Codagnone, C., Karatzogianni, A. and Matthews, J. (2018). *Platform Economics: Rhetoric and Reality in the 'Sharing Economy'.* Bingley: Emerald Publishing Limited.
Couldry, N. and Mejias, U.A. (2018). Data Colonialism: Rethinking Big Data's Relation to the Contemporary Subject. *Television & New Media*, 20(4), pp. 336–349. doi:10.1177/1527476418796632.
Davies, H.C. and Eynon, R. (2018). Is Digital Upskilling the Next Generation Our 'Pipeline to Prosperity'? *New Media & Society*, 20(11), pp. 3961–3979. doi:10.1177/1461444818783102.
Delfanti, A. (2019). Machinic Dispossession and Augmented Despotism: Digital Work in an Amazon Warehouse. *New Media & Society*, 23(1), pp. 39–55. doi:10.1177/1461444819891613.
Delfanti, A. and Frey, B. (2021). Humanly Extended Automation or the Future of Work Seen through Amazon Patents. *Science, Technology, & Human Values*, 46(3), pp. 655–682. doi:10.1177/0162243920943665.
De Moya, J.-F. and Pallud, J. (2020). From Panopticon to Heautopticon: A New Form of Surveillance Introduced by Quantified-Self Practices. *Information Systems Journal*, 30(6). doi:10.1111/isj.12284.
Dietvorst, B.J., Simmons, J.P. and Massey, C. (2015). Algorithm Aversion: People Erroneously Avoid Algorithms After Seeing Them Err. *Journal of Experimental Psychology: General*, 144(1), pp. 114–126. doi:10.1037/xge0000033.
Dietz, D. and Zwick, T. (2020). Training in the Great Recession – Evidence from an Individual Perspective. *Jahrbücher für Nationalökonomie und Statistik*, 240(4), pp. 493–523. doi:10.1515/jbnst-2018-0072.
Doherty, O. and Stephens, S. (2021). The Skill Needs of the Manufacturing Industry: Can Higher Education Keep Up? *Education + Training*, 63, pp. 632–646. doi:10.1108/et-05-2020-0134.
Duggan, J., Sherman, U., Carbery, R. and McDonnell, A. (2020). Algorithmic Management and Appwork in the Gig Economy: A Research Agenda for Employment Relations and HRM. *Human Resources Management Journal*, 30, pp. 114–132.
Durán, J.M. and Jongsma, K.R. (2021). Who Is Afraid of Black Box Algorithms? On the Epistemological and Ethical Basis of Trust in Medical AI. *Journal of Medical Ethics*, 47, pp. 329–335. doi:10.1136/medethics-2020-106820.
Eurostat. (2016). *Classification of Learning Activities.* Luxembourg: Publications Office of the European Union.
Fernández-Macías, E., Bisello, M., Peruffo, E. and Rinaldi, R. (2022). Routinization of Work Processes, De-routinization of Job Structures. *Socio-Economic Review*, mwac044. https://doi.org/10.1093/ser/mwac044.
Fernández-Macías, E. and Hurley, J. (2016). Routine-Biased Technical Change and Job Polarization in Europe. *Socio-Economic Review*, 15(3), pp. 563–585. doi:10.1093/ser/mww016.
Fialho, P., Quintini, G. and Vandeweyer, M. (2019). *Returns to Different Forms of Job Related Training: Factoring in Informal Learning.* [online]. Available at: www.oecd-ilibrary.org, 231. doi:10.1787/b21807e9-en.

Fiser, H.L. and Hopkins, P.D. (2017). Getting Inside the Employee's Head: Neuroscience, Negligent Employment Liability, and the Push and Pull for New Technology. *Boston University School of Law Journal of Science & Technology Law*, 44(1), pp. 59–61.

Ford, J.K., Baldwin, T.T. and Prasad, J. (2018). Transfer of Training: The Known and the Unknown. *Annual Review of Organizational Psychology and Organizational Behavior*, 5(1), pp. 201–225. doi:10.1146/annurev-orgpsych-032117-104443.

Gerber, C. and Krzywdzinski, M. (2019). Brave New Digital Work? New Forms of Performance Control in Crowdwork. In: S. Vallas and A. Kovalainen, eds., *Work and Labor in the Digital Age*. Bingley: Emerald Publishing, pp. 121–143 (Research in the Sociology of Work, Vol. 33).

Gillespie, T. (2014). The Relevance of Algorithms. In: T. Gillespie, P.J. Boczkowski and K. A. Foot, eds., *Media Technologies: Essays on Communication, Materiality and Society*. Cambridge: The MIT Press, pp. 167–194.

Gorwa, R. (2019). What Is Platform Governance? *Information, Communication & Society*, 22(6), pp. 854–871. doi:10.1080/1369118x.2019.1573914.

Gray, M.L. and Suri, S. (2019). *Ghost Work: How to Stop Silicon Valley from Building a New Global Underclass*. Boston: Houghton Mifflin Harcourt.

Hochschild, A.R. (1983). *The Managed Heart: Commercialization of Human Feeling*. Berkeley: University of California Press.

Irani, L. (2013). The Cultural Work of Microwork. *New Media & Society*, 17(5), pp. 720–739. doi:10.1177/1461444813511926.

Irani, L. (2019). *Chasing Innovation: Making Entrepreneurial Citizens in Modern India*. Princeton, NJ and Oxford: Princeton University Press.

Jesuthasan, R. and Boudreau, J.W. (2022). *Work Without Jobs: How to Reboot Your Organization's Work Operating System*. Cambridge: The MIT Press.

Katz, L.F. and Krueger, A.B. (2017). *The Rise and Nature of Alternative Work Arrangements in the United States, 1995–2015*. Cambridge: National Bureau of Economic Research.

Katzenbach, C. and Ulbricht, L. (2019). Algorithmic Governance. *Internet Policy Review*, 8(4). doi:10.14763/2019.4.1424.

Kitchin, R. (2016). Thinking Critically About and Researching Algorithms. *Information, Communication & Society*, 20(1), pp. 14–29. doi:10.1080/1369118x.2016.1154087.

Kovalainen, A., Vallas, S.P. and Poutanen, S. (2020). Theorizing Work in the Contemporary Platform Economy. In: S. Poutanen, A. Kovalainen and P. Rouvinen, eds., *Digital Work and Platform Economy*. New York: Routledge, pp. 31–52.

Krittanawong, C. (2018). The Rise of Artificial Intelligence and the Uncertain Future for Physicians. *European Journal of Internal Medicine*, 48, pp. e13–e14. doi:10.1016/j.ejim.2017.06.017.

Krzywdzinski, M. and Gerber, C. (2021). Between Automation and Gamification: Forms of Labour Control on Crowdwork Platforms. *Work in the Global Economy*, 1(1), pp. 161–184. doi:10.1332/273241721x16295434739161.

Li, L. (2022). Reskilling and Upskilling the Future-Ready Workforce for Industry 4.0 and Beyond. *Information Systems Frontiers*, 16 p. https://doi.org/10.1007/s10796-022-10308-y.

Manokha, I. (2020). The Implications of Digital Employee Monitoring and People Analytics for Power Relations in the Workplace. *Surveillance & Society*, 18(4), pp. 540–554. doi:10.24908/ss.v18i4.13776.

Mayer-Schönberger, V. and Cukier, K. (2013). *Big Data: A Revolution That Will Transform How We Live, Work and Think*. London: John Murray.

McAfee, A. and Brynjolfsson, E. (2017). *Machine, Platform, Crowd: Harnessing Our Digital Revolution*. New York; London: W.W. Norton.

Meijerink, J., Boons, M., Keegan, A. and Marler, J. (2021). Algorithmic Human Resource Management: Synthesizing Developments and Cross-Disciplinary Insights on Digital HRM. *The International Journal of Human Resource Management*, 32(12), pp. 1–18. doi:10.1080/09585192.2021.1925326.

Mejias, U.A. and Couldry, N. (2019). Datafication. *Internet Policy Review*, 8(4). doi:10.14763/2019.4.1428.

Menchik, D.A. (2020). Moving from Adoption to Use: Physicians' Mixed Commitments in Deciding to Use Robotic Technologies. *Work and Occupations*, 47(3), pp. 314–347. doi:10.1177/0730888420919792.

Möhlmann, M., Zalmanson, L., Henfridsson, O. and Gregory, R.W. (2021). Algorithmic Management of Work on Online Labor Platforms: When Matching Meets Control. *MIS Quarterly*, 45(4), pp. 1999–2022. doi:10.25300/misq/2021/15333.

Nedelsky, J. (2013). *Law's Relations: A Relational Theory of Self, Autonomy, and Law*. New York: Oxford University Press.

Neyland, D. (2019). *The Everyday Life of an Algorithm*. Cham: Springer International Publishing. doi:10.1007/978-3-030-00578-8.

Nippert-Eng, C. (2010). *Islands of Privacy*. Chicago: University of Chicago Press.

OECD. (2019). *The Future of Work*. Paris: OECD Publishing.

OECD. (2021). Training in Enterprises. In: *Getting Skills Right*. Paris: OECD Publishing. doi:10.1787/7d63d210-en.

Oxford English Dictionary. (2021). *Oxford English Dictionary*. Oxford: Clarendon Press.

Poutanen, S., Kovalainen, A. and Rouvinen, P. (2020). *Digital Work and the Platform Economy: Understanding Tasks, Skills and Capabilities in the New Era*. New York: Routledge; Taylor & Francis Group.

Rahman, H. (2019). *Invisible Cages: Algorithmic Evaluations in Online Labor Markets*. Stanford: Stanford University ProQuest Dissertations Publishing.

Rosenblat, A. (2019). *Uberland: How Algorithms Are Rewriting the Rules of Work*. Berkeley: University of California Press.

Rosenblat, A. and Stark, L. (2015). Uber's Drivers: Information Asymmetries and Control in Dynamic Work. *SSRN Electronic Journal*, 10(27). doi:10.2139/ssrn.2686227.

Schor, J.B. and Vallas, S.P. (2021). The Sharing Economy: Rhetoric and Reality. *Annual Review of Sociology*, 47(1), pp. 369–389. doi:10.1146/annurev-soc-082620-031411.

Schwab, K. and Zahidi, S. (2020). *The Future of Jobs Report 2020. World Economic Forum*. World Economic Forum. Future of Jobs. Available at: https://www3.weforum.org/docs/WEF_Future_of_Jobs_2020.pdf.

Seaver, N. (2017). Algorithms as Culture: Some Tactics for the Ethnography of Algorithmic Systems. *Big Data & Society*, 4(2). doi:10.1177/2053951717738104.

Shestakofsky, B. (2017). Working Algorithms: Software Automation and the Future of Work. *Work and Occupations*, 44(4), pp. 376–423. doi:10.1177/0730888417726119.

Sienkiewicz, L. (2021). Algorithmic Human Resources Management – Perspectives and Challenges (Universitatis Mariae Curie-Sklodowska). *Annales Oekonomia. Sectio H.*, 55(2), pp. 95–105.

Susskind, R.E. and Susskind, D. (2015). *The Future of the Professions: How Technology Will Transform the Work of Human Experts*. Oxford; New York: Oxford University Press.

Toyoda, Y., Gale, L. and Gratch, J. (2020). The Effects of Autonomy and Task Meaning in Algorithmic Management of Crowdwork. In: *Proceedings of the 19th International*

Conference on Autonomous Agents and Multiagent Systems (AAMAS 2020). Auckland: AAMAS, pp. 1404–1412.

Vähämäki, M., Kuusi, T., Laiho, M. and Kulvik, M. (2020). The Road to Productivity with Automatization: Dialogue Between the Experienced and Measured. In: S. Poutanen, A. Kovalainen and P. Rouvinen, eds., *Digital Work and the Platform Economy: Understanding Tasks, Skills and Capabilities in the New Era*. New York: Routledge, pp. 116–141.

Van Lancker, W. (2012). The European World of Temporary Employment. *European Societies*, 14(1), pp. 83–111. doi:10.1080/14616696.2011.638082.

Walsh, M. (2019). *The Algorithmic Leader: How to Be Smart When Machines are Smarter Than You*. Vancouver: Page Two Books.

Williams, B.A., Brooks, C.F. and Shmargad, Y. (2018). How Algorithms Discriminate Based on Data They Lack: Challenges, Solutions, and Policy Implications. *Journal of Information Policy*, 8(1), p. 78. doi:10.5325/jinfopoli.8.2018.0078.

Willson, M. (2017). Algorithms (and the) Everyday. *Information, Communication & Society*, 20(1), pp. 137–150. doi:10.1080/1369118x.2016.1200645.

Wood, A.J., Graham, M., Lehdonvirta, V. and Hjorth, I. (2018). Good Gig, Bad Gig: Autonomy and Algorithmic Control in the Global Gig Economy. *Work, Employment and Society*, 33(1), pp. 56–75. doi:10.1177/0950017018785616.

World Bank. (2019). *World Development Report 2019: The Changing Nature of Work*. Washington, DC: World Bank. Available at: https://openknowledge.worldbank.org/handle/10986/30435.

World Bank. (2021). TCdata360 – Open Trade and Competitiveness Data. Share of Workforce Employed in Knowledge-Intensive Activities. *Worldbank.org*. [online]. Available at: https://tcdata360.worldbank.org/ [Accessed: 12 Jul. 2021].

Yeung, K. (2017). Algorithmic Regulation: A Critical Interrogation. *Regulation & Governance*, 12(4), pp. 505–523. doi:10.1111/rego.12158.

Zuboff, S. (2019). *The Age of Surveillance Capitalism: The Fight for a Human Future at the New Frontier of Power*. New York: Public Affairs.

3 Introducing platforms as new economic mode

Macro-level background to the rise of platforms

It is increasingly important to analyze the close connections between contemporary forms of platform economies and the new forms of work, both conceptually and empirically, in order to understand how the three interconnected phenomena of work, jobs, and tasks are organized anew in the digital society and economy. The narratives of how contemporary professions and occupations are changing presume a close linkage to societal and economic changes. As described in Chapter 2, the relationship between technologies and work is complex, and warrants detailed analysis to avoid the technological determinism and 'solutionism' that so often governs the debate.

The spread of the global on-demand economy and platform economy has triggered debate among researchers and legal and political decision-makers across the world on the definitions of platform work and the contours of work in general, and paid work in particular. The aspects that relate to the types of employment, and both the wider societal and the individual effects of short-termism and gig work, are part of new platform work – its possibilities and requirements. Short-termism, intermittent jobs, fixed-term contracts, fixed-term employment patterns, part-time jobs, and other deviations from the 'normalcy' of full-time employment have always been part of labor use in the market economy, with the share of these forms of employment to total employment varying. Regulatory aspects are another component of the debate; these relate to increased monitoring through algorithmic management, excessive working hours, overall safety at work, and new types of *contracted dependencies* that platforms use as a form of management for new forms of working in the platform economy. These aforementioned issues also demand a new look at what work 'partnership' with digital monopoly might entail.

There are macro-level patterns that are slow in change, but in the long run, any major change at the macro level in job structures is technology driven. This does not indicate technological determinism, but rather, emphasizes a deeper understanding of how technologies become absorbed into existing

DOI: 10.4324/9781351038546-3

jobs and work, including occupations and professions. Alongside technologies, other drivers of change in employment patterns, structures, and number of jobs include climate change, various forms of migration, and worldwide demographic shifts (ILO, 2021). All these major aspects affect also our ability to earn a living and work and what is possible therein.

In projecting future employment patterns, rather than focusing on technologies' direct effects on the number of jobs across industries or nations, an alternative approach is to consider the overall growth of flexible and temporary work patterns as well as growth in the forms of nonstandard employment. These patterns are expected to prevail in the near future, and are likely to be followed by reduced social protection and growth in job insecurity. As unemployment may grow in some specific occupational groups strongly affected by technological progress, over time, there will be general shifts to other educational fields, leading to other types of work opportunities. The differences in the stability of work positions and employment positions have been relatively persistent at a societal level across educational levels, qualifications, jobs, and occupations, for example. Professional and clerical jobs currently form the largest single occupational stratum in developed economies, and occupations are still strong determinants of which skills, knowledge, and abilities are utilized at work (Tholen, 2019), albeit increasingly affected by technologies. At a societal level, there is an evident correlation between work career and education type. However, increasingly, educational credentials serve also as signifiers of capability to perform multiple roles, rather than as functioning only as a direct sign of work skills. These factors, combined with the macro-level phenomenon of rising precariousness arising from new forms of own-account working, self-employment, and restructuring due to digital transformation, the tapestry of the effects of technologies on employment patterns and future jobs will become more arbitrary than previously.

With the growth of digitalization, an argument has been made that labor markets at large but especially in Europe and North America are polarizing (Autor, 2013; Goos et al., 2014). Employment *polarization* is defined as job growth both in the upper socioeconomic echelon (high-paid occupations) and in the lowest echelon (low-paid jobs), but job declines in mid-paid jobs and occupational groups. One result of this division is the so-called hollowing-out of the middle class (Kurer and Gallego, 2019; Schettino and Khan, 2020). Why are the aspects of polarization and hollowing-out of the middle class of importance for the analysis of platforms and platform work? Especially for expert work, this question relates to the sites of work and their arrangements. Platforms and more generally platformization enable the decoupling of the workplace from provision of work, and organizational belonging and membership from work performance. In that sense, platformization in society changes many of the foundations of the social order.

Looking at macro-level research on polarization and occupational changes in Europe, research analyzing occupational changes in Germany,

Spain, Sweden, and the United Kingdom over a 20-year period, from the 1990s to 2015, shows that there has been general occupational upgrading much due to technology. Research reports analyzing the polarization thesis in European labor markets show that job growth has been by far the strongest in occupations with high job quality and weakest in occupations with low job quality, regardless of the indicator used, but with less of a polarization effect than expected (Oesch and Piccitto, 2019). Still, the polarization of jobs and their qualifications is an ongoing trend, even if the polarization of labor markets in Europe is not as sharp as it is in the US. Nevertheless, there are shared features: the more routine tasks an occupation comprises, the less complex it is and the lower its skill requirements are, which exposes the laborer to replacement (Fernández-Macías and Hurley, 2016; Kurer and Palier, 2019). Recent research from Europe also shows that the macro-level picture is changing, when considering the hollowing-out of the middle class – often but not necessarily following from the polarization of labor markets – in analyses of labor markets and social class. Measured by disposable household income, the middle class is decreasing not only in the US but also in several European countries, partially due to the diminishment of state subsidies of the welfare state (Piketty, 2014).

However, employment polarization happens slowly, over cohorts or even generations (Cortes, 2016; Kurer and Gallego, 2019). Due to the gradual nature of technology-induced occupational change, slowness of polarization, and the complexity of the underlying distributive processes, which are national by nature, it is difficult to forecast the precise impacts of technological change at the macro level. Technology use in general continues to be skills-biased, and in general, as technology spreads, the demand for jobs that require few qualifications shrinks.

What are platforms?

Digital platforms are basically business systems and governing systems that transform, control, innovate, interact, and accumulate. At their core, digital platforms are technological innovations that offer opportunities for other actors to join in. Beneath the surface, which may look like a company, platforms are powerful network actors that transform operations and market systems and make government's activities effective. By platform economy, most researchers refer to the birth, development, and spread of multisided markets, which can have direct (same-side) and/or indirect (opposite-side) network effects (Poutanen et al., 2020a). Due to efficiencies, the platforms can draw other actors into this data-driven ecosystem. All platforms share one commonality, which is the power of the platform owners (Kenney et al., 2020).

Network effects are crucial for understanding how platforms function and why they are so effective in spreading their activities and accumulating monetizable data and thoroughly commodifying the network. Although there is no single agreed-upon definition of the platform economy, the most common definition describes platforms as digital marketplaces where buyers and sellers meet. This definition covers not only economic or monetary actions, but also all types of exchange activities. A more complex definition of the platform economy takes into account the technological aspects that enhance current and create new economic and societal circumstances in which professions and occupations and their societal roles may develop differently than previously expected (Poutanen et al., 2020b). Platforms redefine through the categorical importance of technology the power balances among businesses, between businesses and governments and also between organizations and labor.

The explosion of digital platforms in the economy and society has justifiably raised the discussion of *platformization*, a model or formula of societal and economic development supported by a software-based infrastructure. An ecosystem develops through an assemblage of networked platforms, governed by a particular set of mechanisms, be it laws (the public sector), a market context (companies), or desirability of consumption (users). Thus, platformization may erase some of the distinctions between state, market, and civil society through similarities in operational logics and through leaning on private companies in information delivery, for example. The interoperability of the infrastructures of singular digital platforms brings out the network effects and underlines the understanding of platforms not only as single entities (firms or companies) but also as developing and evolving processes, that is, platformization, in which actors change and are attached to platforms in differing ways (Poutanen et al., 2020b). Within markets, digital platforms automate market exchanges and mediate social actions.

The vital infrastructure that platforms have built and their functions blur boundaries such as those between state and private technology firms. Platform firms have, through huge investments, helped build infrastructures such as data centers, cable systems (Plantin et al., 2016), and support for local and regional energy production and its development toward greener production. Social responsibility is displayed when interests are shared. The global platform corporations are increasingly drawing the attention of governments and supra-national bodies, such as the EU, to exert control over and collaborate within the digital infrastructures, on the one hand, and to strengthen individuals' right to protection in the digital society through data protection laws,[1] on the other.

Platforms create value in two principal ways: through transactions or through innovations (Cusumano et al., 2020; Evans and Gawer, 2016). Transactions are the market places for technologies, people, and services (Poutanen et al., 2020a). The more users sign in to the marketplace, the more successful the platform is. This development is different from the case of the innovation platforms where technology development takes place. Innovation platforms are most often hybrid platforms, open both for innovations and for consumer/product transactions (iPhone). Investment platforms have for their part widened financial technology into cloud computing and human–artificial intelligence (AI) interaction. Platforms evolve to the meta-level, consolidating activities and actions, and sharing and trading data even more efficiently. Platform logic can mean several things but in general refers to the technical capacity of 'unyielding local control and its consequential concentrations of global dominance by a handful of corporate actors' (Andersson Schwarz, 2017, 376). Platform logic can, for its part, trigger emergent effects on a trans- or interplatform scale. As it is no longer appropriate to name these metascales as meta-platforms, due to the renaming of Facebook as Meta Platforms Inc., the term 'trans-platforms' may do.

Platformization is not tied to a specific industry, such as media, nor is it an isolated case among other business logics, suitable best for some industries only. The pervasiveness of platforms is based on the fact that they spread efficiently as a more general business logic based on digitalization, and thus, they also spread the logic of the employment and recruitment models of platforms. For this reason, platformization has transforming power. Platforms reach out and readily include professionals as both core employees and work providers, or partners, working at, on, and through platforms. Additionally, professionalization of platform activities benefits platform companies, but as research shows, it also reinforces existing inequalities (Bosma, 2022).

Due to superior network effects, platforms are indeed considered the most important business model of the 21st century, and this business model is spreading and taking different modes and shapes. In some industries, platforms are becoming the prevailing business logic while in others, platforms are assimilated into existing venture models.

Platforms transforming work and professions

With the growth of the platform economy, new platform hubs and immaterial fields, and the rise of the global platform firms such as Google, Meta, Amazon, and alike, the transformation of work related to platforms is major and irreversible, rocking many of the ideas of what we generally consider as 'work'. 'Platform work' in the literature in general refers to a new form of organizing and mediating paid work and work tasks – gigs – through various digital platforms. Digital platforms include both labor platforms and platforms that mediate expertise and tasks, and enable gig activities but also business-to-business platforms, and sales of material goods and immaterial services. Digital labor platforms transform and organize digital marketplaces for those who seek a suitable worker or job provider, that is, a person with specified and predetermined skills. Equally, the platforms enable marketplaces for those individuals and/or businesses, who seek work tasks/gigs of specified nature. Marked differences between platform work and 'ordinary' work, as we know it, include the specified nature of work tasks, focus on payable and sellable units, whether immaterial or material work or goods and services, and noncommitment to traditional employment patterns, which include work-related practices such as learning and skills development specifically related to the performed work.

Another marked difference to 'ordinary' work is that within platform work, long-term contracts and corporation- or firm-level commitments to work providers, that is, to employees, are not present. Both direct employment and various forms of arms-length employment are part of the complex intertwined jobs, tasks, gigs, and work of whatever type that develop within platforms and relate closely to platforms. Some researchers view the focus only on employment in the platform economy as a 'mistake' (Kenney et al., 2020, 16), as so much of the work at platforms is not at all employment contract–based or related to collective employment. Nor are the platform jobs available regulated by the traditional employer–employee contracts, covering activities such as learning-at-work, holiday breaks, pension saving systems, maternity, and sickness leaves. These are not provided by contractual agreement or facilitated by internalized work culture. As paid employment is the prevailing model for labor demand-and-supply in most societies, many researchers relate the analysis of platform work to the questions of stability of labor markets, individual earning possibilities, and income stability; to work and labor cultures; and to individual earnings, which all direct the analyses closer to traditional work-related contracts, or lack of them. One example of the cost division is the stable costs of work equipment: most digital labor platforms see this as a cost that belongs to the work provider, not the work purchaser. The cost of providing and maintaining the equipment giggers and work providers need in order to work is on themselves (Drahokoupil, 2021).

The overwhelming majority of the research concerning work done at platforms and connected to platforms addresses the various forms of labor platform work, that is, on-line platform work, such as click work, micro-tasking, and expert work, or off-line location-based platform-mediated work, such as delivery work, ride-sharing, servicing, and platform-mediated domestic and care services. Location-based platforms offer services that are delivered and performed in or around local areas, but the mediation of the jobs and gigs takes place online and can thus be global. Digital labor platforms (DLPs) may be driving innovation in the allocation and arrangements of work, but they do change dramatically the earning logic in the labor markets. Digital labor platforms act as intermediaries for a large range and variety of activities, including freelance, contest-based, micro-tasks, taxis, delivery, home services, and professional services.

Why is it important to analyze these forms of work in the frame of and in relation to employment positions and not, for example, entrepreneurial positions? Among the several rationales, two most obvious ones come into focus: information asymmetries and compensation structures. The apps designed by platforms and used by platform companies produce information and power asymmetries between agencies. The asymmetries are constitutive in the business models of platform companies, and also constitutive for the platform business's ability to control its work providers. Second, the lack of transparency in price formation remains for the same reason: the ability to control the price mechanisms is crucial for most platform companies, which in three-sided markets brings forward the need to create and maintain opaqueness.

The contracts between self-employed work providers and purchasers of that work are about the value of the work performed, including the formal expenses. The pricing of work needs to include legally binding payments such as taxes, social security costs, and other formal obligations, which vary nationally but often include pension payments, as one example. When the price of the work follows the seemingly frictionless and presumably transparent market prices, which can be global, there is a tendency to set the price limit lower. As the unit of pricing is most often an hourly rate or a unit-based rate, the unit price should include the risk assessment and its realization in insurance and sick leave costs, or costs covering estimated taxation and insurance payments. Furthermore, any preparation of possible future outcomes, such as unemployment and pension for those in self-employment and in entrepreneurship, should be included in the pricing of work. The estimated value of the skills performed should be covered by the hourly income or per-assignment compensation.

Some digital platforms make the pricing of all service providers visible, thus forcing the work provider to price themself with the markets. While the unit price is comparable for the work purchaser, there are indirect costs that are not visible to the work purchaser, as these costs have no relevance in the transaction. The labor platforms mediate work the price of which does not cover all work-related risks, future costs, and valuation of work. On top of other costs, the person working through platforms is responsible for their own health and safety protection, as well as social and labor protection. Platform algorithms could easily cover such calculations (Adams Prassl et al., 2022), but algorithms are not employed by the work provider or the work purchaser, but by the platform. Those defined as self-employed cannot use the platform algorithms for their own benefit, but have to adjust their 'entrepreneurial freedom' to meet the requirements of the platform.

The autonomy and control that people working through platforms have over their tasks is often low, despite their being defined as self-employed, independent partners. The degrees of flexibility that exist depend on the platform and relate most often to flexibility of work time and schedule. In practice, however, flexibility of working time may still be limited, as labor platforms most often monitor working patterns closely, with more frequent participation often rewarded; as a result, people working through platforms may feel pressured to be constantly available (European Commission, 2021).

According to a recent report, the large majority of digital labor platforms depend on commissions as their primary source of platform revenue. The commission can be either a fee based on the service provider's fee, or a flat rate. The fee based on the service provider's fee is particularly common on freelancing service provision platforms. In simple tasks the platform charges can range between 20% and 35% of the fee, often without additional services, charged by the independent contractor, and on platforms that operate on contests (Rani and Furrer, 2021). In more complex services, skills-based industries, the charges can be higher, but the platforms provide additional services. Some platforms charge clients also an on-board fee and a separate subscription fee, to keep the activities ongoing and avoid ghost service providers and/or ghost service purchasers. In some cases, digital labor platforms generate income by charging customers and/or providers and also by offering additional paid services for people working through platforms, such as accounting services, loans, insurance premiums, etc. (Brancati et al., 2019; Fabo et al., 2017). The business logic of digital labor platforms can give a company a steady flow of income, which consists of various types of income based on three-sided markets, but revenue from commissioned service platformization can also be volatile.

Even if work activities on labor platforms at the European level are still relatively small when compared to volumes in the US or Asia, or indeed to paid employment in Europe, a European Commission report shows that in Europe digital labor platforms have grown rapidly in the last 5 years. The overwhelming power of the US and Asia in the global platforms is visible in the fact that European global on-location service mediating platforms have their offices in Europe, whereas global US- and Asian-based platforms in online services necessarily do not. In Europe, the estimate is that 90% of intermediated labor platform services are on-location services, taxi and delivery being the most important ones, followed by home services and professional services. Online services such as micro-tasking, freelance jobs, contest-based work, and medical consultations are still a small minority in terms of earned income and number of contractors.

For those who work in partnerships – provide their work – in activities that are mediated by the platform, the new types of recognition systems, such as labeling somebody a 'professional host' or 'verified professional', have become increasingly important within the platform ecosystem's value construction (Deboosere et al., 2019; Wachsmuth and Weisler, 2018). With these signifiers and assurances, the platforms are creating their own professional systems and these systems are part of the professionalization taking place on platforms, in different shapes and forms, such as stars, for instance, and also such as naming persons as 'professional hosts', 'five-star hosts', etc. Despite the professionalization processes taking place and qualification stamps given through platform partnering, platform income can be highly unstable and dependent on the forms of work performed on platforms, as well as dependent on external uncontrollable factors.

Digital platforms are indeed integrated at the core of the business or organizational activity in many global platform companies. Platforms are also revolutionizing both business logics and consumer markets (Kenney et al., 2020; Kenney and Zysman, 2019). Platforms are used to aid and make activities more effective, as used in public service logistics, for example (Jesuthasan and Boudreau, 2022). Despite the varied forms and contents of the platforms, they simultaneously organize; build new types of hierarchies; and network, monetize, and govern several activities beyond their core platform business. Thus, all these varieties of platform activities affect the ways in which work at digital platforms is organized and performed. Kenney et al. (2020) extend the idea of platform work and argue that it is a common and a mistake when considering work in the platform economy to consider it only in terms of employment, as the variation in the types of work is much larger than typical employment patterns suggest.

As an example, any sports stadium gigs – be they music, art, or commercial product launches – are huge productions, where social media presence and visibility – as one platform among others – is crucial to the success of the gig and its marketability. Viewers who participate in a gig, for their part, also actively participate in marketing activities and media and visibility spread, most often unintentionally. This participation takes place through participants' active social media accounts, such as Instagram, Twitter, Facebook, and TikTok. Through their active participation, participants plow cultural space for the platforms, and increase their power with their own cultural influencer capabilities. Through their active social media participation, participants simultaneously build brands and produce meanings that are not in the hands of the marketers and advertisers alone. Brands and products are co-produced by the very people who co-consume these branded products (Ritzer, 2015). Platforms capitalize on not only data obtained but also social media activities of individuals.

Categories of platform work

What happens to a profession when the organizing principles of the institutions wherein the profession is practiced are transforming? The privatization of the public services that many traditional professions – such as medical doctors, nurses, and dentists – have provided and the nascence of new organizational forms – such as platforms and entrepreneurship – change how professions are managed and classified within organizations.

Digital platform are new means of organizing professional work. Those who begin to do work done on and through such platforms most often give up salaried positions and the accompanying benefits, such as pensions and health insurance. Such professionals sometimes turn to entrepreneurship or, more often, become own-account or self-employed workers, which involves increased independence and very different kinds of challenges, commitments, control mechanisms, and dependencies compared to waged or salaried positions.

Platform work taxonomies are several (Vallas and Schor, 2020; Kenney and Zysman, 2019). The taxonomy presented by Kenney et al. (2020) draws specifically from the fact that platform ecosystems engage individuals, the vast majority of whom do not receive salaried compensation from platforms. These individuals are not employed by platforms and do not receive a regular salary from platforms, as would be the case in a regular employment position. Thus, measuring existing employment positions at platforms does not reflect income accumulation from work activities at or around platforms. The vast majority of those engaged with platforms and platform-mediated work receive income due to work tasks they perform at platforms or due to platforms. Only for a few is the compensation for the platform work based on an employment contract and salary compensation from the platform company. For the vast majority, the income accumulated at platforms is compensation from tasks and gigs, which can range from micro-tasks and micro-work, hourly work, or single gigs and tasks and their compensation to product or service gifting, for example (Vallas and Kovalainen, 2019).

For this reason, Kenney and Zysman (2019) divided the platform work according to income-earning possibilities and the types of work possibilities existing in the platform ecosystem. In this categorization of platform ecosystem work, three major categories exist, where different types of income possibilities can be differentiated according to their attachment to platformization. First, the actual *platform firms* directly employ and contract different types of work for the development and maintenance of platforms. Part of this work is under employment contracts, part of it is contracted otherwise. Second, as platforms function as three-sided markets, companies and corporations functioning on these markets are subject to platform rules and regulations. *Platform-mediated work* is contracted by firms and companies using platforms, and contracting takes place often as project work or via platform-contracted services and gigs. *Platform-mediated content creation* is a third category of work. It differs from previous ones, consisting of the possibility of creating a person's own or contracted content to media, social media, platforms, and other user-generated content uploaded to platforms for monetization and use.

The employees of platform firms fall into two types of employees: those of venture laborers (Neff, 2015; Neff et al., 2005) and those that can be called the creators of the actual platforms (Kenney et al., 2020). These two groups support and develop the platform firms, and work toward a better revenue model. Venture laborers are also innovators, and through platform venture labor, they monopolize a specific method of invention, such as, for example, the application of deep learning and neural networks to process the big data gathered through platforms, producing new combinations of the existing elements of data (see also Rikap and Lundvall, 2021).

The platform firms also work with contracted individuals that are providing services to the platform firm. Those working on short-term or temporary contracts do not participate in the core business of platforms but work with activities, as *data janitors* (Irani, 2015) doing coding, repairing websites, cleaning data, monitoring data activities, and organizing data. As Kenney et al. (2020) note, these temporary employees and contractors often work remotely, or if they work on-site with venture laborers, nearly always receive lower pay, fewer benefits, and less job security. Most of the platform data janitors are not employees, but work on various types of contracts.

Platform-mediated work differs from the work done by employees of platform firms by being only mediated by the platforms, not essentially attached to the actual platform. Still, it is part of the ecosystem of platforms, and its existence depends upon the platforms. Some researchers call organizations and individuals working closely with the platform and consenting to their rules and regulations as *platform complementators* (Kenney et al., 2020).

The platform-mediated work is dependent on the platform and has two distinctive forms of work activities involved. The first form relates to platform-mediated marketplace activities such as warehouse, logistics, and retailing work. Second, work consists of platform-mediated service activities, such as delivery work, courier work, gig work, or project work. All these forms of work have in common the combination of the features of projectification, short-termism, gigging, and contracted work. The provider can be corporate or individual contractor, and increasingly, digital intermediaries have stepped in to organize the provision of labor. These forms of platform-mediated work can be performed in differing ways, ranging from in-person services performed onsite, online, or offline to contracted services performed offline.

The third category of work, presented by Kenney et al. (2020) could be labelled as platform-mediated content creation. A large part, perhaps the majority, of content creation volume, is uncommissioned and uncompensated. This means that it does not necessarily have monetizable value. Content creation consists of user-generated content, freelancing, consignments, and other forms of data interactions (Kenney et al., 2020). Perhaps even more importantly, though, platform mediated content creation becomes important, as it enhances user interest, and with that, creates data. The data created by users in interactions become a monetizable asset for the platform companies. One example of such monetizable data is social media accounts.

When participating in gigs, the participants, through their active use of social media accounts actively perform (unpaid) work for the platform. The participation also creates data for use by the platform owners. This resembles the ideas of the social factory and the factory without walls (Negri and Newell, 2010). Both these concepts refer to immaterial forms of production by those who both produce and participate in consumption, that is, 'prosume' (Ritzer, 2015, 414). The immaterial forms of production take place in the *immaterial, services-based societal factory* that is run by platforms and social media, and which draws upon the general intellect, consumption power, and cultural interests of the population, relying on the 'swarm intelligence' of the wide population of social media users. Due to the platform logics, the vast majority of individuals receiving income are not employed by the platform firms. Ride-hailing companies do not employ riders as their employees or own cars or bikes, while marketplaces selling consumer products do not employ vendors, and employment platforms do not promise jobs; instead, they act like marketplaces for those seeking services and those offering services. Ritzer (2015) notes that the idea of the prosumer fits well with today's reigning neoliberal philosophy. Indeed, the concept of the prosumer matches well with the epistemic idea of platforms, whereby instantaneous consumption provides the ability to use services where and when needed.

Despite the income-generating effects of platforms for individuals, the stream of income for many is highly unstable. Here, the platforms are crucial, and at the same time uniquely positioned: to survive, platforms are dependent on consumer experiences. Platforms have to provide useful and user-friendly experiences. Not all platform companies are monopolies like Apple, Amazon, Facebook (Meta), and Google. However, building a monopoly is part of the business logic of platforms, when platforms expand from bilateral markets to multilateral markets, and increasingly, the traffic at platforms increases. With that, 'stickiness' becomes part of the platform growth. As Na and Ma (2021) explicate, the transfer costs from one platform to another are high, and therefore, dependence (or stickiness) allows the platform to have more users and grow its market share. Additionally, high-frequency data contribute to monopoly formation, and all platforms bank on the data giving them market superiority in many fields, as network effects. Hence, when platforms become monopolies, such as Uber, Didi (China), and Etsy, they shape the forms of work and the future of work.

All platform companies invest immensely in their technology infrastructure and cloud computing. The investments, combined with the network effects, draw other businesses to collaborate with the platform giants, and also feed into innovation ecosystems that are compatible with and reinforce the giant corporations' platform development. This so-called partner-based strategy allows partners to monetize on the open application programming interfaces, and thus, attract new developers and ideas to flourish. The overall strategy is to bring in new customers to platforms, for example, by making consumption more social (e.g., Instagram).

However, even if consumers are important as the original trigger for the platform economy to grow, for most platform companies, the key strategy is no longer the product or consumer orientation but the platform development and the platform business logic where data are the currency, co-produced by consumers and businesses alike. By making the platform interesting, necessary, expanding, and used, the platform companies monetize the data that streams through their platform. In that process, the elements for monetizing – the data – are brought to platforms by partners, consumers, workers, subcontractors, gig workers, and the self-employed – practically anyone who uses the platforms and works for them.

Earnings at platforms

As the business logic of the platform companies evolves, the work, jobs, and gigs around and within the platforms are bound to transform. Work contents, contracts, and earning logics have already been transformed by and within the platform companies, but also, along with the network effects, a similar type of development broadens into other spheres within the platform ecosystem. The dynamics in the contents of work and in employment patterns are exposed to technology change (Barley, 2020), as are arrangements of income generation due to platformization (Poutanen et al., 2020a).

Income generation for individuals in platform work takes place either through tangible, intangible, and individual work tasks, such as software development projects, or through very specific work tasks, such as the delivery of food, packages, or transfer services. The value of this work is naturally very different to the individual who performs the task and to the platform company. The value differs not only in the income-generation process for individuals and in the value-generation process for businesses, but also, more generally and more importantly, in the scaling of activities. The value of the work differs also according to the tasks, micro-works, or gigs performed. Much of the platform-mediated work is offline or online location-based, such as micro-tasking, home servicing, accommodation offering, or delivery work. All location-based platform work consists of individual tasks and gigs that have within the work process some aspect of freedom, which is in contrast to, for example, online click-work.

Empirical research on the income-generation effects identify insecurity, increased risk resulting from volatile income, lack of stability, and inability to plan for the future (Kessler, 2018; Rosenblat, 2019; Schor and Vallas, 2021). Freedom and possibilities offered by gig work were in some research reports expressed particularly in relation to and as reactions to previous personal life situations and earlier work-related experiences, such as constant traveling and commuting, work–life balance, and status in the previous work organization (Rosenblat, 2019). Some research on gig work and income report the existence of possibilities, opportunities, and freedom in the ways gigs can be performed, but these are not necessarily related to income generation. This flexibility has been reinvented by the rise of technology, and its short-termism is epitomized in the many manifestations of the gig economy.

When analyzing individualized narratives, gig workers' desire for flexibility is evident in many research reports: entrepreneurial aspiration seems to direct gig workers' strategies when they navigate their way through and gather working experience in the gig economy (Yasih, 2022). In a similar fashion to Indonesian gig workers, Spanish riders who deliver food and goods articulate their constant availability on platforms, agility, dependence of the platforms, and simultaneous freedom from regular work as adaptive individual strategies (López-Martinez et al., 2022). This echoes corporation advertising messages that platform partners are self-actualizing entrepreneurs, free to choose and work whenever they wish. In this conceptualization, there is no mention of the precarious work or worker associated with the gig economy. The individualized strategies play out as possible self-exploitation when individuals end up holding multiple jobs and working extra hours without rest in between shifts, as the case is for many online transportation drivers and riders globally, especially in the global South.

Taking a wider viewpoint to include workers who work as experts at platforms, the crucial question is whether the organization pays the income – or salary. From work providers' (workers') point of view, the question becomes reformulated as to whether the individual is seen by the company merely as a jobholder, a cost liability for the organization, and a holder of set qualifications for the job, which are bound to become outdated over time and which require updating from time to time. Alternatively, the question of who pays the worker might be reformulated as follows: is the worker regarded as having an array of possible skills/capabilities rather than being just a holder of a job (or a degree)? If the answer is the former, the individual has a more flexible identity and isolated entrepreneurialism, which is an admired quality in the process of neoliberal economic globalization. We discuss this in Chapter 6 in more detail.

In contemporary labor relations, new technologies create jobs, or rather, gigs, such as platform work. Labor platforms blur the legal notion of an employer–employee relationship (De Stefano, 2015). Work at and through platforms is not comparable to job contracts, and the labor market position is not the same either. Gigs differ and carry hidden or explicit educational qualification structures and employment experiences. Platform gigs based on high competence and specialized qualifications usually require skills obtained through education or long experience at work, which has provided in-house training for the tasks. These types of digital work platforms are web-based, often global, and offer freelance gigs or micro-tasks. Gigs for technical experts, software engineers, translators, or graphic designers may be deadline driven and require long waiting times without pay, endless bidding for gigs, and short-termism as structural features within the platform. There is often some resemblance between the gig offered and the skills and qualifications obtained, but not always. Click-work, for example, mechanical Turk type of work, does not necessarily require particular skills and classification of materials, but is often tedious with repetitive patterns and takes a lot of time.

Platforms, professions, and consumption

Why is the middle class and its position of any importance when the position and future of professions and occupations are addressed? There are several linkages between middle class, professions, and technological development. Macro-level labor market developments are connected to several other societal trends that, in turn, affect how the roles of professions and occupations develop in societies. First, the societal and economic importance of the middle class is everywhere connected to overall investments in education and the importance of education in society (Acemoglu and Zilibotti, 1997; Thewissen et al., 2015).

Second, the middle class, its size and wealth, is tightly connected to changing consumption patterns in societies, that is, first and foremost to the consumption of services. Consumption of services is the basis of most platform company service provisions, corporate and individual partnerships, and emergence of project and gig work. The importance of immaterial work is obvious in any social media and physical events, where participants are increasingly not passive participants but an active part of the value-creation process. However, to become a participant in value-creation process, there has to be consumption power. Work through active participation in social media accounts, etc. could be labeled as active production-and-consumption, 'prosumption', by which the platform economy offers value creation through prosumption for those who can afford it, mostly, the middle class. Purchasing power requires also some stability of income and jobs, overall trust in upward mobility, and an ability to plan future consumption.

Third, the importance of the middle class for societal stability is reflected in the national political climates and voting behaviors. This may seem at first far-fetched but the polarization of employment and decline of jobs in some sectors, prompted by technology development, profoundly concerns white-collar, middle-class occupations that consist of jobs in support office work (back-office jobs, e.g., personal assistants) and administration (HR, marketing, and accounting). If these jobs are less stable, it has been predicted that there will be political repercussions (Cortes, 2016). A large part of routine jobs consists of occupations that require formal education and some, or even ongoing, training. One of the questions for these routine jobs is whether they can be replaced by robots or not. Routine work tends to disappear also through 'natural' turnover, that is, there are fewer entry jobs for routine occupations and jobs, and higher exit rates from these jobs and occupations over time. These are the jobs at the 'fringes of the lower-middle class', as Kurer and Palier (2019, 5) note.

Research has shown that expanding middle-level occupations in many countries include the lower end of skilled workers in the service sector, and very often also low-quality jobs with precarious working conditions in routine skilled jobs and service sector jobs. It is assumed that the strongest political response at the macro level in societies might not be among those who are hardest hit in the labor market but among those who are most concerned about their abilities to maintain their status, economic wellbeing, and future prospects in the labor market (Im et al., 2019). Thus, the specific effects of technological innovations – stability of jobs and stable consumption power – are key to understanding their possible mediated political implications for the middle class. In this respect, platforms represent both possibilities and threats.

The complex macro-level picture of the connections between the future of work, the development of labor markets, and technologies does not change overnight. The shift may be gradual and it will most likely not be linear: there are forms of work that change, also without a technological nudge, and several factors from education to demographics have an effect on the labor market developments. Furthermore, the contemporary societal trend of blurring boundaries between workers, consumers, and digital markets reflect the micro-processes of what happens within the world of work, which has wider percussions and is connected to the macro level described earlier.

Why technology development is a threat to some jobs and not all jobs? One explanation relates to the routine tasks, such as invoices, payments, and account handlings that can be handled with machine learning and digitalization, as described earlier. Another explanation is more complex and relates to the ways technology becomes rooted in our everyday lives. Production and consumption become intertwined in many ways. We follow somebody, often a celebrity or social media influencer on social media accounts such as Twitter, Instagram, or Facebook, and often like or show our support to actions and activities of that person. Seldom do we come to think that by following and liking, and consuming the social media sites of a social media influencer or celebrity, we produce – without knowing – income to that person. Usually the social media person earns income or receives products or services based on numerical measures such as number of followers, likes, comments, and such. Inadvertently, we work as consumers – for our own pleasure – and as producers of income for the person we follow digitally.

This blurring of boundaries between consumer and producer has brought about co-creation ideologies and co-production thinking, visible especially in the rise of the *prosumption* and *prosumer*, interrelationships between production and consumption, and co-productive consumers and producers (Ritzer, 2015; Simon, 2015). This ideological turn of joint consumption and production blurs the boundaries between the production mode and the consumption mode.

The idea of prosumption echoes platform business logic in which those who need to earn an income through platforms are billed as business partners to platform companies. In this rhetoric, platform workers' skills, such as driving or cleaning, and owning a bike or a car have become gateways to entrepreneurial freedom and possibilities at platforms. Platform economy businesses, when targeting consumers and work providers whom they wish to have as partners, advertise with the idea of democratizing entrepreneurial possibilities, by making entrepreneurship ostensibly available for everybody. However, do platforms create entrepreneurs and incubate new businesses, and through them, create wealth, economic growth, and prosperity in ways that market economy theories assume? Does driving a car or riding a bike as a partner to a ride-hailing or food delivery monopoly corporation, or flat-renting as a partner to a global property-renting corporation create actual entrepreneurship in societies, sustainable businesses, and reasonable living income in the economies? Or is the platform economy about monetizing the data obtained by the platforms and reorganizing the capitalization of ownership anew, with low or no responsibilities for the work providers attached to platforms?

When we analyze the skilled group of work providers at platforms, professionals, and those with specialized skills and professional experience, we find slightly differing answers to the question of why they work at platforms compared to lower-skilled work of riders or cleaners. Research reports, as expected, show vast diversity of experiences among platform workers: in many interview-based studies, the results echo the view that some benefit while some suffer due to autonomy and flexibility (ILO, 2021; Piasna et al., 2022; Poutanen et al., 2020b; Wood et al., 2018). Autonomy and flexibility mean entirely different things to work providers with differing life situations. The varieties in individual responses, as described earlier, may reflect many issues ranging from life situation, work experiences, and prior labor market career to income needs and possibilities for alternative earnings. Surveys and job offer analyses (European Commission, 2021; Kässi et al., 2021) offer significant analyses of platform jobs offered and gigs available. However, snapshot surveys and one-country analyses often cannot be compared or lack longitudinal analysis by educational background, income, and work history.

The current transformations in the social, cultural, and economic modes of work reflect the complexity of income creation and work performance trajectories. How is it possible to secure updated skills for knowledge workers who do not work within the parameters of traditional jobs and work careers but undertake freelancing, gig work, and intermittent or fixed-period types of jobs? Loose commitments may mean that corporations do not get the best possible outcome from work; for workers, there is a huge discrepancy in working hours and actual hours used to search for the next gig differentiate hugely, and the notion of work–life balance, or a 5-day working week comprising 8 h a day, is not possible in platform work. Indeed, the financialization of immaterial work may require new types of corporations where capable and skilled individuals are attached only loosely, as they become social agents of their own commodification.

Financialization is here understood not as a single social process but rather as a means by which a social agency is transformed and reoriented (Haiven, 2014) toward platformization. Thus, financialization does not refer to the financial sector or financial corporations, nor to what political economists call the FIRE (financing, investments, and real estate sectors) sectors of the economy. Moreover, financialization does not refer to a discrete, single process; rather, it refers to processes that take form in rhizomatic manifestations in people's everyday lives. This aspect emphasizes the analysis of social and cultural practices, as bottom-up processes. The narratives, expressions, and metaphors used when talking about platform work, own identity, and position in that work are based on the cultural and social resources workers have as their repertoires. That there is resemblance in platform workers' and platform firms' repertoires comes as no surprise, as the language and rhetoric that platforms use is both persuasive and powerful. The strength of the persuasive invitation to partnership work is built on messages that distance the practices of platform work, such as zero waiting hours, online monitoring, dependencies of various sorts, constant bidding for gigs, etc., and that induce the entrepreneurial freedom to master own time and decisions. Income insecurity and fluctuation of the cash flow are two aspects that are not easily controlled in the entrepreneurial position, but they are seldom mentioned in the invitations for partnership.

New digital work at platforms

Almost all contemporary forms of work in the digital society include features originating from digital platforms, from the sharing economy to the gig economy, to the extent that these features have become almost intrinsic features of jobs, work, labor, and the everyday lives of individuals, shaping both work lives and everyday lives. Common digital markers of contemporary digital work are entrepreneurialism, micro-entrepreneurialism, self-employment, own-account working, holding multiple jobs, gig work, and hybrid work through various platforms. These features are united in the aim to reallocate and individualize risks related to the cost of work and labor, social security costs of workers, and training requirements and renewal of individuals' skills and human capital.

These features have been absorbed as part of the ordinary working life in many organizations, to the extent that management research and managerial practices have adopted the concept of *intrapreneurialism*, which is that some employees in organizations are considered as entrepreneurial by nature, or at least endowed with an entrepreneurial mindset. The normative traits and classifications are related to a desired 'intrapreneurial person' ranging from 'being active and forward-looking' to being 'passionate and exciting' (Jones, 2014, 40–41). These constructed features are assumed to lead to behavior that is desirable from a managerial point of view.

Many of these entrepreneurial postures and individualistic expressions have earlier been seen as contradictory and contrasted with the traditional positions in large organizations, and with that, shunned in managerial practices of corporations, unless they serve the greater corporate culture. However, with the erosion of 'standard' employment and the cultural processes accompanying the projectification of work and shifts in the roles and definitions of expertise in large corporations, the new labor market conditions emphasize self-branding as necessary and virtuous (Gershon, 2016, 2011; Vallas and Hill, 2018, Weil, 2009).

The concept of the 'intrapreneur' garners and epitomizes the neoliberalist ideas of self-branding within an organization and the idea of organizational entrepreneurialism within the organization. Individualism in this respect turns the self-branding that takes place within the limits of the organization into hyper-individualism (Hay, 2003; Lavrence and Lozanski, 2014;

Rose et al., 2006). In hyper-individualism, self-branding shifts the focus from *negative liberty*, which is seen as freedom from external restrictions, toward positive liberty, which is seen as freedom to enact one's potential in markets. This self-governance emphasizes how neoliberalism governs, by creating internalized control (Watts, 2021). The internalized control mechanism values certain elements such as self-sufficiency and personal freedom. Individuals are assumed to develop an *agency* within which they are encouraged to develop self-responsibility and self-discipline, skills, and capabilities that will help them to navigate economic and social precarity and internalize active agency positionality. The research in entrepreneurial studies is impregnated with assumptions that emphasize individual and agency within any organizational and institutional settings.

The conceptualization of self-branding presented earlier, as capitalized *currency of agency* within the larger organization, reformulates the understanding of work within the organization or corporation as a constant project-based selling of oneself to project teams. Within projects, team formation can resemble the formation of a baseball team at school: the best scorer gets picked first, and someone who never hits the ball remains lowest in the internal hierarchy. This conceptualization takes any organization expert work logic a step closer to platform logic for work, and raises the following questions. Why stay as an employee if you can become a partner? Why work for the goals of others in a large organization when you can work for yourself and your own goals alone?

Working at digital platforms is not all about working at online labor platforms. Nor does work at platforms consist solely of gig work. The hybrid work arrangements located in the ambiguous space between self-employment and standard employment have been labeled 'the gig economy' at large (Woodcock and Graham, 2020). As Woodcock and Graham (2020), and Poutanen et al. (2020b) note, as an elusive concept, the gig economy has come to manifest a variety of aspects to changing labor conditions: flexibility, additional income, short-termism, deteriorating labor conditions, and opportunities. First and foremost, these changing labor conditions share the transfer of the risk related to work, be it injury insurance, sick leave, pensions, parental leave entitlement, training and updating qualifications, or social security costs. Within the platform economy and gig economy, short-termism usually means that employees as gig workers or 'platform partners' receive only limited social benefits and entitlements, and the longevity of these relationships cannot be challenged by the work provider, gigger, or partner.

There are features that unite the work at platforms, and these are tightly entangled with the forms and varieties of value creation at platforms. One of these features is the *new precarity*, which is contrary to the idea of 'traditional' precarity being bundled with low or no educational and skills qualifications and weak work-related trajectories and labor market positions. The new precarity is often tied to the gig economy, but is relevant to all those who work or provide their expertise at platforms. Contracts for experts and nonskilled providers of work are based on single tasks, not continuity or the same known purchasers of the expertise in question. Bidding for jobs has to be undertaken separately for each gig. The individualization of the contracted work means that under the new precarity, everyone prepares their resume, makes a presentation, takes care of and buys the tools for the work, and takes care of any necessary retraining or skills update needed for the gigs.

The investment of own money into the entrepreneurial actions and activities incurs a risk but does not really encourage entrepreneurial and personal aspects of entrepreneurial effort – the service provisioning takes place at the platform, under the platform's guidance and format, and in the end, the platform has the final say whether the entrepreneurial individual is accepted to the platform or not. The personal profile does not guarantee activities, work, or gigs, as the competition for gigs is immense and often global by nature.

Another common feature of online work providers is *micro-entrepreneurialism*. Many online work providers perceive themselves as micro-entrepreneurs, not just because they use their own laptops and vehicles, and cover other costs, from office space to pensions and social security costs, but also for other reasons related to identity politics. In several studies in countries with low or nonexistent worker protection and little possibility for manual labor, micro-entrepreneurialism is found to be a better option than waged work. One of the reasons for the favorable attitude toward micro-entrepreneurialism in relation to gig work is that it is connected to the digital platform corporations through which services and expertise are offered.

The assumed status of a micro-entrepreneur may subjectively be valued higher than that of a manual laborer, for example, especially among those who work as micro-entrepreneurs, despite their low income and nonexistent work-related protection, for example (Yasih, 2022; Rosenblat, 2019; Prentice, 2017). Often times the entrepreneurial narratives that emphasize the individual agency, inadvertently promote the empowerment of micro-entrepreneur that is nowhere to be seen with gig work. Micro-entrepreneurship promotion encapsulates the neoliberal disposition of the self-regulating citizen-subject: entrepreneurial, adaptive, and self-reliant (Prentice, 2017). The research results are highly contextually dependent, but several ethnographic studies show the problems connected to micro-entrepreneurialism, and no conclusion can be drawn that those positions of micro-entrepreneurialism would be better by the objective standards for work (Hann and Parry, 2018; Parry, 2018). In an interview study of Indonesian motor-cycle drivers, they were more willing to define themselves as micro-entrepreneurs and partners rather than defining themselves as unskilled labor in an uncertain employment relationship, despite equally grim struggles for earnings in both positions (Yasih, 2022). This type of individual denunciation of the subordination position calls attention to the formation of entrepreneurial identity, in alignment with neoliberal tenets. The lack of opportunities is not solely about the necessity for entrepreneurial activity, but cuts deeper into the earning possibilities and identity formation of those who work, and seek an income. App-based economies often reduce wages, even if new opportunities for workers are created.

One of the reasons that platforms are assumed to have such a pervasive position is the strength and size of the *informal economy* and the lucrative potential platforms may have among those seeking jobs. The pervasiveness of the informal economy means not only a lack of formal employment but also the absence of unionism, as shown by Yasih (2022) in an analysis of Indonesian couriers, and by Zickuhr (2021), Callaci (2021), and Amrute et al. (2021a, 2021b) in studies on US cases of fissured workplaces. The term *fissured workplace* was introduced by Weil (2017) in his analysis of increasing short-termism and contracting out of jobs in firms. Following Weil's (2017) notion of the fissured workplace, it is obvious that the platform economy strengthens the erosion of the Fordist firm model. In this model, mass production required large corporations, and with it, the relative stability of employment contracts, clear hierarchies, and supervisory structures. These were more or less the normal business structure, and the firm gained its strength from developing a competent core workforce, even with unionized activities.

Platforms and apps operating at platforms have for their part eradicated these Fordist hierarchies within corporations and with that, the stability of jobs and positions in firms. With outsourced work, there are no internal training paths available for capable workers, and upward mobility within firms through training is no longer emphasized. When apps mediate work tasks and gigs, and allocate tasks and gigs through algorithms, and when they also control the performance of workers, giggers, and task performers, the organizational mediators, such as middle management and supervisors, are missing. Algorithmically governed structures and feedback have given entirely new features to the ideas of work and employment. The direction, allocation, and evaluation of work at platforms are accomplished digitally, with very little or no transparency and only very few opportunities for information negotiation.

Furthermore, geo-politics matters: the discrepancy between the global South and global North is growing with platform work. The platform work and new forms of work differ unambiguously in outcomes and in possibilities for earnings. Most of the job growth in many countries since the 2010s has been in nonstandard employment arrangements, part of a widening of job insecurity and worsening quality (Katz and Krueger, 2017). For many migrants, work at platforms may offer new possibilities for earning a living and working close to, or at the formal economy, as studies on cleaning work show (Gruszka et al., 2022). Meanwhile, many of the couriers of ride-hailing apps are migrants, or working-class people from the local area, and the majority perform such work full-time, as no other jobs are available (Greenhaus,

2019; Kessler, 2018). Gig work extends from any basic service to expert jobs and tasks, and refers increasingly to all types of app-based jobs and gigs.

Varieties of platform work

Prior to the growth of platformization and the development of app economies, technologies that transformed or changed industrial or service production did not 'decouple' work and workers from the organization where they worked. Because workers were connected to their organizational or institutional structures through their positions (Brynjolfsson and McAfee, 2014), their work changed – with the technologies – within the companies.

Platforms function differently from what we know of corporate businesses' business models, in particular regarding the division of work within organizations: platforms and apps mediate work tasks and gigs digitally, divide tasks in novel ways, and enable the performance of workers/task performers to be controlled through algorithmically governed structures that give work and employment entirely new features. In platform companies, the direction, allocation, and evaluation of work are all accomplished digitally, with very little transparency for the worker and only very few opportunities for information negotiation, for example.

Thus, platforms change work, both internally and externally, through marketplace interactions. In doing so, platforms reshape local and national economy structures. For example, the increasing centrality of platforms in the delivery of goods and services is changing the sectoral composition of local economies, such as shops, and may have hitherto unknown effects (Kenney et al., 2020; Kenney and Zysman, 2019). Digital platforms thus change the organization of work, and consumption – and thereby the essential parts of modern society. Even if these effects are mainly confined to the local and national levels, the repercussions are global.

More profoundly, platforms are also changing the cultural–societal foundations of the ideas of work, education, professions, and occupations. If work generated by platform companies is separated from the idea of a specific job or task, and employment contract within a given platform company and widened to include value creation, the concept of work would also expand to fields of value creation that either directly depend on the value of the work performed at platform, or depend on the value of the work performed to other users and advertisers around the platform. Hence, the work within the platform ecosystem and that done at the outskirts of the platform ecosystem are part of the value-creation system within and around platforms. In this way, the idea of platform work widens from direct income generation within the platform to value generation in and around the platform ecosystem (Kenney et al., 2020).

Platform-mediated work depends on the platform and its structure, rules, and regulations. In the value-creation ecosystem, platforms mediate work and generate income first through the marketplace sale of goods and services, and second, through contracting for labor activities. The income generated within the platform-mediated work depends on several matters that are not within the influence of the worker. Thus, earnings are precarious and subject to changes by the platform owner.

Platforms that mediate labor or work differ in terms of whether the work is online or offline. Either way, the work contracted through labor platforms can be considered temporary work or gig work. Both forms are without any of the characteristics of typical job contracts. Gig work at platforms is commissioned or contracted as own-account work or as work done by a partner who is assumed to work as a self-employed or own account worker. The partner can be referred to with a role-based term such as driver, or contractor, or more generally, as the case with experts, as freelancer. The gigs differ and can range from ride-hailing or delivery services to expert tasks mediated by expert platforms that either are or come close to profession-based platforms.

The temporariness of many work requirements, uncertainty about the need for continuity, and avoidance of indirect labor costs leads to gigs then to a gig economy. For the individual, the income from gigs most often is unstable, contingent, market driven, and dependent on the market situation. The gigs may require some formal qualifications, but the pay is not directly dependent on formal qualifications, rather on the nature of the task or gig as well as the market situation: where and which capable work providers are available and at what price.

The ecosystem around all the largest platforms includes, for example, gig workers who do not work directly for the platform but who may work as content creators for a company that needs a platform for visibility. This group of workers participates directly in content creation for the ecosystem companies, and indirectly create value for the platform company. This takes place with several variations of the income-generating processes, ranging from content uploads to user-generated content and data created through the use of the Internet and platforms, and also covering uncompensated user-generated content and data. Much of this work is done through gigs, partnering as an own-account worker or as a self-employed person. Among others, Cutolo and Kenney (2019) refer to the platform ecosystem members as *dependent entrepreneurs*. The concept of a dependent entrepreneur is somewhat problematic, as entrepreneurial freedom is highly limited and the dependency is in principle limitless, as no collaborative ties exist if the platform does not agree to accept the content produced. Thus, renaming gig work, freelancer work, contracts, and own-account working with different, perhaps more entrepreneurial titles does not change the categorical aspects of the work and its nature.

What happens to work in the platformization?

What happens when work is no longer tightly connected to a job, organization, or institution, but rather, to individuals and their marketable skills and capabilities? It is correct to say that platforms are currently reorganizing the economic world and, by extension, work (Poutanen et al., 2020b). Platforms have already dramatically enhanced opportunities for all types of freelancing and for freelancers with new content delivery platforms, lowering entry barriers and widening markets. In so doing, global inequalities of different kinds are becoming more visible with research on digital globalization. The effects extend even to occupations and professions that have been considered 'traditional'. While it is important to distinguish skills, expertise, and knowledge from technologies, it is skills, expertise, and knowledge that have become used in differing ways on platforms; by contrast, in 'ordinary' organizational jobs and careers, length of tenure may be a key career builder and maintainer of jobs, more than individual skills maintenance.

Especially in relation to technology development, a persistent but largely misplaced argument in the literature states that jobs tend to disappear with technology (McAfee, 2019). This argument has been proved problematic by several empirical studies discussed in Chapter 2. Taking the technology and jobs argument further, what at first glance may look like a replacement of people by robots and AI may actually be about new combinations and new reconfigurations of previous tasks. As pointed out earlier, technologies do not necessarily replace people, but rather, speed up the renewal and reorganizing of old tasks and jobs, creating new optimizations, sometimes combined with so-called automation potential. Automation in jobs usually falls into three broad categories: robotic process automation (whose aim is to reduce variance or minimize potential errors), cognitive automation or AI (e.g., language understanding), and social robotics (e.g., physically working with people). For each task, in principle, people can be substituted (repetitive factory work, mechanical Turk type of work) and augmented and their work replaced with technologies.

Work without jobs requires a detailed organizational analysis of the needs, jobs, and talents within the organization, in order to create a flow of skills to work, instead of positions. Matching such a skills pool with employers' needs may create a major reorganization of activities and internal markets within the organization, based on the assumption of a sufficient amount of internal projects and assignments. This type of 'deconstruction' and disintegration of work, skills, and workers into tasks and smaller units is prone to price setting and thus, can be sold to various projects and activities (Gilarsky et al., 2020; Jesuthasan and Boudreau, 2022). This is addressed in research on talent management, which more generally asks whether the focus should be on jobs or individuals (Cappelli and Keller, 2017; Wiblen and Marler, 2021).

It is difficult to foresee whether this deconstruction of work – and worker – will become a prevalent model, even though algorithms that can advance such development are already partially or fully integrated into human resource management (HRM) and decision-making (Ajunwa and Greene, 2019). Algorithmic HRM is profoundly shaping how labor is managed and human resource practices are performed in corporations. Algorithmic HRM is based on generating and using digital data, deployment of software algorithms that process data, and partial or full automation of HRM-related decision-making (Kuhn et al., 2021). While the full use of skills and talents is and remains the aim of algorithmic HRM, the growing use of outsourcing, contracts, and contractors, such as temporary workers, extras doing gigs, or self-employed with contracts, seems to be governed first and foremost by budgetary regulations and restrictions in most organizations. Thus, the questions of 'skill management' and 'deconstructing jobs' within the digital and algorithmic HRM become mainly questions of cost-saving policies. The highly relevant aspects of the algorithmic governance of HRM activities, such as contracts and selection of personnel, could remove some cultural biases, but should not replace them with other, more hidden biases that may be part of the algorithmic governance and decision-making.

The algorithmic HRM within organizations requires a minimum stability and predictability in terms of the skills pool for workers, and future skills needed. If that cannot be achieved, the selection of individuals to work, based on their skills, has some resemblance to human job markets. From workers' perspective, income generation based on skills and not jobs needs to be stable and predictable, so that unintended consequences, such as emptying of the talent pool, can be avoided within the organization. However, an untouched field in the HRM literature is the question of biases within algorithms, such as ethnicity, age, and gender-related biases, and their effects on decisions made based on algorithmic HRM (Ajunwa and Greene, 2019, Kuhn et al., 2021), such as personnel selection. Technology development and algorithms do not unavoidably push employers to adopt such metrics and views of the workforce. Rather, in any competitive labor market situation, firms allocate resources for employees through the benefits of organizational citizenship (Crain, 2011).

As noted in Chapter 2, the impact of the value created by specific digital technological developments, such as AI, is difficult to measure or locate, for example, when looking into patent data (Brynjolfsson and Kahin, 2000). Implicit in many taxonomies is the difficulty of determining how work should be measured, because measurement difficulties are proliferating: do we measure number of contracts, length of such contracts, variety in income sources, or value created?

With digitalization, the arrival of the platform economy is changing the ways in which living wages are formed in specific fields, especially in developed economies, but also in developing economies (measured, e.g., by gross domestic product or human development index). In this context, platforms shape the ways and forms through which individuals are connected to the formal economy. Generally, platforms are changing the ways in which work is regarded as attached to organizational practices. For many organizations, this is fissuring the workplace (Amrute et al., 2021a, 2021b; Weil, 2017) and reorganizing work – employee–employer relations anew. It is unclear whether these developments are in real life creating new work possibilities and expanding the set of arrangements and alternatives through which individuals can generate income and income security.

Note

1 The most stringent data protection legislation – the General Data Protection Regulation, GDPR – is in Europe. In the US, there are several consumer protection laws in some state jurisdictions but no nationwide law, and none as broad as that in Europe.

References

Acemoglu, D. and Zilibotti, F. (1997). Was Prometheus Unbound by Chance? Risk, Diversification, and Growth. *Journal of Political Economy*, 105(4), pp. 709–751. doi:10.1086/262091.

Adams Prassl, A., Boneva, T., Golin, M. and Rauh, C. (2022). Work That Can Be Done From Home: Evidence on Variation Within and Across Occupations and Industries. *Labor Economics*, 74, p. 102083. doi:10.1016/j.labeco.2021.102083.

Ajunwa, I. and Greene, D. (2019). Platforms at Work: Automated Hiring Platforms and Other New Intermediaries in the Organization of the Workplace. In: S.P. Vallas and A. Kovalainen, eds., *Work and Labor in the Digital Age: Research in the Sociology of Work*. Bingley: Emerald Publishing Ltd, pp. 61–91.

Amrute, S., Rosenblat, A. and Callaci, D. (2021a). The Robots Are Just Automated Management Tools. Post-Pandemic Automation Part II. *www.datasociety.net*. Available at: https://points.datasociety.net/the-robots-are-just-automated-management-tools-b9bf28c4434 [Accessed: 14 Jun. 2022].

Amrute, S., Rosenblat, A. and Callaci, D. (2021b). *Why Are Good Jobs Disappearing If Robots Aren't Taking Them? Post-Pandemic Automation Part I*. Available at: https://points.datasociety.net/why-are-good-jobs-disappearing-if-robots-arent-taking-them-9f8d4845302a [Accessed: 1 Jul. 2022].

Andersson Schwarz, J. (2017). Platform Logic: An Interdisciplinary Approach to the Platform-Based Economy. *Policy & Internet*, 9(4), pp. 374–394. doi:10.1002/poi3.159.

Autor, D.H. (2013). The 'Task Approach' to Labor Markets: An Overview. *Journal for Labour Market Research*, 46(3), pp. 185–199. doi:10.1007/s12651-013-0128-z.

Barley, S.R. (2020). *Work and Technological Change*. Oxford: Oxford University Press.

Bosma, J.R. (2022). Platformed Professionalization: Labor, Assets, and Earning a Livelihood through Airbnb. *Environment and Planning A: Economy and Space*, 54(4). doi:10.1177/0308518x211063492.

Brancati, C., Pesole, A. and Fernández-Macías, E. (2019). *Digital Labour Platforms in Europe: Numbers, Profiles, and Employment Status of Platform Workers*. Luxembourg: Publication Office of the European Union, ISBN 978-92-76-08955-1, doi:10.2760/16653, JRC117330.

Brynjolfsson, E. and Kahin, B. (2000). Introduction. In: E. Brynjolfsson and B. Kahin, eds., *Understanding the Digital Economy: Data, Tools, and Research*. Cambridge: The MIT Press, pp. 2–12.

Brynjolfsson, E. and McAfee, A. (2014). *The Second Machine Age: Work, Progress, and Prosperity in a Time of Brilliant Technologies*. New York: W.W. Norton & Company.

Callaci, B. (2021). *Puppet Entrepreneurship*. Data & Society. Technology and Control in Franchised Industries. Available at: https://datasociety.net/people/callaci-brian/ [Accessed: 1 Feb. 2022].

Cappelli, P.C. and Keller, J.R. (2017). The Historical Context of Talent Management. In: D.G. Collings, K. Mellahi and D.G. Cascio, eds., *The Oxford Handbook of Talent Management*. Oxford: Oxford University Press, pp. 23–41.

Cortes, G.M. (2016). Where Have the Middle-Wage Workers Gone? A Study of Polarization Using Panel Data. *Journal of Labor Economics*, 34(1), pp. 63–105. doi:10.1086/682289.

Crain, M. (2011). Arm's-Length Intimacy: Employment as Relationship. *Washington University Journal of Law and Policy*, 35, pp. 163–212.

Cusumano, M.A., Yoffie, D. and Gawer, A. (2020). *The Future of Platforms*. Cambridge, MA: The MIT Sloan Management Review.

Cutolo, D. and Kenney, M. (2019). *Dependent Entrepreneurs in a Platform Economy: Playing in the Gardens of the Gods*. [online]. Available at: https://brie.berkeley.edu/sites/default/files/brie_working_paper_2019-3.pdf [Accessed: 15 Mar. 2021].

De Stefano, V. (2015). The Rise of the 'Just-in-Time Workforce': On-Demand Work, Crowd Work and Labour Protection in the 'Gig-Economy'. *SSRN Electronic Journal*, 71(3). doi:10.2139/ssrn.2682602.

Deboosere, R., Kerrigan, D.J., Wachsmuth, D. and El-Geneidy, A. (2019). Location, Location and Professionalization: A Multilevel Hedonic Analysis of Airbnb Listing Prices and Revenue. *Regional Studies, Regional Science*, 6(1), pp. 143–156. doi:10.1080/21681376.2019.1592699.

Drahokoupil, J. (2021). The Business Models of Labour Platforms: Creating an Uncertain Future. In: J. Drahokoupil and K. Vandaele, eds., *A Modern Guide to Labour and the Platform Economy*. Cheltenham: Edvard Elgar Ltd, pp. 33–48.

European Commission. (2021). *Digital Labour Platforms in the EU: Mapping and Business Models*. Final report. Publications Office. Available at: https://data.europa.eu/doi/10.2767/224624 [Accessed: 14 Apr. 2022].

Evans, P.C. and Gawer, A. (2016). *The Rise of the Platform Enterprise: A Global Survey 2016*. Surrey: The Center for Global Enterprise, Surrey Business School.

Fabo, B., Karanovic, J. and Dukova, K. (2017). In Search of an Adequate European Policy Response to the Platform Economy. *Transfer: European Review of Labour and Research*, 23(2), pp. 163–175.

Fernández-Macías, E. and Hurley, J. (2016). Routine-Biased Technical Change and Job Polarization in Europe. *Socio-Economic Review*, 15(3), pp. 563–585. doi:10.1093/ser/mww016.

Gershon, I. (2011). 'Neoliberal Agency'. *Current Anthropology*, 52(4), pp. 537–555. doi:10.1086/660866.

Gershon, I. (2016). 'I'm Not a Businessman, I'm a Business, Man'. *HAU: Journal of Ethnographic Theory*, 6(3), pp. 223–246. doi:10.14318/hau6.3.017.

Gilarsky, M., Nunn, R. and Parsons, J. (2020). *What Is Work Sharing and How Can It Help the Labor Market?* Brookings Institution. [online]. Available at: www.brookings.edu/blog/upfront/2020/04/16/what-is-work-sharing-and-how-can-it-help-the-labor-market [Accessed: 10 Mar. 2021].

Goos, M., Manning, A. and Salomons, A. (2014). Explaining Job Polarization: Routine-Biased Technological Change and Offshoring. *American Economic Review*, 104(8), pp. 2509–2526. doi:10.1257/aer.104.8.2509.

Greenhaus, S. (2019). False Freedom: Sharing the Scraps from the Perilous Gig Economy. *Literary Hub*. [online]. Available at: https://lithub.com/false-freedom-sharing-the-scraps-from-the-perilous-gig-economy/ [Accessed: 12 Feb. 2022].

Gruszka, K., Pillinger, A., Gerold, S. and Theine, H. (2022). *(De) Valuation of Household Cleaning in the Platform Economy* (Working paper No 2022). WU Vienna University of Economics and Business. Available at: ideas.repec.org [Accessed: 7 Mar. 2022].

Haiven, M. (2014). *Cultures of Financialization: Fictitious Capital in Popular Culture and Everyday Life*. Basingstoke: Palgrave Macmillan.

Hann, C. and Parry, J.P. (2018). *Industrial Labor on the Margins of Capitalism: Precarity, Class and the Neoliberal Subject*. New York: Berghahn Books.

Hay, J. (2003). Unaided-Virtues: The (Neo)Liberalization of the Domestic Sphere. In: J. Bratich, J. Backer and C. McCarthy, eds., *Foucault, Cultural Studies and Governmentality*. Albany: University of New York Press, pp. 165–206.

Im, Z.J., Mayer, N., Palier, B. and Rovny, J. (2019). The 'Losers of Automation': A Reservoir of Votes for the Radical Right? *Research & Politics*, 6(1). doi:10.1177/2053168018822395.

International Labor Organization (ILO). (2021). *The Role of Digital Labour Platforms in Transforming the World of Work. World Employment and Social Outlook*. New York: ILO.

Irani, L. (2015). *Justice for 'Data Janitors'*. Public Books. [online]. Available at: www.publicbooks.org/justice-for-data-janitors [Accessed: 16 Mar. 2021].

Jesuthasan, R. and Boudreau, J.W. (2022). *Work Without Jobs How to Reboot Your Organization's Work Operating System*. Cambridge, MA: The MIT Press.

Jones, S. (2014). How to Build an 'Intrapreneurial' Culture – An Entrepreneurial Culture Within an Organization. *Effective Executive*, 17(2), pp. 40–45.

Kässi, O., Lehdonvirta, V. and Stephany, F. (2021). How Many Online Workers Are There in the World? A Data-Driven Assessment. *Open Research Europe*, 1, pp. 53–67. doi:10.12688/openreseurope.13639.4.

Katz, L.F. and Krueger, A.B. (2017). The Role of Unemployment in the Rise in Alternative Work Arrangements. *American Economic Review*, 107(5), pp. 388–392. doi:10.1257/aer.p20171092.

Kenney, M., Rouvinen, P. and Zysman, J. (2020). Employment, Work, and Value Creation in the Era of Digital Platforms. In: S. Poutanen, A. Kovalainen and P. Rouvinen, eds., *Digital Work and the Platform Economy*. New York: Routledge, pp. 13–20.

Kenney, M. and Zysman, J. (2019). Work and Value Creation in the Platform Economy. In: S.P. Vallas and A. Kovalainen, eds., *Work and Labor in the Digital Age* (Research in the Sociology of Work, Vol. 33). Bingley: Emerald Publishing Ltd, pp. 13–41.

Kessler, S. (2018). *Gigged: The End of the Job and the Future of Work*. New York: St. Martin's Press.

Kuhn, K.M., Meijerink, J. and Keegan, A. (2021). Human Resource Management and the Gig Economy: Challenges and Opportunities at the Intersection Between Organizational HR Decision-Makers and Digital Labor Platforms. *Research in Personnel and Human Resources Management*, 39(1), pp. 1–46. doi:10.1108/s0742-730120210000039001.

Kurer, T. and Gallego, A. (2019). Distributional Consequences of Technological Change: Worker-Level Evidence. *Research & Politics*, 6(1). doi:10.1177/2053168018822142.

Kurer, T. and Palier, B. (2019). Shrinking and Shouting: The Political Revolt of the Declining Middle in Times of Employment Polarization. *Research & Politics*, 6(1). doi:10.1177/2053168019831164.

Lavrence, C. and Lozanski, K. (2014). 'This Is Not Your Practice Life': Lululemon and the Neoliberal Governance of Self. *Canadian Review of Sociology/Revue canadienne de sociologie*, 51(1), pp. 76–94. doi:10.1111/cars.12034.

López-Martinez, G., Haz-Gómes, F.E. and Manzanera-Román, S. (2022). Identities and Precariousness in the Collaborative Economy, Neither Wage-Earner, nor Self-Employed: Emergence and Consolidation of the Homo Rider, a Case Study. *Societies*, 12(1). doi:10.3390/soc12010006.

McAfee, R.P. (2019). Review of AI Superpowers: China, Silicon Valley and the New World Order, by Kai-Fu Lee. *Business Economics*, 54(3), pp. 185–190. doi:10.1057/s11369-019-00128-5.

Meijerink, J., Boons, M., Keegan, A. and Marler, J. (2021). Algorithmic Human Resource Management: Synthesizing Developments and Cross-Disciplinary Insights on Digital HRM. *The International Journal of Human Resource Management*, 32(12), pp. 1–18. doi:10.1080/09585192.2021.1925326.

Na, X. and Ma, Y. (2021). *Analysis of Monopoly in Platform Economy and Suggestions for Countermeasures*. Paper presented at 2021 International Conference on Society Science (ICoSS2021). Available at: http://proceedings-online.com/proceedings_series/proceeding/ICoSS2021 [Accessed: 3 Dec. 2021].

Neff, G. (2015). *Venture Labor: Work and the Burden of Risk in Innovative Industries*. Cambridge: The MIT Press.

Neff, G., Wissinger, E. and Zukin, S. (2005). Entrepreneurial Labor Among Cultural Producers: 'Cool' Jobs in 'Hot' Industries. *Social Semiotics*, 15(3), pp. 307–334. doi:10.1080/10350330500310111.

Negri, A. and Newell, J. (2010). *The Politics of Subversion: A Manifesto for the Twenty-First Century*. Cambridge: Polity Press.

Oesch, D. and Piccitto, G. (2019). The Polarization Myth: Occupational Upgrading in Germany, Spain, Sweden, and the UK, 1992–2015. *Work and Occupations*, 46(4), pp. 441–469. doi:10.1177/0730888419860880.

Parry, J. (2018). Introduction. Precarity, Class and the Neoliberal Subject. In: C. Hann and J.P. Parry, eds., *Industrial Labor on the Margins of Capitalism. Precarity, Class and the Neoliberal Subject*. New York; Oxford: Berghahn Books.

Piasna, A., Zwysen, W. and Drahokoupil, J. (2022). *The Platform Economy in Europe: Results from the Second ETUI Internet and Platform Work Survey* (Working Paper 5/2022). Brussels: ETUI.

Piketty, T. (2014). *Capital in the Twenty-First Century*. Cambridge: Harvard University Press.

Plantin, J.-C., Lagoze, C., Edwards, P.N. and Sandvig, C. (2016). Infrastructure Studies Meet Platform Studies in the Age of Google and Facebook. *New Media & Society*, 20(1), pp. 293–310. doi:10.1177/1461444816661553.

Poutanen, S., Kovalainen, A. and Rouvinen, P. (2020a). *Digital Work and the Platform Economy: Understanding Tasks, Skills and Capabilities in the New Era*. New York: Routledge, Taylor & Francis Group.

Poutanen, S., Kovalainen, A. and Rouvinen, P. (2020b). Digital Work in the Platform Economy. In: S. Poutanen, A. Kovalainen and P. Rouvinen, eds., *Digital Work and the Platform Economy: Understanding Tasks, Skills and Capabilities in the New Era*. New York: Routledge, pp. 3–12.

Prentice, R. (2017). Microenterprise Development, Industrial Labour and the Seductions of Precarity. *Critique of Anthropology*, 37(2), pp. 201–222. doi:10.1177/0308275x17694944.

Rani, U. and Furrer, M. (2021). Digital Labour Platforms and New Forms of Flexible Work in Developing Countries: Algorithmic Management of Work and Workers. *Competition & Change*, 25(2), pp. 212–236. doi:10.1177/1024529420905187.

Rikap, C. and Lundvall, B.-Å. (2021). *The Digital Innovation Race*. Cham: Springer International Publishing. doi:10.1007/978-3-030-89443-6.

Ritzer, G. (2015). Prosumer Capitalism. *The Sociological Quarterly*, 56(3), pp. 413–445. doi:10.1111/tsq.12105.

Rose, N., O'Malley, P. and Valverde, M. (2006). Governmentality. *Annual Review of Law and Social Science*, 2, pp. 83–104.

Rosenblat, A. (2019). *Uberland: How Algorithms Are Rewriting the Rules of Work*. Berkeley: University of California Press.

Schettino, F. and Khan, H. (2020). Income Polarization in the USA: What Happened to the Middle Class in the Last Few Decades? *Structural Change and Economic Dynamics*, 53, pp. 149–161. doi:10.1016/j.strueco.2019.12.003.

Schor, J.B. and Vallas, S.P. (2021). The Sharing Economy: Rhetoric and Reality. *Annual Review of Sociology*, 47(1), pp. 369–389. doi:10.1146/annurev-soc-082620-031411.

Simon, P. (2015). *The Age of the Platform: How Amazon, Apple, Facebook, and Google Have Redefined Business*. Mumbai: Embassy Books.

Thewissen, S.H., Kenworthy, L., Nolan, B., Roser, M. and Smeeding, T. (2015). *Rising Income Inequality and Living Standards in OECD Countries: How Does the Middle Fare?* (LIS Working Paper Series No. 656). Luxembourg: Luxembourg Income Study (LIS). Available at: http://hdl.handle.net/10419/169217.

Tholen, G. (2019). Degree Power: Educational Credentialism Within Three Skilled Occupations. *British Journal of Sociology of Education*, 41(3), pp. 283–298. doi:10.1080/01425692.2019.1690427.

Vallas, S.P. and Hill, A.L. (2018). Reconfiguring Worker Subjectivity: Career Advice Literature and the 'Branding' of the Worker's Self. *Sociological Forum*, 33(2), pp. 287–309. doi:10.1111/socf.12418.

Vallas, S.P. and Kovalainen, A. (2019). Taking Stock of the Digital Revolution. In: S.P. Vallas and A. Kovalainen, eds., *Work and Labor in the Digital Age*. Bingley: Emerald Publishing, pp. 1–12.

Vallas, S.P. and Schor, J.B. (2020). What Do Platforms Do? Understanding the Gig Economy. *Annual Review of Sociology,* 46(1), pp. 273–294. https://doi.org/10.1146/annurev-soc-121919-054857.

Wachsmuth, D. and Weisler, A. (2018). Airbnb and the Rent Gap: Gentrification Through the Sharing Economy. *Environment and Planning A: Economy and Space*, 50(6), pp. 1147–1170. doi:10.1177/0308518x18778038.

Watts, G. (2021). Are You a Neoliberal Subject? On the Uses and Abuses of a Concept. *European Journal of Social Theory*, 25, pp. 458–476. doi:10.1177/13684310211037205.

Weil, D. (2009). Rethinking the Regulation of Vulnerable Work in the USA: A Sector-Based Approach. *Journal of Industrial Relations*, 51(3), pp. 411–430. doi:10.1177/0022185609104842.

Weil, D. (2017). *Fissured Workplace: Why Work Became So Bad for So Many and What Can Be Done to Improve It*. Cambridge: Harvard University Press.

Wiblen, S. and Marler, J.H. (2021). Digitalised Talent Management and Automated Talent Decisions: The Implications for HR Professionals. *The International Journal of Human Resource Management*, 32(12), pp. 1–30. doi:10.1080/09585192.2021.1886149.

Wood, A.J., Graham, M., Lehdonvirta, V. and Hjorth, I. (2018). Good Gig, Bad Gig: Autonomy and Algorithmic Control in the Global Gig Economy. *Work, Employment and Society*, 33(1), pp. 56–75. doi:10.1177/0950017018785616.

Woodcock, J. and Graham, M. (2020). *The Gig Economy: A Critical Introduction*. Bristol: Polity Press.

Yasih, D.W.P. (2022). Normalizing and Resisting the New Precarity: A Case Study of the Indonesian Gig Economy. *Critical Sociology*. [online]. doi:10.1177/08969205221087130.

Zickuhr, K. (2021). *Workplace Surveillance Is Becoming the New Normal for US Workers*. Institute for Research on Labor and Employment University of California, Berkeley. https://equitablegrowth.org/research-paper/workplace-surveillance-is-becomingthe-new-normal-for-us-workers/ [Accessed: 5 Feb. 2022].

4 Reconfigurations of professions and professionalism

Evolving images of professions

The position of professions in the societal and economic tapestry has primarily been based on the importance of expert knowledge. This remains the case as societies are continually building on expertise and evolving knowledge-intensive activities. Societal and economic developments are enabled by the contemporary, complex, and entangled knowledge structures. Expert knowledge, thus, has a profound position in the trajectories of societies. Expertise and the possession of expert knowledge are being recognized and acknowledged in societies, not only through societal status ranking but also through specific legitimizing processes. More specifically, the legitimation of professions occurs through several processes of restricted, limited, or controlled access to formal education, through education and further training procedures, and eventually through the licensed practicing of the profession.

All these processes result in growing and intensifying knowledge reserves and the continuity of knowledge in the respective field. More importantly, these processes do the identity work for the profession and are impregnated with the importance of social networks and linkages with expertise, positions, and professional practices. The building process of a profession is multidimensional, since professions, for their part, play a fundamental role in building up, maintaining, and shaping societal institutions. Research on professions has highlighted the crucial aspects of this 'construction' work undertaken by and through the activities of professions. Identity studies (Fitzgerald, 2020) have shown how *professional identity* is most often defined in the literature as what professionals do, that is, the behaviors and activities (knowledge base, skills) of the profession. Another field of research has emphasized *subjectivity* over *identity*, as it is considered to capture the conceptualization of what directs and motivates individuals' engagement in something (learning the profession) (Billett, 2017). A third field of research has foregrounded *identity work* as an ongoing processual activity, in which identities are narrated by individuals, groups, and surroundings, rather than being constituent within a person. In this field of research, professionals may be interpreted as self-disciplining subjects who produce themselves through technologies of the self as subjects (Brown and Coupland, 2015).

DOI: 10.4324/9781351038546-4

The vast amount of analyses of legal, educational, and medical professions and institutions, as well as the increased understanding of the roles and positions of professional work in a globalized world, have created an evolving image of the connections between professions and the state and institutional professional work (e.g., Dent et al., 2016; Abbott, 1988). There is a general consensus among researchers of professions that the positions and roles of professions in societies transform over time and that the institutional arrangements related to professions are not fixed. What remains unclear, however, are the ways this transformation changes professions, and how professions are shaped through constant interaction and collaboration with other professions and occupations.

However, more powerful and overarching social and market forces such as globalization and global competition on the one hand, and supranational institutions, new types of collaborations and coalitions, and other agencies, on the other, have come to the forefront of all the activities of states and state institutions. These new types of ties also influence the ways states operate through their own institutions and legitimate bodies and impact the jurisdictional relationships within and between professions and the state. The relationships between professions and the state are not directly or immediately connected, but mediated and arbitrated through several layers of institutions, organizations, and procedural practices.

When professions were defined mainly as builders, maintainers, and developers of the state, they were also regarded as configured and attached to the state apparatus and its public institutions, such as its legal structures and institutions, healthcare institutions, and higher education institutions, all of which function outside the realm of markets, providing the key services for society. The demarcations between state and the market were interpreted to mean that professions had their independence from the means of production in and for the market (Faulconbridge et al., 2021), while the state provided the operational space for professions. To put it rather simplistically, professions were regarded as governing societies, and the importance of this ideal image of professions for the state and state development remained relatively stable and rigid for a long time.

The role of professions in the research was, to a large extent, treated as untouched by the complexities of social forces such as conflicts, power displays, and intersectionalities of various kinds. This 'intact' or isolated development in the research on professions has led a few researchers to call for an end to traditional research on the sociology of professions (Evetts, 2016; Nolin, 2008; Noordegraaf, 2007), even though new, interesting questions and avenues for research have also emerged, blurring and crossing the boundaries between traditional disciplinary fields.

One such field in which intersectionality became part of the analyses straddling professions and other crosscutting conceptualizations was gender studies on professions. In the 1980s and 1990s, several gender researchers remarked that male-dominated professions had served as role models for theories on professions, and that those professions that were considered 'semi-professions' were dominated by women (Witz, 1990). Professional projects were described first and foremost as projects of occupational closure. Another growing field is the critical analysis of professionalism, considered partially as a legitimizing process of power in defining problems and controlling available solutions. A more recent field that has opened up the research on professions relates to market developments, in terms both of professions working in markets and of the emergence of markets within the state and its institutions. The growth of managerial control in the public sector and the general loss of the autonomy of professions are often connected to both the rise of technological control mechanisms and market forces such as efficiency and auditing. Both of these factors have led to questions regarding the increasing subjugated control and audit cultures that have 'invaded' professions (e.g., medical doctors who have managerial, HR, and economic responsibilities for a unit) and organizational settings where effective managerial control is overpowering professional expertise. These factors, together with several intersecting analyses of gender, race, age, and forms of social closure within professions, have introduced new aspects of professions to research.

As discussed briefly in Chapter 1, the traditional delineation between professions and occupations was based on the Weberian–Parsonsian ideas of professions, that is, that professions generally serve a beneficial function for society, are self-regulating, and hold some power (Saks, 2012; Adams and Saks, 2018). Occupations, for their part, were seen as not fully yielding to this function of professions. The normative element in the state-building functions is understandable, given the state formation phase in Western societies, the building up of societies, and governance structures. With the growth of higher education institutions, the abundance of professions and occupations led to difficulties differentiating between the status of each. As higher education has expanded, educational shifts from technical and vocational training toward university education have taken place in several fields, including healthcare and nursing, media and communications, teaching and education, and technical occupations, to mention a few.

Revisiting the idea of professions, Evetts (2016) redefined them as being closer to the knowledge-based category of service occupations and requiring a period of tertiary education and work experience. This rather loose definition allows for shifts and changes within the professional groups. As the boundaries between occupations and professions become more porous, the question of ethical responsibilities in both categories has come to the fore (Noordegraaf and Schinkel, 2011). Research has suggested a more open and flexible approach to professions, featuring the idea of tasks that require the collaboration of a diversity of professions and occupations. For example, as described in Chapter 1, pathologists and radiologists, who read and interpret images, work closely with nurses and technicians, who are crucial in imagining and tissue sample digitization practices. The qualifications pathologists and radiologists need for their work are partially achievable through education processes, but perhaps more importantly, through practice and teamwork, since a variety of tasks and processes undertaken among team members can make a marked difference to the outcome. Hence, in this example, a set of occupational groups, not just doctors as professionals, bring forward their expertise and can influence the outcome of care. Since such a great variety of tasks is performed through the procedures and sophisticated judgments that occur within teams, the idea of a profession may change from that of a rigid entity to that of a more fluid and collective entity.

Professions, expertise, and occupations

The differences and divisions between professions, semi-professions, and occupations in society arose as one result of the ways in which social classes and closures of expertise were organized and marked. The status differences between occupations and professions grew through many mechanisms, including educational requirements for jobs. The divisions between professions and occupations have not been entirely delineated: Why can some occupations enter the sphere of professions while others cannot? The importance of the state in the birth of professions, as well as the crucial role of professions in supporting state institutions – and functioning mainly or entirely within the state – is well documented and recognized (Dent et al., 2016). Are these elements still sufficient for differentiating occupations from professions? With the rise of the importance of financial and economic aspects and institutions in societies, as well as the shifting position of the state, we may ask if not only the character of occupations but also, more importantly, the character and nature of professions, have changed over time. Do professions entertain such an influential permanency in societal and state developments? Do professions still maintain a special relationship with the state, as inscribed earlier? Institutional ties connect some professions to formal institutions and to the state; however, this is not the case for all contemporary professions.

The idea of professions as a societal cornerstone establishes their connection with formal institutions. This connection is not so well established nor visible between most occupations and the state. State and formal institutions reinforce the social closure of professions through formal documentation such as certificates, licenses to operate as members of the profession, and professional associations. Very early on, professions shared some characteristics, such as the required higher education qualifications and formal ethical codes of conduct. These characteristics were some of the defining demarcation lines between professions and 'lesser-valued' occupations; thus, the state was seen as accepting of professions and their privileges as part of a consensually oriented social system.

Yet, there is complexity in state–profession relations, which comes forward in the analyses of relations between professions and other parties in society. Employment status, determined by the contract of employment, is not the only aspect that defines the status and position of professions. Indeed, the more critical analyses of professions have explored them as part of the class structure, based on the ownership of the means of production, in contrast simply to the relations of the market (Saks and Adams, 2019; Adams and Saks, 2018). In most professions, knowledge is the only means of production, and as the price (of knowledge) is determined by the market, the view of professions as part of the class structure calls for critical analysis and scrutiny. Not all knowledge has exchange value as a commodified means of exchange.

In their attempt to monopolize knowledge, professions – from professional guilds to institutions such as universities – have faced new types of organizational demands in society that have eroded some of their authority. According to several researchers, as early as the 1970s, the emergence of computing technology was claimed to be partially 'eroding the professions' control over expert knowledge' (Suddaby and Muzio, 2015, 29); that is, technology was claimed to deskill the professions, as well as other work groups. In a parallel fashion, the shift among professions toward large bureaucracies and corporations was claimed to enhance the commodification of professional work. However, research has also shown the problematic nature of these types of deterministic claims (Spence et al., 2017), especially in relation to the role of technology.

The growth in the overall amount of expert work and expert occupations has taken place globally, especially in professional services such as management, accountancy, consulting, software engineering, programming, and legal services. These expert occupations function mainly or solely in markets, that is, they operate as market-based professions. They also share a common feature in that their significance extends far beyond their scale or importance. Indeed, the 'freedom of profession' is exercised within the realm of markets, not only within the state. The understanding of expertise has diversified, with the number of new occupations and level of new expertise growing, and with the diversification and specialization within occupations, giving further rationale for broadening the focus of the study of professions.

Weber saw professions as more specifically attached to Protestantism (Weber, 1917/2004, translated by Owen and Strong, 2004), partly because the concept of a profession, in its original meaning, had strong resonances of a 'calling' or 'vocation'. As Owen and Strong aptly noted in their preface of the translation of Weber's 1917 lecture, both meanings were active in Weber's thinking and writings on the fundamental position of professions in societal state formation and development. In its original meaning, thus, 'profession' did not have instrumentality built into it: Professions and their knowledge reserves were the ends, not the means, for achieving something in society. This notion had an almost moral calling in Weber's thinking and writings, which has been repeated as a subtext in many ideals of the research on professions. The Weberian view has been and remains influential within this research, although it has been partially replaced by other – for example, neo-Weberian and Foucauldian – analyses of professions.

Weber's classical notion of a profession as a 'calling' has been contested and disputed in modern-day empirical and theoretical studies: Ample research has challenged the idea of the altruistic 'calling' by demonstrating the elitism, barrier formation, monopolistic protection, and allied occupations working in practice to shield the achieved privileges (Suddaby and Muzio, 2015). Professions do not necessarily share core attributes, other than that – through their expertise – they all exert power and control over their clients, be they the state, institutions, or individuals. For some researchers, professions represent a privileged position in the labor markets, governed by those within the profession (Empson et al., 2015). However, with the shift of professional work toward bureaucracies, a concomitant loss of privilege and social status followed. This loss often relates to the threat of deskilling: In the 1970s and 1980s, several research papers reported the occurrence of deskilling due to the emergence of computing technology.

As discussed earlier, the deskilling of professions or occupations is by no means a straightforward process, nor is it caused by technology; rather, it emerges as a result of a complex group of interwoven causes and effects, as well as connections to societal development and even to globalization processes. The permeation of technology into occupations and jobs has, in fact, caused two major trends: It has created entirely new occupations and professions that did not previously exist, and it has retooled the content of old professions to the extent that new technologies now permeate the skills the occupation requires.

Given the views on the origins of 'professions' as callings, it is understandable that the sociological literature on professions as societal cornerstones has specifically addressed their normative aspects. This is described and visible, on the one hand, in the gravity of professions (lawyers as nation-builders, judges and priests as moral guardians, medical doctors as lifesavers, university professors as guardians of knowledge, etc.), which has been seen as important in the research. On the other hand, the exclusionary practices of professions in maintaining that gravity, such as hierarchy battles and power struggles between doctors and nurses, have received attention in the research and have found new interpretations in the analyses of work practices, for example (Nancarrow and Barthwick, 2016).

The focus of the research on professions has shifted over time from analyses of the 'structural-functional' type of questions to questions of power and privilege and of process and practice, to mention a few new areas of interest (Suddaby and Muzio, 2015, 26). Johnson (1972) famously remarked that professions have developed over time as a means of controlling an occupation, rather than as a means of altruistic service to others. This argument contrasts Weber's definition of a profession as a calling – even if these two processes, control and service, are not mutually exclusive. With this shift, new occupations and professions, such as business and corporate consultants, managerial controllers, and accountants, have also entered the focus of analyses as examples of new 'fluid' professions, where professions form an occupational organizing pattern; with expertise, these occupations have ascended to the category of professions.

The autonomy and status of professions in the state machinery originate from their special relationship with the state and its institutions, much more so than their relationship with the private sector, especially in Europe and Scandinavian countries. The flux and connections between the state machinery and the private business sector did not emerge through professions but, rather, mainly through legislative instruments; this also concerned the career transitions from the public to the private sector and vice versa – these were scarce and did not follow a usual pattern for careers.

The special relationship of professions with the state no longer resides in the state alone: Other forms of organizing and attaching have become more prominent and more important, to the extent that researchers now challenge the analyses of single professions that lack sufficient contextualization. From higher education institutions to the early years of professional identity formation, the modern 'guild system' with its associations and clubs is part of the process of socialization to a profession, and these contexts and social contracts continue to have importance. Professional organizations were originally guilds, where the symbolic value of being part of the profession is strengthened. The idea of the guild, whether a professional guild or another type, is by its nature exclusionary, rather than following the modern liberal style of inclusive and open membership. Professional guild members, that is, professionals, hold and transfer specific cultural, social, and economic capital and renew it in their networks. Professional guilds have always been instrumental in organizing further education and courses to renew their members' skills, as well as to build and maintain networks.

The research on professions has been under critical scrutiny over the last few decades due to the strong ethnocentricity it features; this research has long focused on the American and British contexts, and the societal arrangements and class structures also influenced how the professions were studied. Studies of professions have often been concerned only with one country (Burrage and Torstendahl, 1990). With the global shifts and changes in states' roles, the connections of professions to the state have changed: in some countries, professions have become mobilized by political and ideological forces, while in others, the shaping of professions has not been politically induced. Given the many approaches to analyzing professions, the 'research on professions' has most recently focused on examining them not as static entities or fixed social structures but as ongoing processes of professionalization. In this process of professionalization, several types of competitive processes emerge, such as attempts to monopolize expertise and knowledge.

Some researchers have underlined the characteristics differentiating the so-called *corporate professions* from *collegial professions* (Brock, 2021; Hodgson et al., 2015). The difference between the two is carved in the ways the networks are accessed and used. Corporate professions have developed their own enclosure mechanisms that emphasize corporate competences and industry knowledge and experience, in contrast to collegial professions (Muzio et al., 2011, 451). The distinction between these two groups is based on their abilities to draw on and recombine different elements in order to create professional identities and groups. These new types of professionalism could be called 'hybrid' forms. Hybrid professions differ from traditional professions, where the main emphasis is on the mastery of formal knowledge, which is proven by traditional examination (Muzio et al., 2011).

Globalization operates mainly through international firms, supranational organizations, and professional bodies. Through its operational channels globalization also heavily influences the shape of corporate professionalism (Sabini and Paton, 2021). The contemporary organizational environment acknowledges increasingly fewer national state boundaries in their actions and activities; thus, the attachment to the state and its institutions plays a smaller role in professions and in the formation of professionalism. More importantly, though, hybrid professionalism follows shifting mechanisms of attachment to professions. Increasingly, managerial tasks are stitched into the job descriptions of professions, organizing the services of these professions based on economic aspects and rendering professions as managerial devices for economic purposes. Indeed, new forms of expertise establish a specific culture and professional identity and compete to maintain their position by working closely with clientele. With hybrid professionalism, the dynamics and implications of hybridized professional knowledge step into the limelight. The two methods of building professional identity are often called hybridization. The hybridization concept presumes that professions evolve according to social change, and up-to-date theoretical concepts such as that of hybridization can capture these changes more appropriately. The ambivalence between power and vulnerability is one key to understanding contemporary professions and professionalism (Schnell, 2017); questions of power and vulnerability become prevalent in the new platform professions, which are addressed in the next chapter.

Professional work faces different types of pressures. These pressures partially arise from the ecosystem and partially from governance systems within and around professions. As presented earlier, professions are not immutable, nor do they have inherent characteristics of the governance of professional work and organizations. Professional expertise signifies power and autonomy. While autonomy and self-regulation are fundamental for expertise, they may not cover all aspects of governance at work. The basis of autonomy and self-regulation at work resides in the applicability of knowledge and practical problem-solving ability (Reed, 2018; Evetts, 2002).

Working with clientele means, in practice, using professional skills to identify and develop new services and tailoring these services to the unique circumstances of each client (Hodgson et al., 2015). For these types of new occupations, traditional professional closures are neither achievable nor desirable when compared to other strategies for professionalization. The 'new' occupations and individuals in these occupations navigate their paths to professionalization among the traditional, collegial routes and newer, corporate, and market-logic-oriented routes. Cross and Swart (2020) suggest that this new form of professionalism requires the kind of 'professional fluidity' that is co-constructed and an agentic position in relation to customers, be they patients, businesses, or the state. The legitimacy of the fluid position is established through the clientele and through constantly active relations with clients and collaborators, rather than through institutions or employing organizations. The question of the role of fluidity is two-fold: if the fluidity of professionalism is first and foremost defined and governed through relations with customers, how does it differ from customer relations management and risk and reputation management?

Re-introducing technology into the research on professionalism

The increase in digitalization and AI, as well as the introduction of digital platforms, and their effects on professions and on the birth of completely new and societally influential professions (such as influencers!) may provide enough reasons to warrant a recalibration of the analyses of professions. Adding to this, revisiting the classical definition of professions (lawyers, doctors, etc.) becomes a necessity, since this definition leaves an increasing number of occupational groups outside of it. This scenario gives further impetus for a reconceptualization that would take into account the dynamism brought into the fields of both professions and occupations by technological development.

The integration of technology (AI included) into professions does not automatically mean or signify major changes in the profession or a potential redefinition of professional borders. Technologies become part of the skills and tasks of a profession in many subtle ways. In fact, professions and professionalism seem to 'always' have gone through changes, and so it is also with technologies (Alvehus et al., 2021). The question of what happens to professions and within professions as a result of technological transformation may need to be refocused on the practices within the profession, rather than on the profession itself (see Faulconbridge et al., 2021). When states adopt and accept market-type activities and elements in their activities and institutions, the position of a profession is bound to change as well. Many of the practices within a profession actively undertake boundary work, that is, developing new delineations and protective shields. This work reproduces economic elites while also strengthening differences within the elite groups in organizations.

As noted, professionalism is a contested concept, not least due to the new professions in social media described in Chapter 3. The 'ideal' type of professionalism, which carries within it the notions of vocation and calling, may be the subtexts of Weberian definitions but, as such, do not encapsulate the positions and roles of professions today. Professions are no longer sole institutions nor based on callings, closed guilds, or associations for professions alone. Neither do professions represent the only or key institutions for the modernization of society, even if they hold cultural authority and cultural legitimation. It is indeed interesting to note that professions ascribed to specific times in the development of Western societies have not had a similar role in state formation in developing countries (Dent et al., 2016). Several cross-country comparisons show, for example, how professions are organized differently in developing economies and developed economies.

The configuration of professions is often built into learning from others in the work context. Sennett (2009) describes this type of learning as a certain kind of *craftsmanship*, that is, learning professional expertise gradually by practicing; repeating the techniques or knowledge until they are mastered; learning the features, patterns, and deviations of professional practices; and devoting time and effort to the learning process. Sennett breaks the phenomenon into several components, from learning the tricks of the trade to mastering craftsmanship. Sennett also differentiates crafts from arts because, according to him, arts refer specifically to individualized endeavors that are 'unique and at least distinctive' (p. 66), while crafts form a collective and continuous practice based on work by many and the collaborative learning that proceeds from that. When defining craftsmanship, Sennett describes connections between material consciousness and ethical values and challenges received ideas about what constitutes good work (Sennett, 2009). This view, to some extent, echoes the Weberian idea of professionalism as a 'calling': good work has value in itself, not solely in relation to its market value.

In the learning processes, either through education, training, or learning through the actual practicing of the profession, professionals today engage with digitalized repertoires of their crafts. Most jobs and work tasks assume some mastery of digital technologies, which often takes place in collaborative teams, such as in healthcare settings or on construction and building sites. Still, professional education is, to a large extent, designed to keep the professions separate until the completion of the training process, even though the working lives of most professionals feature constant intersections with other professions. As the complexity of technology in almost every work task grows, greater attention to the quality of the learning environments would be beneficial for the in-depth learning of craftsmanship. Such systems are already in place in several professions, such as in the legal profession, where algorithms are shaping and reorganizing professional decision-making; for example, predictive machine learning classifies data materials and organizes them according to the litigation procedure.

As one result of the rise of digitalization and AI and their roles in both businesses and the public sector, new divisions, hierarchies, and cracks have subtly emerged within professions, within professional groups, and among those who practice professions. The question of how technologies transform professions is not one-dimensional nor easy to answer. As discussed in Chapter 1, the traditional professions transform with technological development, and some of the qualifications needed within these professions change drastically. These changes often take place without visible changes from the outside or, indeed, in the hierarchy of professions in society. For example, dentists are similarly recognizable to their customers now as they were in the years before digitalization, despite the radical renewal of the materials and methods they use at work, their machinery, and the myriad ways digitalization has helped them in widening the knowledge space and by offering specialization.

Some changes within professions and professional practices are visible: within the legal profession, new professionals have emerged who operate with digital tools, programs, and machinery. In this process, the construction of legal argumentation and presentation are also changing as a result of constantly evolving technologies. Machine-learning-based technologies have brought new professions into the legal ecosystem, which was previously governed by legal professions alone. The number of other than lawyers working on legal materials, such as technicians using machine-learning technologies, and the overall possibilities of outsourcing these services have increased in legal firms. With the widening specter of professionals working on cases, the reconfiguration of social relations within legal firms, and more widely within the legal profession and educational institutions, is taking place. Research on the increasing technology use in procedural matters has found that legal professionals rely on the evaluations and judgments of a range of new technical experts within law firms. This reliance increasingly also extends to third-party vendors and their technical experts (Kluttz and Mulligan, 2019). Consequently, as technology takes a larger bite of the core activities of law firms, the selection of technical systems upon which lawyers rely to make professional decisions is under pressure. The question of which algorithmic tools are suitable for decision-making is, thus, critical.

Relatedly, because predictive coding systems are used to inform lawyers' professional judgments, some researchers have argued – aptly so – that these systems must be designed for greater transparency and interactions (Kluttz et al., 2022). Machine learning models rely on patterns identified in the data; thus, these models also reinforce both the identified patterns and those already in use. Machine-learning programs ingest data, produce an updated model, and then quickly feed the outputs back into the model in a recursive manner, without evaluating the correctness of the data. Many researchers have demonstrated that data analytics programs are value-laden in many ways; most importantly, technologies that should help professionals in their work but also create moral consequences, which are not necessarily beneficial, solvable by a professional themselves, or within the jurisdiction of the profession (Kluttz et al., 2022).

Technology, including AI and digitalization, encapsulates several values and forms of capital in society, such as symbolic capital. The governance of forms of capital, symbolic capital included, relates to the distinctive authority to define the boundaries and contents of a profession, which may entail struggles and re-negotiations concerning the authority over legitimate substance within the profession.

Both the boundaries and content of professions are also constantly at stake in wider societal fields of power (Noordegraaf and Schinkel, 2011). This type of approach to the analysis of professions de-essentializes the discussion of professions and professionalization. The recognition of professions as constructed categories, and their repertoires and resources as discursive, addresses the symbolic capital that is written into them and the reconstruction of symbolic capital in different fields.

Toward hybrid professions?

Classical professions and professionalism were defined by their embeddedness in and closeness to state bureaucracy and its structures, and less by their aptitude for controlling or managing others through their labor. The new professions and hybrid professionalism have emerged as tightly connected to the rise of knowledge societies, together with the increasing importance of services and new occupations. The rise of the service sector has also meant that the traditional idea of professions and professionalization is no longer about knowledge so much as it is about the strategy of socially excluding other occupations from upward mobility in society. With the expansion of educational institutions and fields and the growth of demand in the labor markets, this strategy is no longer sustainable from a societal perspective. Instead of controlling for social closure and operating autonomously, professionals and professions are increasingly entwined in various types of performance measures and follow-ups and continuous evaluation, not by peers but by managers. Coping with the ambiguities and opacities of managerial activities is part of working life. One example of this type of profession is consultants, who through their actions and work mold institutions and their settings in politics, as well as the organizational practices of corporations.

Some researchers (e.g., Adams and Sawchuk, 2020) have remarked that while occupational autonomy and control allow more space for a recognition of the interests and procedures of organizational and managerial imperatives, they have always been, in some form, part of the organizational or institutional settings of professions. This argument implies that professional knowledge itself can be altered through the practices of a profession. Professional knowledge can, thus, undergo a hybridization in the course of organizational life, despite the relatively immutable nature of professions. This raises the question of how professional knowledge may change in relation to changing autonomy, independence, managerial control, and accountability aspects. The subtle managerial control mechanisms may not necessarily relate to the content of professional knowledge; however, they are prone to addressing the efficiency and effectiveness of professional actions.

Hybrid professions today do not have one shape but several; thus, the term hybridization may best describe the processes by which the description of new requirements for expertise and structural and cultural changes in societies become part of contemporary professions. The *hybridization of professions* is not an unproblematic mixing of perspectives at work. Rather, it has been argued that hybridization produces contradictions in the uses of professional knowledge in practice, often with implications for de-professionalization (Adams and Sawchuk, 2020). The *economization* of professional activities and the *monetization* of knowledge are at the core of these processes as the logic of managerialism is juxtaposed with the logic of traditional professionalism. This is especially relevant when professional expertise and economic power are at stake, and the complexity of expert knowledge is in danger of becoming translated into one-dimensional economic value. Beyond changes in autonomy, the economization of professions may also mean shifts in workload, work processes, and procedures that impact the development and uses of professional knowledge and the future of traditional professions.

Research that has analyzed commercialized drug development and patenting has demonstrated the complexity of the relations between traditional professions and managerially oriented professions. In her examination of the relations between basic research, clinical studies, and drug development, Schnell shows how the professional roles of medical doctors who hold several positions alternate between science, medical practice, and managerialism. Medical professions display the complexity of hybridity as the roles are being drawn closer to each other in the hybridized field of the pharmaceutical industry (Schnell, 2017). The interdependence of these professions and pharmaceutical companies is built through several layers of knowledge construction, which include research, drug experiments, measurement, and the reporting of results, and extend to eventual drug development and patenting. This scenario exemplifies a few of the assemblages, intervals, and alliances involved in the development of hybrid professional positions.

Other processes of new professionalization occur alongside hybrid development. Technology and its adoption comprise one feature that widens skills development outside of the regulated formal educational institutions. This draws attention to organizations, which in many cases have taken control over more formal skills training in specific technologies, and which engage the necessary competences and services for this skills training. Technologies cause professions to cross boundaries. This process takes place in several ways, for example, technologies create new means of connecting and, thus, draw the different occupational groups to work together. Technologies may also create demand for knowledge that is only accessible outside of the traditional professional realms.

Let us take the example of lawyers, discussed in Chapter 1. Technologies such as machine learning systems and AI change the profession and bring about new occupations, which develop into new professions. But how does technology then change these new professions? The early research and discovery phase of any litigation system can use technology-assisted review or predictive coding. Both are examples of machine-learning-based decision support systems that lawyers can and do increasingly use in their practice (Kluttz and Mulligan, 2019). It is largely unclear how professional identities and interactions with clients are transformed by the machine-learning systems within an established profession. It has been reported that when technologies such as machine-learning systems rearrange practices and sequences of work, some loss of human agency and skill occurs. The heightened accountability becomes a question in situations where workers (professionals) correct the mistakes made by machines but cannot rewrite the machines' programs; thus, they are unable to practice full control over machine-learning systems (Elish, 2019).

Kluttz and Mulligan (2019) analyzed the relations between lawyers, new professionals that support the litigation procedure, and predictive coding technologies. The power relations between different types of professionals and the core activities related to technology reveal some of the forthcoming struggles that will follow technology absorption and its governance. Their research results show that many of the traditional professions do not have the expertise to use, adopt into practice, or evaluate the practicality and use of complex algorithmic tools. This seems to be one of the key challenges for traditional professions in the near future. The boundaries between professions within science-based and research-intensive fields and sectors are becoming more permeable, as the aforementioned examples show. These closer assemblages may also create avenues for new types of conflicts, such as a loss of professional power, and address new types of questions regarding the knowledge closures and knowledge sharing that are encountered in hybrid professionalism more often than in traditional professionalism.

Societies are not comprised of the singular actions of their individual members but of complex and historically developed layers, relations, networks, and structures that develop and shape rationales and relations, including actions and institutions. Moreover, societies are not immutable, nor are they a result of autonomous haphazard processes: The existing structures and institutions also evolve, develop, and change, and the materiality shapes the concomitant understandings of professions and professionalism (Poutanen et al., 2020; Collins, 2020). For traditional professions that rely on the autonomy of the knowledge realm and freedom of space for maneuvers, the widening fields of professionalism may result in shrinkage, while for hybrid professions, this expansion may open up the fields of operation, often toward both managerialism and technologies.

The previous chapters discussed the importance of the platforms and platform work, and the ways platforms transform all work. One previously untouched aspect, which is the focus of this chapter, is how established professions and the idea of professionalism fit into these ideologies and practices of the platform market, as well as how new professions are being made, defined, and conditioned by platforms and platform markets and, increasingly, within the organizations and institutions in which they reside. These organizations most often follow or imitate the logic of markets in their structuring.

Technology and its digital features, such as the software and apps used by consumers, can indeed be a powerful new actor that connects 'old' professions to new ones and establishes new possibilities for new professions. The next chapter will discuss the mechanisms that connect work and skills in new ways and enable new professional groups to be established. These new professions are fully dependent on the business models of platforms. Orlikowski (1992) noted that the reformulation of the technology concept allows a deeper understanding of the interactions between technologies, organizations, and humans. This understanding also provides insights into new professions and their formation in the platform economy.

References

Abbott, A. (1988). *The System of the Professions: An Essay of the Division of Expert Labour.* Chicago: University of Chicago.

Adams, T. and Sawchuk, P.H. (2020). Professional-Organizational Contradictions and Hybridization of Knowledge: Insights from the Study of Engineering and Nursing in Canada. *Vocations and Learning*, 14(1), pp. 75–93. doi:10.1007/s12186-020-09253-1.

Adams, T.L. and Saks, M. (2018). Neo-Weberianism and Changing State – Profession Relations: The Case of Canadian Health Care. *Sociologia, Problemas e Práticas*, (88), pp. 61–77. doi:10.7458/spp20188814798. Available at: http://journals.openedition.org/spp/5013.

Alvehus, J., Avnoon, N. and Oliver, A.L. (2021). 'It's Complicated': Professional Opacity, Duality, and Ambiguity – A Response to Noordegraaf (2020). *Journal of Professions and Organization*, 8(2), pp. 200–213. doi:10.1093/jpo/joab006.

Billett, S. (2017). Subjectivity and Human Resource Development A Quest for Intersubjectivity. In: M. Lee, K. Black, R. Warhurst and S. Corlett, eds., *Identity as a Foundation for Human Resource Development.* New York: Routledge.

Brock, D.M. (2021). Research on Professional Organizations: A Review of Theoretical Traditions, Themes, Methods and Locations. *Canadian Review of Sociology/Revue canadienne de sociologie*, 58(4), pp. 569–586. doi:10.1111/cars.12364.

Brown, A.D. and Coupland, C. (2015). Identity Threats, Identity Work and Elite Professionals. *Organization Studies*, 36(10), pp. 1315–1336. doi:10.1177/0170840615593594.

Burrage, M. and Torstendahl, R. (1990). *The Formation of Professions: Knowledge, State and Strategy.* London: Sage; Uppsala: Kollegiet för Samhällsforskning.

Collins, B. (2020). Defining the Employee in the Gig Economy: Untangling the Web of Contract. In: R. Page-Tickell and E. Yerby, eds., *Conflict and Shifting Boundaries in the Gig Economy: An Interdisciplinary Analysis*, pp. 23–43. doi:10.1108/978-1-83867-603-220201003.

Cross, D. and Swart, J. (2020). Professional Fluidity: Reconceptualising the Professional Status of Self-Employed Neo-Professionals. *Organization Studies*, 42(11), pp. 1699–1720. doi:10.1177/0170840620964985.

Dent, M., Bourgeault, I.L., Denis, J.-L. and Kuhlmann, E. (2016). General Introduction: The Changing World of Professions and Professionalism. In: M. Dent, I.L. Bourgeault, J.-L. Denis and E. Kuhlmann, eds., *Routledge Companion to the Professions and Professionalism*. London; New York: Routledge, pp. 1–10.

Elish, M.C. (2019). Moral Crumple Zones: Cautionary Tales in Human-Robot Interaction. *Engaging Science, Technology, and Society*, 5(40), pp. 40–69. doi:10.17351/ests2019.260.

Empson, L., Muzio, D., Broschak, J.P. and Hinings, C.R. (2015). *The Oxford Handbook of Professional Service Firms*. Oxford: Oxford University Press.

Evetts, J. (2002). New Directions in State and International Professional Occupations: Discretionary Decision-Making and Acquired Regulation. *Work, Employment and Society*, 16(2), pp. 341–353. doi:10.1177/095001702400426875.

Evetts, J. (2016). Hybrid Organizations and Hybrid Professionalism: Changes, Continuities and Challenges. In: A. Wilkinson, D. Hislop and C. Coupland, eds., *Perspectives on Contemporary Professional Work. Challenges and Experiences*. Cheltenham: Edward Elgar Ltd, pp. 16–33.

Faulconbridge, J., Henriksen, L.F. and Seabrooke, L. (2021). How Professional Actions Connect and Protect. *Journal of Professions and Organization*, 8(2), pp. 214–227. doi:10.1093/jpo/joab008.

Fitzgerald, A. (2020). Professional Identity: A Concept Analysis. *Nursing Forum*, 55(3), pp. 447–472. doi:10.1111/nuf.12450.

Hodgson, D., Paton, S. and Muzio, D. (2015). Something Old, Something New? Competing Logics and the Hybrid Nature of New Corporate Professions. *British Journal of Management*, 26(4), pp. 745–759. doi:10.1111/1467-8551.12105.

Johnson, T.J. (1972). *Professions and Power*. London: Routledge.

Kluttz, D. and Mulligan, D.K. (2019). Automated Decision Support Technologies and the Legal Profession. *SSRN Electronic Journal*, 34(3), pp. 853–890. doi:10.2139/ssrn.3443063.

Kluttz, D.N., Kohli, N. and Mulligan, D.K. (2022). Shaping Our Tools: Contestability as a Means to Promote Responsible Algorithmic Decision Making in the Professions. In: K. Martin, ed., *Ethics of Data and Analytics. Concepts and Cases*. Boca Raton: CRC Press Taylor & Francis, pp. 420–429.

Muzio, D., Hodgson, D., Faulconbridge, J., Beaverstock, J. and Hall, S. (2011). Towards Corporate Professionalization: The Case of Project Management, Management Consultancy and Executive Search. *Current Sociology*, 59(4), pp. 443–464. doi:10.1177/0011392111402587.

Nancarrow, S. and Barthwick, A. (2016). Interprofessional Working for the Health Professions. From Fried Eggs to Omelettes? In: M. Dent, I.L. Bourgault, J.-L. Denis and E. Kuhlmann, eds., *Routledge Companion to the Professions and Professionalism*. London; New York: Routledge, pp. 343–353.

Nolin, J. (2008). *Science for the Professions. University of Borås Report 4*. Borås: University of Borås Press.

Noordegraaf, M. (2007). From 'Pure' to 'Hybrid' Professionalism. *Administration & Society*, 39(6), pp. 761–785. doi:10.1177/0095399707304434.

Noordegraaf, M. and Schinkel, W. (2011). Professionalism as Symbolic Capital: Materials for a Bourdieusian Theory of Professionalism. *Comparative Sociology*, 10(1), pp. 67–96. doi:10.1163/156913310x514083.

Orlikowski, W.J. (1992). The Duality of Technology: Rethinking the Concept of Technology in Organizations. *Organization Science*, 3(3), pp. 398–427. doi:10.1287/orsc.3.3.398.

Poutanen, S., Kovalainen, A. and Rouvinen, P. (2020). Digital Work in the Platform Economy. In: S. Poutanen, A. Kovalainen and P. Rouvinen, eds. *Digital Work and the Platform Economy: Understanding Tasks, Skills and Capabilities in the New Era*. New York: Routledge, Taylor & Francis Group.

Reed, M.I. (2018). Elites, Professions, and the Neoliberal State: Critical Points of Intersection and Contention. *Journal of Professions and Organization*, 5(3), pp. 297–312. doi:10.1093/jpo/joy010.

Sabini, L. and Paton, S. (2021). Professional Regulatory Entanglement: The Curious Case of Project Management in Italy. *Journal of Professions and Organization*, 8(1), pp. 51–69. doi:10.1093/jpo/joab001.

Saks, M. (2012). Defining a Profession: The Role of Knowledge and Expertise. *Professions and Professionalism*, 2(1). doi:10.7577/pp.v2i1.151.

Saks, M. and Adams, T.L. (2019). Neo-Weberianism, Professional Formation and the State: Inside the Black Box. *Professions and Professionalism*, 9(2). doi:10.7577/pp.3190.

Schnell, C. (2017). Proliferations and Vulnerabilities: Hybridization of Professionalism in the Field of Cancer Medicine. *Professions and Professionalism*, 7(1), p. 1707. doi:10.7577/pp.1707.

Sennett, R. (2009). *The Craftsman*. New Haven: The Yale University Press.

Spence, C., Zhu, J., Endo, T. and Matsubara, S. (2017). Money, Honour and Duty: Global Professional Service Firms in Comparative Perspective. *Accounting, Organizations and Society*, 62, pp. 82–97. doi:10.1016/j.aos.2017.09.001.

Suddaby, R. and Muzio, D. (2015). Theoretical Perspectives on the Professions. In: L. Empson, J.P. Broschack and B. Hinings, eds., *The Oxford Handbook of Professional Service Firms*. Oxford: Oxford University Press, pp. 25–47.

Weber, M. (1917/2004). *Vocation Lectures – 'Science as a Vocation'; 'Politics as a Vocation'*. R. Livingstone, trans., D. Owen and T.B. Strong, eds. Indianapolis: Hackett Publishing Co, Inc.

Witz, A. (1990). Patriarchy and Professions: The Gendered Politics of Occupational Closure. *Sociology*, 24(4), pp. 675–690. doi:10.1177/0038038590024004007.

5 Platformized work, entrepreneurship, and professions

Varieties within platform work

The ways in which work is organized in platform ecosystems differ widely and take various forms, based on the business logic of the platform company and the type of work done. Most of the work contracted and offered on platforms is atomized, taskified, and surveyed closely – such as online gig and transport work – and/or sliced into smaller units than ever before – such as micro-tasks and microjobs. Such work gigs do not usually offer a decent income and do not support any type of skills development or maintenance of competence. Despite there are exceptions in earnings, they are a minority. Instead, they come close to and resemble poorly paid, monotonous, repetitive industrial assembly line work and precarious forms of labor, where one laborer is replaceable by the next one online. The marked difference is the lack of an employer. At the other end are platforms where gigs and offers call for suitable expertise and professionals. The work offered requires specialized and even highly skilled, crafted, and customized expertise, entailing the use of skills and allowing some time or performance related autonomy in the execution of the job offer. These varieties allow some degree of freedom in practical solutions pertaining to the work outcome. Such platform jobs resemble self-employment and relate to entrepreneurial activities through actual freedom, if not necessarily income-generation possibilities.

Yet, global competition, made possible by technological development and algorithms, does not conform to the image of creative online platform work that would carry any features of craftmanship in itself, in relation to skills and their upkeep, as outlined by Sennett (2009), for example. The time pressures for the highest-skilled labor in online platform markets are intense, and capitalizing on giggers' skills and creativity requires a large number of creative giggers. From the perspective of an individual gigger, this means constantly selling one's own capabilities and skills, without the possibility of updating or renewing those skills during work. Platforms do not offer automatic continuity for contracts, nor do they offer security expectation for the next gig to emerge. They do not guarantee the same or better contract terms for subsequent gigs. Markets have decisive power and purchase a final

DOI: 10.4324/9781351038546-5

product or service, and not the learning process. On platforms, offers and bids may come at unsuitable times, or with impossible deadlines, or with scopes that are not possible to meet. At worst, tech-enabled bidding on platforms may work as a market-based algorithmic activity, meaning that all offers can be curtailed by the algorithmic selection process while calculating the best price efficiency of the offers available.

Most platform work is located between these two ends of the continuum vis-à-vis the content of and conditions for work. Diverse forms of platform work share several features with temporary work and traditional self-employment (De Stefano, 2015; Kovalainen, 1995). Freedom and autonomy in performing gig work, and the ability to learn or update one's skills while performing work tasks, for example, seldom if ever exist in relation to unskilled work tasks offered on platforms. This is, again, in contrast to professionals and highly professional work where skills provide possibilities to choose and work flexibly, whether the work is done through platforms or traditional contracting. When compensation is based on the activity or task performed, and not on the standard of salaried compensation in the field overall, it may affect standardized salary levels in the long run. Comparisons between platform compensation and paid salaries in employment positions do not compare easily. The compensation received on platforms does not allow room for learning while at work, as the case is in many professional jobs, or for using compensated work time to update one's skills toward enhancing work performance.

At a larger scale, as mediators of activities, platforms do not recognize freelancers, that is, the platform work contractors, as workers, but only as own-account working partners or self-employed collaborators, whose provision is mediated to the purchaser. Platforms do not create value in their business model from the actual outcome of their mediating activity, that is, the work done in the market. Platforms do not recognize benefits, that is, paid work-related entitlements or labor-related compensation, either. The final outcome of a business activity, exchange of labor skills and capabilities against compensation, that is, the work done, is not part of the business model of platform companies. They mediate services and goods and bring together those who want to sell their labor skills and capabilities and those who want to purchase them based on algorithmic functions (Poutanen et al., 2020). The data from these transactions, the service commissions of the actual contracts, and overall activity on platforms form the core of their business model, even if there is a lot of variation to this basic model, depending on the ways the platform company needs to tie the resources to provision of services, etc.

Thus, ordinary labor-related and work contract–based agreements on issues such as sick and maternity leave, compensation for overtime or injury at work, and minimum wages do not exist in the context of platformized work, as there is no formal employment contract where an employer would cover these compensations. Platform partners provide their own health insurance, retirement savings, and other benefits. They are classified under several formal contexts, such as own-account and self-employed workers, for the sake of taxation. Own-account work contracts concern all practical aspects of contracted activity, apart from the freedom to choose the tech platform, the ability to set prices, and the freedom to enjoy full autonomy while performing the task or work they have contracted for. The performance of work on many platforms is highly regulated, ranging from partner uniforms and clothing to the use of certain sets of phrases while servicing customers.

In platformization, self-employment becomes seemingly regulated as a 'normal' employment contract, with formal behavioral rules, sometimes with uniforms, often with guidance for scripts, and even surveillance. Recommendations for price-setting for work are given indirectly on platforms, by other contractors, who are also potential competitors for the same bid. Contracting as an individual partner on platforms is seldom seen as a free business activity like other types of self-employment contracts. Qualitative and quantitative platform studies show that while platform workers are not a homogenous population, most platform workers combine their online platform work with paid work in the traditional labor market (Kristiansen et al., 2022; Conen, 2020). Thus, the structural features of labor markets affect how and into what the labor market develops. The interlinkages between online and traditional labor markets, and the ways in which corporations and companies use platforms to recruit and use labor, bring about variations in hybrid forms of work. These may have major roles to play in the development of national labor policies.

Platform work is not a single category of work, contractual form, or mode of operation subject to specific types of work, gigs, or conditions. However, platformization transforms and extends beyond traditional categories of work, and transforms the ways in which we use and analyze typical categories of work, and explain changes brought forth by digitalization. As platforms diversify, the gigs they offer also expand, which leads to individualized settings where none of the platform workers are similar. The traditional classification of 'employed population' as is often the case in most labor market research, does not capture platform workers unless students, pensioners, additional income earners, and unemployed people are included in the analyses.

Platform work as self-employment and own-account work

Research shows that digital platforms shape markets and bring about novelty in three ways: First, in terms of how platforms structure and govern a variety of markets with a tendency toward platform and data monopolies; second, through intermediate actions and activities among multiple actors with unilaterally imposed rules and conditions of operation; and finally, they bring novelty both to markets and consumers by constructing new digital user subjectivities with new consequences in material lives (e.g., Poutanen et al., 2020; Van Doorn, 2022). Work and its arrangements are integral in all these aspects of the platform economy. However, work and its arrangements on platforms differ from 'ordinary' work arrangements in several ways. The novelty of platforms extends to different kinds of work situations.

As shown in Chapter 3, work connections to platforms are seldom based on normal employment relations, that is, paid employment. For most people who actively work on platforms, income generation takes place through contracted assignments, gigs, rental payments, and taskified microjobs and activities, and not as salaries. The crucial difference is that institutional forces, that is, the structure of platforms compels individuals to engage in self-employment or own-account work, to earn an income through platforms. There, an individual choice is not about whether one wishes to become an entrepreneur, own-account worker, or self-employed, but is between earning income on platforms or not earning an income at all.

The birth of platform work has several interpretations but it is inherently related to the digitalization and growth of the Internet as a business platform. Some studies have called it 'uberization'. Platform work manifests in several ways. It is also seen as an entrepreneurial activity (Baron, 2018). However, entrepreneurship is vast and more integrally related to business activities rather than to earning possibilities. It disguises more rather than opens up the 'disruptive' nature of platforms as economic activity. Studies (Aloisi and De Stefano, 2022; Schor and Vallas, 2021; Aloisi, 2020; De Stefano and Aloisi, 2018) show that uberization as a sociocultural phenomenon marks a more general shift from a hierarchical bureaucratic control over work to a technologically derived and enabled control mechanism that extends to work, and does not just refer to ride-services type of work. The use of such control mechanisms is not restricted to platform work alone, but the roles of the control mechanisms become far more prevalent with the atypical nature of platform work: not only do they control the work and task assignments, but also the performance and overall access to the platforms. The control mechanisms and metrics controlling platform work are changing the logics of work performance. Metrics are transforming even those professions that were earlier unknown to adapt to such measures, and this transformation is often unintentional, as seen in Christin's (2020) ethnography on the development of journalism in the US and France, and deeply transformative, as described by Aldredge et al. (2020) in their analysis of changes in accounting as a highly skilled profession.

For any platform work, metrics are a default in all work scripts. They are fundamental for platforms in several ways. First, the very existence of the platform depends on metrics. On social media platforms, the number of visitors is crucial for income generation and platform value creation, while in other platforms, the testimonials of the customers play a bigger role in reputation building (Arora et al., 2019; Bollmer, 2018). On labor platforms, the metrics of work gather information for the assessment of time, tasks, and availability, for example. On business-to-business platforms, metrics relate to contractual trust-building among firms. Most people working through digital labor platforms are considered self-employed, or sole proprietors. Second, those working on and through platforms probably have several types of contracts with platforms and customers, which can include full-time, part-time, and/or temporary work, or address the outcome and offer a lesser role to the hours worked. These aspects are governed by metrics provided by the platform company on specific issues relevant to both the purchaser and provider of work. Third, algorithmic calculations form the basis of control and metrics for any activity on platforms. As mentioned in Chapter 2, algorithms used in metrics evaluation and decisions made based on those algorithms remain opaque to those under evaluation or control. Despite the critique against algorithmic surveillance and control mechanisms (Zuboff, 2019), they have become a defining element for any work, even expert work, performed on and through platforms.

Own-account and self-employed workers are statistical categories that share the income generation model and classification of economic activity. Both do their work on their 'own account', with their own devices and tools, at their own risk, based on their skills and capabilities, and do not employ others. The legal basis for activities can be a limited liability firm or, often, sole proprietorship. Those categorized as self-employed or own-account workers differ from those in paid employment positions based on income generation and means of production. In the latter, the risks related to work are contracted by an employer and not an employee. The means of production and surplus of contracting them are owned by the employer. Both self-employed and sole proprietors are conceptually far from the original idea of entrepreneurship, as it relates more to the idea of ownership of a firm, company, or business and creation of new enterprise and growth, rather than to an earning model of self-employment or own-account work based on one's skills. Self-employment or own-account work may be creative and innovative, but do not aim to see the growth of their idea into an entrepreneurial hub or innovations in a similar fashion. The literature refers to serial entrepreneurs and venture capitalists who are entrepreneurs who start new ventures or purchase existing ones through a management buy-out or buy-in (Dabić et al., 2021; Wright et al., 1997). In Western countries, approximately 50% of new entrepreneurial ventures are made by those who already have had some prior entrepreneurial experience with previous businesses (Ucbasaran et al., 2010), either through their own business or by working as freelancers in another's business. The use of a programmatic or one-size-fits-all conceptual model to analyze economic transformation such as platformization and its earning models is in this sense problematic.

Why should those working on and through platforms not be classified as business owners, own-account, or self-employed workers, when all three categories belong to the entrepreneurial category, according to labor market statistics, and enjoy entrepreneurial freedom, individuality, and flexibility of work? Platform workers do not fall under the classical categories of self-employed and own-account workers, and do not have entrepreneurial status because their roles do not involve risk-taking and they do not enjoy the freedom to set the price for their work. Business start-ups differ from own-account work and self-employment through a range of measures starting from business and financial plans, to performance measurements and investments needed, among others. There are important theoretical threads that are crucial to follow-up while tracing the possible connections/disconnections between professionalism and entrepreneurialism in contemporary society.

Entrepreneurship theories meet profession theories

Given that digitalization and platforms are powerfully changing the economic landscape globally, it is interesting to see how the theoretical aspects of such functions in the economy, especially in the case of highly skilled experts, act in a new complex environment. Do professionals choose self-employment and own-account work via platforms, instead of paid employment? Are they able to choose both? Or, do they instead become entrepreneurs, which offers them more possibilities, given their high skills and capabilities, in digital markets? We may ask how established theories of entrepreneurship resonate with the theoretical approaches that explain the role and position of professions in society. Starting with the classics offers tools to reflect on the current economy where entrepreneurs and professionals navigate technological transformation.

The emergence and crucial role of entrepreneurs as catalysts of economic transformation in the wake of industrialization is well documented (Mason and Harvey, 2013; Casson, 2010; Norlander, 1992). Entrepreneurship can be the driving force for the growth of the firm and a factor limiting its rate of growth (Casson, 2010). Academic analyses of entrepreneurial phenomena in the economy have a long and rich history. Entrepreneurs as exceptional individuals, and entrepreneurship as a knowledge field concerning economic change, growth, and development, have been the subjects of research since Adam Smith, John Stuart Mill, Joseph Schumpeter, Ludwig von Mises, and John Maynard Keynes, to mention a few classical scholars who have been canonized as forefathers of the theoretical corpus in entrepreneurship as a multidisciplinary field of research (Kovalainen, 1995; Swedberg, 2000; Mason and Harvey, 2013). Mainstream economics has had very little to say about entrepreneurship, and most often, has considered its business activities and management only a part of the market (Swedberg, 2000). The concept and phenomenon of entrepreneurship revolve around economic activities – entrepreneurship is defined through its 'economic function', which is other than a paid employment position. Contemporary economics relate entrepreneurship to market development based on a favorable institutional environment, but the question of the legitimacy of entrepreneurship as an academic discipline lingers on (White et al., 2021). Despite this critique, canon-building in entrepreneurial theory construction has drawn from the aforementioned classics; the focus is still relatively often on individuals as entrepreneurs, despite the volume of research devoted to and failure to identify distinctive traits of an entrepreneurial personality (Kovalainen, 1995).

Entrepreneurship has been and is about the ideas of economic livelihood and business activities in society and the economy. A central focus of the literature on entrepreneurship was, for a long time, on similarities and differences between entrepreneurial roles and paid employment. As entrepreneurship research has developed in fields of science such as psychology, social psychology, education, and business studies, it is therefore only natural that the entrepreneurship research field or domain has developed subfields and pockets for new theoretical approaches (Neff et al., 2005). Among these new topics, entrepreneurs, businesses, and economic livelihoods are no longer the sole focus of analyses; topics such as individual lives, subjectivist approaches, and alternative livelihoods, for example, have emerged as legitimate in entrepreneurship research. The roots of knowledge that formed a basis for the theories of entrepreneurship have ranged from early disequilibrium theories of economies to psychology of entrepreneurs, covering elements such as characteristics, reactions, mindsets, and personality features. In disequilibrium theories, the economic actor or entrepreneur was considered a crucial igniter for economic change, dynamic nature, and development, instead of the state or other institutions that sought to maintain economic equilibrium (Arrow, 1971). In psychological and social-psychological theories of entrepreneurship, analyses continue to address the distinctive features that characterize and differentiate entrepreneurs from nonentrepreneurs, such as by attempting to understand the entrepreneurial mindset from various cognitive, behavioral, and emotional perspectives (Kuratko et al., 2020).

Entrepreneurial research is constructed alongside various types of divisions, such as quantitative, psychologically oriented, and comparative studies, and qualitative, historically, or locally embedded studies. Nonpaid employment positions are at the core of all analyses. The entrepreneurial value creation theory, for example, aims to explain the entrepreneurial experience from the intention and discovery of an entrepreneurial opportunity to the development of competences and rewards and to general economic development (Hébert and Link, 2012; Ozkazanc-Pan et al., 2022).

When the disciplinary field researching professions and developing theories on profession formation vis-à-vis economic or social development is compared with the disciplinary field of entrepreneurship, it is obvious that entrepreneurship is relatively young and addresses slightly differently questions on power, institutions, and society. This is evident in numerous texts, books, and articles reflecting on the field and simultaneously building its legitimacy. The narrative of the discipline has been built through canonical forefathers and journals in the field. As a disciplinary field, entrepreneurship has been able to fill the void within business studies by analyzing 'real economy' actions and activities, in contrast to other business disciplines. The multidisciplinary approach to entrepreneurship as a catalyzing force for economies has widened and spread from Austrian economics, focusing on individuals' roles in economic disequilibrium, to business studies and management, addressing individual and business start-ups from a business economics perspective. Analysis has explicitly or implicitly focused on questions such as how and why business and entrepreneurial opportunities arise and why they are detected and taken advantage of by certain individuals or entrepreneurs to make the business function (Lundström and Halvarsson, 2006; Gupta et al., 2016). Nonetheless, the variations in the overall research approaches, methods, and methodologies used, and data gathered on entrepreneurs and their activities, have stretched the disciplinary boundaries.

Most entrepreneurship theories and empirical studies on entrepreneurship have analyzed risk, dependency, and freedom in the market (e.g., Schumpeter, 1934; Gupta et al., 2016). Market conditions have been analyzed in relation to economic activities initiating something new (Bridge et al., 1998; Bridge and O'Neill, 2018). Although research on entrepreneurship has long recognized that entrepreneurs are not a homogenous group research has continued to address several person-, firm-, or family-related aspects of entrepreneurial activities, and to a lesser extent, the relation between professions and entrepreneurship, including professional qualifications enabling entrepreneurial activities (Gupta et al., 2016). The field of entrepreneurship studies and theories is expanding, with differentiations in question-setting and diversity in results, often also addressing other-than-entrepreneurial questions. One strand among the new and diverse openings in research on entrepreneurship is the emphasis on everyday developments and locally embedded analyses, where the focus is on activities channeled as economic entrepreneurship (Ozkazanc-Pan et al., 2022; Lou, 2021; Lobato, 2016). Entrepreneurship research has expanded and borrowed conceptual tools from cultural studies, for example, Levi-Strauss' concept of bricolage (Stinchfield et al., 2012; Baker and Nelson, 2005) and concepts from feminist studies such as gender essentialism and constructions of gender (Javadian, 2022; Mirchandani, 1999). There are very few studies that analyze and differentiate actual value creation in entrepreneurial and paid employment work. The linkages are few between professional work and integrity, and entrepreneurial work and market orientation, for example. Methodologically, entrepreneurial studies cover a variety of similar methods, as do studies on work, professions, and professionalism.

Weber (1864–1920) has not often been recognized as one of the founding forefathers of entrepreneurship, unlike his contemporary Josef Schumpeter. An obvious reason for this may be that Weber never wrote one specific text or piece of analysis on entrepreneurship; instead, his ideas on the topic were diffused over several of his texts. According to him, entrepreneurs can be found in an exchange economy, where value creation is possible. He stated that entrepreneurship mattered most not as economic operations of a single individual or individuals, but as a general direction of economic action and activities (Swedberg, 2000). For Weber, entrepreneurship as a vocation to make money, was first set free when religion lost its grip with the growth of secularization. With his writings on bureaucracy, Weber laid the foundation for theories on profession, and thus, his views on entrepreneurship are highly interesting. They raise interest independently from profession theories from at least two perspectives. First, Weber's early definition of entrepreneurship helps put Schumpeter and his followers' solipsistic and individualistic entrepreneur-idea within a wider societal context (Swedberg, 2000). For an entrepreneur to exist, for Weber, an enterprise, institution, or organization is needed to take advantage of market profit opportunities. For Weber, this was crucial for a viable business, as a creative individual alone was insufficient. This latter perspective crystallized the Weberian ideas of the economy and the role of the community. Second, redressing Weber's 'visible absence' from the canon of entrepreneurship classics can add a new dimension to prior research by drawing attention to less visible features of the differences between approaches (Gupta et al., 2016), and hidden fractures in the knowledge formation of the theoretical canon, in particular as regards the early emphasis on the individualistic view on entrepreneurship, instead of the collective one emphasized by Weber (1922/1978).

Modern societies and economies have been characterized by continuous technological and organizational progress. This has meant, in practice, major changes over time in the ways in which economies function, and with that, entrepreneurship has come to mean other things than described in the classics. As Swedberg (2000) noted, the processes of industrialization are globally too variegated to allow simple generalizations concerning entrepreneurial activities. Blaug (1986) elaborated on the epistemological basis and failure of mathematical economics and its differences in building the knowledge base for the 'new disciplinary field.' Multidisciplinarity may pose problems that become obvious later when theorization takes place. The debates and disputes on the idea of an entrepreneur as a rational actor as against a constructed and constrained actor is a long-term, unintended consequence of the differences in epistemic approaches.

Epistemic and value differences reveal a larger gap in the mode of knowledge production between theories on entrepreneurship and professions. Despite the spread of the disciplinary field of entrepreneurship, the differences between actual entrepreneurship and business success are seldom analyzed through a focus on professionalism. This is evident in analyzing the prevalence of topics that relate to the market aspects of own work, or professional integrity in the market. Very few studies on entrepreneurship and self-employment have discussed the market aspects of actual work, that is, what the constant market value evaluation does to one's creativity, skills, and capabilities, which are the core issues in platform work. In research on entrepreneurship, it is important to understand what happens when the economic function of the entrepreneur as the intermediator in the market is replaced by platforms and algorithms, and new types of dependencies of work and income generation become visible at the global level. The analyses of the rise or decline of entrepreneurial activities globally do not offer a full picture of the new scheme of global digital connections.

Global dependencies of skills, work, and platforms

There are several ways to visualize and analyze the global flows of digital demand for work and supply of production that make the new types of global flows visible and tangible. Perhaps the most comprehensive one was developed by Oxford University's Online Labour Index (OII, 2020). The overall picture is that the global digital flows of work demand and supply have strengthened over time. New configurations of digital platformized work have emerged globally. Some of these configurations pertain to dependencies of different kinds, despite specialized skills sold on global and local platforms. Being the sole proprietor of your own skills may not lead to independence, even despite global demand for your skills. One indication of the lack of independence among platform partners is the payment system. Independence in terms of contracted compensation for work performed is assumed in self-employed and entrepreneurial positions in the market.

Compensation and payment systems vary globally. Work done through platforms is not necessarily compensated monetarily, but can also consist of various types of credit points, credits, gift cards, and vouchers, tying the independent partner-contractor to the platform. These dependent currency forms may vary and be tied to specific types of consumption through the platform (Rani and Furrer, 2021). According to International Labor Organization (ILO) researchers, for example, workers in less-developed countries seem more likely to get compensation for provisional work with gift cards or vouchers instead of cash payments (Berg and de Stefano, 2018; Rani and Furrer, 2021). Such payments do not allow economic independence in any entrepreneurial or self-employed manner, but rather signify contractual and financial dependency on the platform company. At a larger scale, the nationally introduced aims to increase flexibility in labor markets have been associated globally with the simultaneous rise of part-time, temporary, and contingent work, as through projectification, freelancing, or gig work with insecurity around payments, and at the labor market level, often with few or no benefits (IMF, 2021; Chen et al., 2021).

The form of payment is not the only distinguishing feature between those in paid employment contracts and those in self-employment. The status of self-employment in terms of being shielded from the loss of economic activities or unemployment, is weak in comparison to those in paid employment (Manza, 1992; Mackert, 2012). If the own-account or self-employment work is based on one contractual relation, for example, subcontracting, the taxation laws of many countries do not see it as an independent activity but rather, as a dependent activity from that contractor, and thus see it as a disguised employment relationship. The position of platform workers is complex under the national labor laws of different countries, and various interpretations have been challenged in the courts by platform workers and labor unions. The fundamental issue in most court cases concerns the difference between being an independent contractor and a dependent employee. The extent of control a platform company exercises over a worker is usually the test. Similarly, the question of economic dependency on the platform company has been scrutinized in many cases (Caplan and Gillespie, 2020; Childers et al., 2019).

The rise in the number of self-employed individuals in many countries has raised the question of identifying ways to understand the wide spectrum of dependencies and independencies that exist under this category. The categorization of individuals lacking paid employment contracts as self-employed disguises much of the working conditions and possibilities for independence in their working relations (Conen and Schippers, 2019). This is not a new phenomenon and is not driven by technology alone. Research has shown how self-employment comprises various types of own-account working categories, and often, the uniting features for those classified as being in self-employment, relate to precarity and vulnerability in the labor markets, alongside qualifications pertaining to low education levels, heavy caregiving responsibilities, and lack of state support and skills demanded in the most competitive parts of labor markets (OECD, 2021). These, combined with low national income levels, and the rapid technological transformation of the service sector, may create marginal positions within employment. One example are women (and men) who engage in subcontracting and piecemeal work at home for small- and medium-sized businesses (Bhatt, 2011; Mezzadri and Fan, 2018). Work may comprise micro tasks, or simple production, such as sewing for garment or textile industries at home. Most such work has been transferred to the Global South and takes place without formal contracting. Thus, it constitutes a part of the informal or black economy.

Platforms may have transformed social media corporations and delivery companies into visible manifestations to an ordinary consumer, but such enterprises are only a part of the platformized economy and responsible for only some effects. With technological developments, platforms have entered global production chains and modes rather early on, and have, owing to skillful and rapid network effects, entered service and production modes globally, transforming them in the process. Platforms have transformed formal and informal economies at the national level. In the informal sector economic activities take place at a smaller scale, adjacent to but often hidden from the formal economy, and on many occasions, organized through own-account work or small business activities, and where the correlation between poverty and informality is strong (ILO, 2021). Platforms have entered and transformed the informal economy and its functions and work practices.

Why do platforms give such importance to the analyses of the global redistribution of work and/or wealth? Owing to their network effects and efficient global or local functions, platforms are prime movers in societal and economic transformations. The factors are many and show the ways in which platforms constitute infrastructure that can be used by the public in several ways. Digital technologies and data are the key components of platformization (Poell et al., 2019), and can have positive impacts with equalizing measures concerning wealth and income accumulation, and increase the development of marginalization in societies.

Own-account workers seldom, if ever, have opportunities for business activities in any traditionally idealized and intended entrepreneurial sense. Despite the problems pertaining to platforms and their functioning, they can constitute and be used as part of the infrastructure of public institutions. A good example is Togo, in West Africa, during the COVID-19 crisis. Togo is one of the poorest countries in Sub-Saharan Africa. Over 80% of its population earns livelihood through various activities in the informal economy. Through low-tech mobile technologies such as USSD, a cash transfer platform that does not require an Internet connection for users to enroll and receive payments, was developed with the help of ministries. The state was able to transfer social assistance to citizens' mobile money accounts, once they were declared eligible through the platform (Behsudi, 2022). When the state develops such platforms, it can have powerful, transformational effects. Existing platforms can be used to alleviate challenges during crises, as the collaboration for food aid between the UN's World Food Program (WFP) and Uber in Ukraine shows. Uber developed a customized version of its online platform for the WFP to deliver food in Ukraine (UN News, 2022). Both examples highlight the possibilities of platforms in addressing crises.

The contemporary rise in self-employment in many countries offers insight into the flexibilization of the labor markets and growth in digital solutions channeling low-paid service work possibilities mainly or solely through platforms, instead of through traditional employment contracts. It also talks about the problems with consolidated statistical categorizations in capturing the multidimensionality of work, especially on platforms.

Unruly categories

Despite the global nature of platforms, national contexts as operative landscapes matter for global platforms and platform companies. This is not to imply that transnational professions and global professional standards and practices do not align with or matter at the national level. Liminal and legally privileged spaces allow transnational professional standards and practices to flourish within national borders, and national borders matter less today than before (Harrington and Seabrooke, 2020). The increase in international organizations and their prominence, ranging from global NGO-type organizations to collaborative supranational bodies such as the EU and its layers of governance mean that the state level is no longer the only connection for professions; instead, increasingly, professions and expertise work through supranational bodies (Moats, 2021). This is not to say that the national level does not matter. For platform companies, national legislations set operative frames, especially for labor platforms. This means that national laws still affect and dictate the ways in which new platform companies can function and adjust to their surroundings (Frenken et al., 2019).

Workers' rights and entitlements vary between countries and the strength of national laws has been tested in cases concerning the employment/self-employed position in Europe and the US. In some countries, on-location operating platform companies partner with insurance companies, to cover some of the platform workers' security benefits. National contexts reflect differences in the collective bargaining systems and their power (Reskin, 2005). In Germany, for example, many workers are employees on different types of flexible contracts, and this means that they are not always covered by collective agreements covering some unemployment benefits, sickness, and parental leaves, for example (Rani and Furrer, 2021), whereas in Nordic countries, collective agreements offer a blanket, overall status for employees, irrespective of their individual or personalized contracts with their employers.

The workforce is bound to local and regional contexts. When on-location platform work is not included, much of the online platform work is global. Global platform work also means a global-level competition of work offers and requests for work, as well as in generic and global competence and skills standards spreading globally. These aspects become most noticeable in work prices. People can compete for online services. Such work can be executed anywhere the world over, including in jurisdictions with lower labor costs and purchasing power. Owing to these global imbalances and differences, the global flow of work provision and offers for work and skills tends to take place between the US or Europe and Asia, and to a much lesser degree, between the US and Europe (OII, 2020).

The most common way to enter platforms that operate as a marketplace for work and labor is to register. Platform-mediated work is allocated through open-calls rather than by designed and individualized job calls, which may set individualized parameters for jobs. The mechanism of selecting work providers varies from platform to platform, but direct job offers require bids from everyone willing to take the job, or the automated matching of offers and requests by an algorithm. The time taken to participate in bidding, preparing to bid, and engaging in competition for work is not compensated. Platform dependence experienced by work providers is financial (compensation) and organizational (instructions, supervision, and control) in nature. In contest-based platforms, clients can either create a contest or search for providers themselves. In contest-based digital labor platforms, the number of contests that participants can enter is limited by the platform (Rani and Furrer, 2021).

A major change introduced in labor markets owing to platforms is the rapid growth of online platform work and its global nature. According to the ILO the number of location-based platforms increased close to tenfold during 2010 and 2020, and the number of online platforms tripled (ILO, 2021). Online platform work has become part of the labor market mechanisms that are available globally, but not with the same pace and market strength everywhere. However, it is gaining importance everywhere, and is present in policy and regulatory discussions. This phenomenon puts pressure on the more general regulatory responses and demands collective reactions against new types of inequalities, insecurities, and social problems that have emerged with platform-mediated work. The benefits of platform work, reported by platform workers and worker-partners, relate to time freedom, flexibility, and ability to work as one's own boss (ILO, 2021).

The experience of work differs across platforms, and depends highly on skills and capabilities, career prospects in other than platform labor markets, and several other factors. Whereas time freedom exists, the unpredictability of working hours owing to waiting time while making deliveries or going on rides, and preparation time for job bids imply that presence and preparation are obligatory, but not compensated. Winning bids are the only ones that receive monetary compensation. The volatility of the market is evident in the number of job offers and bids available from time to time. Most ride fares fluctuate or change without workers having any control over pricing, making remuneration unpredictable (De Stefano and Aloisi, 2018). Jobs accepted and declined have effects on evaluations and ratings, and the algorithms are not free of error. Various nonstandard working arrangements are part of the 'over-flexibilization' that takes place in labor markets. Platform-based work falls under the ambit of app-driven casual work arrangements, which constitute a subgroup of nonstandard forms of work, if we use traditional classifications. Several activities are mediated through platforms, and different labels and definitions are used, such as gig and on-demand work, work-on-demand via apps, platform work, digital labor and (gig) economy, crowdsourcing, piecework, and collaborative consumption (Drahokoupil, 2021; Kovalainen et al., 2020; Codagnone et al., 2018; Florisson and Mandl, 2018).

Algorithmic surveillance

Technologically derived and boosted control mechanisms can comprise monitoring and controlling algorithms without human interference. In such cases, humans no longer control operations on platforms; instead, algorithms are in control of work. Such control is centered on time, activity, or procedures, and does not tend to concern content. Through the adoption of technology, experts and workers allocate tasks and decisions to automated systems, machines, and artificial agents. These automated systems and algorithmic adaptations of AI mediate human relationships and make decisions and act on behalf of humans. The output may be defined by an individual who has transformed organizational wishes into algorithms, which, for their part, if possible, transform data into the desired format. Mistakes and misinterpretations may happen during translation.

Control through technology raises several ethical questions. For instance, digital metrics are universally used in all forms of digital traffic; however, they have not yet been thought of as a form of control, even when used to monitor employees and workers. Those who were not assessed through quantitative evaluation earlier are now meeting assessments based on masses of data on their performance. The scale of digitalization has multiplied evaluative practices and managerial efforts, and the development of standardized knowledge of performance has led to the effective use of corporation metrics. The quantification of evaluations is not new, given the rise of Taylorism in the 1930s and the cost–benefit analysis tools of the 1980s. The transformation of qualities into quantities has always been a part of productive capitalism. In the course of delegating decisions and evaluations to automated systems, guided by algorithmic procedures and applications, the criteria that guide the actions of automated systems become invisible, with less or no scrutiny. Often, accountability in decision-making algorithms is incomplete and there is no clarity on who holds the responsibility for the decisions made by or with the support of algorithms. Transparency promotes accountability; however, transparency and auditing do not necessarily suffice in achieving accountability. Algorithmic decision-making processes may lead to more objective and therefore potentially fairer decisions than those made by humans influenced by several factors and biases (Lepri et al., 2018). Algorithmic procedures may indeed promote efficiency, but also prompt power asymmetries, technological normativities, and restrictions on reflexive or evaluative analyses (Scholz, 2012; D'Agostino and Durante, 2018; Lepri et al., 2018).

In evaluating platform work, the algorithm routinely offers information on possible deviations according to preset parameters, and takes pre-determined and anticipated decisions following deviations thereafter. However, algorithms do not ask for explanations for deviations a posteriori, and do not make deliberate choices to allow for unanticipated exceptions to algorithmic rules. Does an algorithm make a better boss? According to one study, access to human contact point is important as it can significantly affect working conditions for those working on and through platforms, especially labor platforms (Florisson and Mandl, 2018; Fuchs, 2017). Research has shown that reliance on algorithmic ratings have negative consequences for the working conditions of people working through platforms (Möhlmann and Teubner, 2020; Schor and Vallas, 2021). If workers do not meet preset rules and/or regulations, or receive low rankings from customers, algorithms automatically reject them from the platform.

In search of reconceptualizations for work, professions, and entrepreneurship

Useful definitions of platform work address digitalization, as platforms depend fully on digital tools and their use for the mediation of work.

Mediated platform jobs differ from the traditional employer model, where the employer is responsible for the tools, salaries, and other forms of compensation as part of the salary, such as health insurance coverage. Platforms mediate work tasks and bids for them, but do not mediate employment relations, and do not directly offer employment or employ workers. They connect individuals to gigs and tasks through technologies and create new types of assemblies and relations among individuals willing to use the services provided and companies offering their services, and finally, the platform firms between both. The ownership and agency processes merge into each other. Platforms function as a three-sided architecture or market (Kenney et al., 2020). Despite the unique content, platforms are not unique in terms of structural qualities or the use of algorithms, as they are similar in terms of visual and functional structures, and bank on familiarity with the functions of other platform webpages.

By creating new assemblies and connections, platforms create new markets and opportunities, and for that reason alone, many definitions of platform work are inaccurate as they fail to take into account work that exists fully or partially because of platforms. This myopia concerns several debates on professions that have not addressed relationships among professions, non-professionals, and institutions in specific environments (Faulconbridge et al., 2021). Examples of such work include renting and retailing, which have exploded with the introduction of digital platforms. Platform-based and mediated work, such as renting out homes, cottages, flats, and rooms (e.g., Airbnb host/hostess activities) and online retailing (e.g., Ebay and Amazon sellers), are based on the ownership of means for work, such as renting out homes/rooms, or manufacturing and retailing. Both forms are ownership-driven and pre-date platforms. Ownership-based rental/selling activities have used traditional means and variations in pricing. Sales and other exchange-related activities have always existed. By creating global markets, all forms of platforms, through companies such as Airbnb, Etsy, and Amazon, have standardized and homogenized economic activities in relation to assets in ways that were not possible earlier (Adams Prassl, 2022; Gray and Suri, 2019). Transnational corporations have strived and sometimes succeeded in such standardization, but have most often differentiated activities across different nation-states.

The emergence and proliferation of the platform economy have changed the world of work, production, and consumption and its patterns vis-à-vis platform-mediated work arrangements. The content of work has changed, and the legal status of platform-based and mediated work and work providers has become so complex that the interpretation is that in many cases, new realities of work have outgrown the formal legal concepts that regulate the world of work (de Stefano and Aloisi, 2018). The effects on work and work contracts, conditions, and aspects such as supervision may vary based on whether the platform is operating globally or locally. For this reason alone, the analysis of platforms as a unified or single business model may be inappropriate and misleading given the difference in the content of work, tasks provided, supervision carried out, and relations nurtured. Apart from being a crucial part of the new immaterial platform economy industry, social media enables new possibilities for consumption by billions of users through personalized feeds comprising images, news, and games. Social media has opened up a plethora of marketing possibilities, involving the promotion of products and services by influencers who enjoy authority over consumers (Ye et al., 2021; Yeomans, 2019; Yuan and Lou, 2020; Ge and Gretzel, 2018; Schaefer, 2012).

The cultural, social, and economic transformations taking place via social media and platforms are profound. Technology has enabled greater immersion and interactions across digital systems, and the generational shift is visible in the influence of digital social life on consumption patterns and life choices the world over (Danziger, 2022; Aggrawal et al., 2018; Ritzer, 2015). Large shifts in the everyday use of technology are brought about through all-encompassing procedures, such as transforming the national taxation systems into a web-based service, for example. Nation-states use and develop their online services, and transfer many of their earlier labor-intensive services into algorithmically maneuvered web-based services, taxation being one example. Institutions use digital means to communicate and advertise their services. Thus, businesses and nation-states exist and function online and offline. Digital social media has become an integral part of both the economy in general and the platform economy monetization process in particular. Thus, social media influencers are no longer merely celebrities working as campaign promotors or media ambassadors but are often serious professionals and long-term business partners for global and national brands. The grassroots entrepreneurial elements, which ranges from celebrities to people running cottage industry–type influencer accounts are signs of new emerging professions, discussed in details in the next Chapter 6.

Collaborative ties with influencer partners can range from single endorsement posts to long-term ambassadorships and brands. New social media influencers are 'opinion leader[s] in digital social media who communicate[s] to an unknown mass audience' (Gräve, 2017, 1; Bishop, 2021; Cotter, 2018; Uzunoğlu and Misci Kip, 2014). To consumers, the influencer is not strategic, calculating, or business-minded (O'Meara, 2019; Semaan et al., 2019). Much due to – assumed and alleged – sharing of personal lives on their platform channels, many influencers mediate themselves as accessible and reliable, peers or next-door neighbors who offer unbiased, trustworthy opinions and therefore radiate high credibility.

For these reasons, fixating on just two concepts alone – either paid employment or self-employment – and assuming similarities within these categories, while describing the existing forms of work models on platforms, offers a narrow view into work and income generation possibilities in the platform economy. Several controversies vis-à-vis global platform companies highlight the power of global firms and national and supranational policies, when several recent legal disputes and battles over worker positions are analyzed (Aloisi and De Stefano, 2022; Kovalainen et al., 2020; Poutanen et al., 2020). Thus, a better understanding and detailed analysis of the ways in which the platform economy transforms work are necessary. The power of platform owners may not become clear at the outset, but the platform-labor fixture exposes the imbalance in power relations.

References

Adams-Prassl, J. (2022). Regulating Algorithms at Work: Lessons for a 'European Approach to Artificial Intelligence'. *European Labour Law Journal*, 13(1), pp. 30–50. doi:10.1177/20319525211062558.

Aggrawal, N., Arora, A., Anand, A. and Irshad, M.S. (2018). View-Count Based Modeling for YouTube Videos and Weighted Criteria – Based Ranking. In: M. Ram and J.P. Davim, eds., *Advanced Mathematical Techniques in Engineering Sciences*. Boca Raton: CRC Press, pp. 149–160.

Aldredge, M., Rogers, C. and Smith, J. (2020). The Strategic Transformation of Accounting into a Learned Profession. *Industry and Higher Education*, 35(2), pp. 83–88. doi:10.1177/0950422220954319.

Aloisi, A. (2020). Platform Work in the European Union: Lessons Learned, Legal Developments and Challenges Ahead. *European Labour Law Journal*. [Forthcoming]. Available at: SSRN: https://ssrn.com/abstract=3556922 or http://dx.doi.org/10.2139/ssrn.3556922.

Aloisi, A. and De Stefano, V. (2022). *Your Boss Is an Algorithm: Artificial Intelligence, Platform Work and Labour*. London: Bloomsbury Publishing.

Arora, A., Bansal, S., Kandpal, C., Aswani, R. and Dwivedi, Y. (2019). Measuring Social Media Influencer Index – Insights from Facebook, Twitter and Instagram. *Journal of Retailing and Consumer Services*, 49(49), pp. 86–101. doi:10.1016/j.jretconser.2019.03.012.

Arrow, K.J. (1971). The Firm in General Equilibrium Theory. *The Corporate Economy*, pp. 68–110. doi:10.1007/978-1-349-01110-0_3.

Baker, T. and Nelson, R.E. (2005). Creating Something from Nothing: Resource Construction Through Entrepreneurial Bricolage. *Administrative Science Quarterly*, 50(3), pp. 329–366. doi:10.2189/asqu.2005.50.3.329.

Baron, D.P. (2018). Disruptive Entrepreneurship and Dual Purpose Strategies: The Case of Uber. *Strategy Science*, 3(2), pp. 439–462. doi:10.1287/stsc.2018.0059.

Behsudi, A. (2022). *Technology-Driven Development. Finance & Development*. Washington: IMF Publications. [online]. Available at: www.imf.org/en/Publications/fandd/issues/2022/03/Technology-driven-development-Lawson.

Berg, J. and De Stefano, V. (2018). Employment and Regulation for Clickworker. In: M. Neufeind, J. O'Reilly and F. Ranft, eds., *Work in the Digital Age: Challenges of the Fourth Industrial Revolution Identifying the Challenges for Work in the Digital Age*. London; New York: Rowman & Littlefield, pp. 175–184.

Bhatt, E.R. (2011). *We Are Poor But So Many: The Story of Self-Employed Women in India*. Oxford: Oxford University Press.

Bishop, S. (2021). Influencer Management Tools: Algorithmic Cultures, Brand Safety, and Bias. *Social Media + Society*, 7(1). doi:10.1177/20563051211003066.

Blaug, M. (1986). *Economic History and the History of Economics*. New York: New York University Press.

Bollmer, G. (2018). *Theorizing Digital Cultures*. London: Sage Publications.

Bridge, S. and O'Neill, K. (2018). *Understanding Enterprise: Entrepreneurs & Small Business*. Basingstoke: Palgrave Macmillan.

Bridge, S., O'Neill, K. and Cromie, S. (1998). *Understanding Enterprise, Entrepreneurship and Small Business*. 2nd ed. Basingstoke: Palgrave Macmillan.

Caplan, R. and Gillespie, T. (2020). Tiered Governance and Demonetization: The Shifting Terms of Labor and Compensation in the Platform Economy. *Social Media + Society*, 6(2). doi:10.1177/2056305120936636.

Casson, M. (2010). Entrepreneurship: Theory, Institutions and History. Eli F. Heckscher Lecture, 2009. *Scandinavian Economic History Review*, 58(2), pp. 139–170. doi:10.1080/03585522.2010.482288.

Chen, C.C., Garven, S.A., Jones, K.T. and Scarlata, A.N. (2021). Is Career Guidance Sending the Right Message About Accounting Work? Comparing Accounting with Competing Professions. *Accounting Education*, 30(4), pp. 355–384. doi:10.1080/09639284.2021.1913615.

Childers, C.C., Lemon, L.L. and Hoy, M.G. (2019). #Sponsored #Ad: Agency Perspective on Influencer Marketing Campaigns. *Journal of Current Issues & Research in Advertising*, 40(3), pp. 1–17.

Christin, A. (2020). *Metrics at Work*. Princeton; Oxford: Princeton University Press.

Codagnone, C., Karatzogianni, A. and Matthews, J. (2018). *Platform Economics: Rhetoric and Reality in the 'Sharing Economy'*. Bingley: Emerald Publishing Limited.

Conen, W. (2020). *Multiple Jobholding in Europe: Structure and Dynamics*. WSI Study, No. 20. Dusseldorf: WSI.

Conen, W. and Schippers, J.J. (2019). Self-Employment: Between Freedom and Insecurity. In: W. Conen and J.J. Schippers, eds., *Self-Employment as Precarious Work*. Cheltenham: Edward Elgar Publishing, pp. 1–22.

Cotter, K. (2018). Playing the Visibility Game: How Digital Influencers and Algorithms Negotiate Influence on Instagram. *New Media & Society*, 21(4), pp. 895–913. doi:10.1177/1461444818815684.

Dabić, M., Vlačić, B., Kiessling, T., Caputo, A. and Pellegrini, M. (2021). Serial Entrepreneurs: A Review of Literature and Guidance for Future Research. *Journal of Small Business Management*, pp. 1–36. doi:10.1080/00472778.2021.1969657.

D'Agostino, M. and Durante, M. (2018). Introduction: The Governance of Algorithms. *Philosophy & Technology*, 31(4), pp. 499–505. doi:10.1007/s13347-018-0337-z.

Danziger, P.N. (2022). Social Commerce is a $1.2 Trillion Opportunity and the Next Global Shopping Revolution. *Forbes*. 27 Jan. [online]. Available at: https://www.forbes.com/sites/pamdanziger/2022/01/27/social-commerce-is-a-12-trillion-opportunity-and-the-next-global-shopping-revolution/?sh=4bfeb9101d98 [Accessed: 7 Oct. 2022].

De Stefano, V. (2015). The Rise of the 'Just-in-Time Workforce': On-Demand Work, Crowd Work and Labour Protection in the 'Gig-Economy'. *SSRN Electronic Journal*, 71(3). doi:10.2139/ssrn.2682602.

De Stefano, V. and Aloisi, A. (2018). *European Legal Framework for Digital Labour Platforms*. Luxembourg: European Commission. doi:10.2760/78590, JRC112243.

Drahokoupil, J. (2021). The Business Models of Labour Platforms: Creating an Uncertain Future. In: J. Drahokoupil and K. Vandaele, eds., *A Modern Guide to Labour and the Platform Economy*. Cheltenham: Edward Elgar Publishing, pp. 33–49.

Faulconbridge, J., Folke Henriksen, L. and Seabrooke, L. (2021). How Professional Actions Connect and Protect. *Journal of Professions and Organization*, 8(2), pp. 214–227. doi:10.1093/jpo/joab008.

Florisson, R. and Mandl, I. (2018). *Digital Age: Employment and Working Conditions of Selected Types of Platform Work*. Eurofound Working Paper WPEF18004. Dublin: European Foundation for the Improvement of Living and Working Conditions.

Frenken, K., Waes, A., Pelzer, P., Smink, M. and Est, R. (2019). Safeguarding Public Interests in the Platform Economy. *Policy & Internet*, 12(5). doi:10.1002/poi3.217.

Fuchs, C. (2017). *Social Media: A Critical Introduction*. Los Angeles: Sage.

Ge, J. and Gretzel, U. (2018). Emoji Rhetoric: A Social Media Influencer Perspective. *Journal of Marketing Management*, 34(15–16), pp. 1272–1295. Doi:10.1080/0267257x.2018.1483960.

Gräve, J.-F. (2017). Exploring the Perception of Influencers vs. Traditional Celebrities. In: *Proceedings of the 8th International Conference on Social Media & Society – #SMSociety17*. New York: ACM Press. doi:10.1145/3097286.3097322.

Gray, M.L. and Suri, S. (2019). *Ghost Work: How Amazon, Google, and Uber Are Creating a New Global Underclass*. New York: Houghton Mifflin Harcourt Publishing Company.

Gupta, V.K., Dutta, D.K., Guo, G., Javadian, G., Jiang, C., Osorio, A.E. and Ozkazanc-Pan, B. (2016). Classics in Entrepreneurship Research: Enduring Insights, Future Promises. *New England Journal of Entrepreneurship*, 19(1), pp. 7–23. doi:10.1108/neje-19-01-2016-b001.

Harrington, B. and Seabrooke, L. (2020). Transnational Professionals. *Annual Review of Sociology*, 46(1), pp. 399–417. doi:10.1146/annurev-soc-112019-053842.

Hébert, R.F. and Link, A.N. (2012). *A History of Entrepreneurship*. London: Routledge.

ILO. (2021). *The Role of Digital Labour Platforms in Transforming the World of Work. World Employment and Social Outlook*. New York: International Labor Organization.

IMF. (2021). *Measuring the Informal Economy. IMF Policy Paper*. New York: International Monetary Fund. Available at: www.imf.org.

Javadian, G. (2022). Gendered Perspectives on Organizational Creation: Lessons from the Past and Insights for the Future. In: B. Ozkazanc-Pan, A.E. Osorio, D.K. Dutta, V.K. Gupta, G. Javadian and G. Chun Guo, eds., *Modern Classics in Entrepreneurship Studies: Building the Future of the Field*. Cham: Springer International Publishing, pp. 15–33.

Kenney, M., Rouvinen, P. and Zysman, J. (2020). Employment, Work, and Value Creation in the Era of Digital Platforms. In: S. Poutanen, A. Kovalainen and P. Rouvinen, eds., *Digital Work and the Platform Economy*. New York: Routledge, pp. 13–20.

Kovalainen, A. (1995). *At the Margins of the Economy: Women's Self-Employment in Finland, 1960–1990*. Aldershot: Avebury.

Kovalainen, A., Vallas, S.P. and Poutanen, S. (2020). Theorizing Work in the Contemporary Platform Economy. In: S. Poutanen, A. Kovalainen and P. Rouvinen, eds., *Digital Work and the Platform Economy*. New York: Routledge, pp. 31–52.

Kristiansen, J.H., Larsen, T.P. and Ilsøe, A. (2022). Hybrid Work Patterns: A Latent Class Analysis of Platform Workers in Denmark. *Nordic Journal of Working Life Studies*, 10, pp. 1–26. doi:10.18291/njwls.133721.

Kuratko, D.F., Fisher, G. and Audretsch, D.B. (2020). Unraveling the Entrepreneurial Mindset. *Small Business Economics*, 57(4). doi:10.1007/s11187-020-00372-6.

Lepri, B., Oliver, N., Letouzé, E., Pentland, A. and Vinck, P. (2018). Fair, Transparent, and Accountable Algorithmic Decision-Making Processes. *Philosophy & Technology*, 31(4), pp. 611–627. doi:10.1007/s13347-017-0279-x.

Lobato, R. (2016). The Cultural Logic of Digital Intermediaries. *Convergence: The International Journal of Research into New Media Technologies*, 22(4), pp. 348–360. doi:10.1177/1354856516641628.

Lou, C. (2021). Social Media Influencers and Followers: Theorization of a Trans-Parasocial Relation and Explication of Its Implications for Influencer Advertising. *Journal of Advertising*, 51(1), pp. 1–18. doi:10.1080/00913367.2021.1880345.

Lundström, A. and Halvarsson, S. (2006). Entrepreneurship Research: Past Perspectives and Future Prospects. *Foundations and Trends® in Entrepreneurship*, 2(3), pp. 145–259. doi:10.1561/0300000009.

Mackert, J. (2012). *Social Closure*. Oxford: Oxford University Press.

Manza, J. (1992). Classes, Status Groups, and Social Closure: A Critique of Neo-Weberian Social Theory. *Current Perspectives in Social Theory*, 12, pp. 275–302.

Mason, C. and Harvey, C. (2013). Entrepreneurship: Contexts, Opportunities and Processes. *Business History*, 55(1), pp. 1–8. doi:10.1080/00076791.2012.687542.

Mezzadri, A. and Fan, L. (2018). 'Classes of Labour' at the Margins of Global Commodity Chains in India and China. *Development and Change*, 49(4), pp. 1034–1063. doi:10.1111/dech.12412.

Mirchandani, K. (1999). Feminist Insight on Gendered Work: New Directions in Research on Women and Entrepreneurship. *Gender, Work & Organization*, 6(4), pp. 224–235. doi:10.1111/1468-0432.00085.

Moats, J. (2021). Preparing for the Future of Work and the Development of Expertise. In: M.L. Germain and R.S. Grenier, eds., *Expertise at Work*. London; Cham: Palgrave Macmillan, pp. 179–224. https://doi.org/10.1007/978-3-030-64371-3_10.

Möhlmann, M. and Teubner, T. (2020). Navigating by the Stars: Current Challenges for Ensuring Trust in the Sharing Economy. *NIM Marketing Intelligence Review*, 12(2), pp. 22–27. doi:10.2478/nimmir-2020-0013.

Neff, G., Wissinger, E. and Zukin, S. (2005). Entrepreneurial Labor among Cultural Producers: 'Cool' Jobs in 'Hot' Industries. *Social Semiotics*, 15(3), pp. 307–334. doi:10.1080/10350330500310111.

Norlander, K. (1992). Entrepreneurs During the Early Industrialization in Sweden. *Scandinavian Economic History Review*, 40(1), pp. 89–94. doi:10.1080/03585522.1992.10408241.

OECD. (2020). *The Emergence of Alternative Credentials. OECD Education Working Paper No. 216 by S. Kato (OECD), V. Galán-Muros (Global Institute on Innovation Districts) and T. Weko (OECD)*. Paris: OECD.

OII. (2020). Oxford Internet Institute, ILO, Oxford University: Online Labour Observatory. *onlinelabourobservatory.org*. [online]. Available at: http://onlinelabourobservatory.org/ [Accessed: 5 Sep. 2022].

O'Meara, V. (2019). Weapons of the Chic: Instagram Influencer Engagement Pods as Practices of Resistance to Instagram Platform Labor. *Social Media + Society*, 5(4). doi:10.1177/2056305119879671.

Ozkazanc-Pan, B., Osorio, A.E., Dutta, D.K., Gupta, V.K., Javadian, G. and Chun Guo, G. (2022). *Modern Classics in Entrepreneurship Studies: Building the Future of the Field*. Cham: Springer International Publishing.

Poell, T., Nieborg, D. and van Dijck, J. (2019). Platformisation. *Internet Policy Review*, 8(4). doi:10.14763/2019.4.1425.

Poutanen, S., Kovalainen, A. and Rouvinen, P. (2020). *Digital Work and the Platform Economy: Understanding Tasks, Skills and Capabilities in the New Era*. New York: Routledge; Taylor & Francis Group.

Rani, U. and Furrer, M. (2021). Digital Labour Platforms and New Forms of Flexible Work in Developing Countries: Algorithmic Management of Work and Workers. *Competition & Change*, 25(2), pp. 212–236. https://doi.org/10.1177/1024529420905187.

Reskin, B.F. (2005). Including Mechanisms in Our Models of Ascriptive Inequality. In: L.B. Nielsen and R.L. Nelson, eds., *Handbook of Employment Discrimination Research*. Dordrecht: Springer, pp. 75–97. https://doi.org/10.1007/1-4020-3455-5_4.

Ritzer, G. (2015). Prosumer Capitalism. *The Sociological Quarterly*, 56(3), pp. 413–445. doi:10.1111/tsq.12105.

Schaefer, M. (2012). *Return on Influence: The Revolutionary Power of Klout, Social Scoring, and Influence Marketing*. New York: McGraw-Hill.

Scholz, T. (2012). *Digital Labor: The Internet as Playground and Factory*. New York: Routledge.

Schor, J.B. and Vallas, S.P. (2021). The Sharing Economy: Rhetoric and Reality. *Annual Review of Sociology*, 47(1), pp. 369–389. doi:10.1146/annurev-soc-082620-031411.

Schumpeter, J.A. (1934). *The Theory of Economic Development: An Inquiry into Profits, Capital, Credit, Interest, and the Business Cycle*. Cambridge: Harvard University Press.

Semaan, R.W., Ashill, N. and Williams, P. (2019). Sophisticated, Iconic and Magical: A Qualitative Analysis of Brand Charisma. *Journal of Retailing and Consumer Services*, 49, pp. 102–113. doi:10.1016/j.jretconser.2019.03.011.

Sennett, R. (2009). *The Craftsman*. New Haven: The Yale University Press.

Stinchfield, B.T., Nelson, R.E. and Wood, M.S. (2012). Learning from Levi-Strauss' Legacy: Art, Craft, Engineering, Bricolage, and Brokerage in Entrepreneurship. *Entrepreneurship Theory and Practice*, 37(4), pp. 889–921. doi:10.1111/j.1540-6520.2012.00523.x.

Swedberg, R. (2000). *Entrepreneurship: The Social Science View*. Oxford: Oxford University Press.

Ucbasaran, D., Westhead, P., Wright, M. and Flores, M. (2010). The Nature of Entrepreneurial experience, Business Failure and Comparative Optimism. *Journal of Business Venturing*, 25(6), pp. 541–555. doi:10.1016/j.jbusvent.2009.04.001.

UN News. (2022). Ukraine: WFP Teams Up with Uber, in Boost for Pinpoint Aid Deliveries. *United Nations News*. [online]. https://news.un.org/en/story/2022/06/1119952.8 [Accessed: 18 Oct. 2022].

Uzunoğlu, E. and Misci Kip, S. (2014). Brand Communication Through Digital Influencers: Leveraging Blogger Engagement. *International Journal of Information Management*, 34(5), pp. 592–602. doi:10.1016/j.ijinfomgt.2014.04.007.

Van Doorn, N. (2022). Platform Capitalism's Social Contract. *Internet Policy Review*, 11(1). doi:10.14763/2022.1.1625.

Weber, M. (1922/1978). *Economy and Society: An Outline of Interpretive Sociology*. Berkeley: University of California Press.

White, J., Saurav, S. and Gupta, V.K. (2021). Entrepreneurship Research After Chiles, Bluedorn, and Gupta: Has the Field Delivered on the Promise of Good Scholarship? In: B. Ozkazanc-Pan, A.E. Osorio, D. Dutta, V.K. Gupta, G. Javadian and C. Guo, eds., *Modern Classics in Entrepreneurship Studies: Building the Future of the Field*. Cham: Palgrave Macmillan, pp. 35–64.

Wright, M., Robbie, K. and Ennew, C. (1997). Venture Capitalists and Serial Entrepreneurs. *Journal of Business Venturing*, 12(3), pp. 227–249. doi:10.1016/s0883-9026(96)06115-0.

Ye, G., Hudders, L., De Jans, S. and De Veirman, M. (2021). The Value of Influencer Marketing for Business: A Bibliometric Analysis and Managerial Implications. *Journal of Advertising*, 50(2), pp. 1–19. doi:10.1080/00913367.2020.1857888 [Accessed: 11 Oct. 2022].

Yeomans, L. (2019). *Public Relations as Emotional Labour*. Abington, Oxon; New York: Routledge.

Yuan, S. and Lou, C. (2020). How Social Media Influencers Foster Relationships with Followers: The Roles of Source Credibility and Fairness in Parasocial Relationship and Product Interest. *Journal of Interactive Advertising*, 20(2), pp. 1–42. doi:10.1080/15252019.2020.1769514.

Zuboff, S. (2019). *The Age of Surveillance Capitalism: The Fight for a Human Future at the New Frontier of Power*. New York: Public Affairs.

6 Social media influencer as a new platform profession

Elements of the platform profession

Social media influencers represent an entirely new type of profession in comparison to traditional ones. The profession is mainly built on digital media, markets, and platforms. The construction of professional ties and networks takes place mainly or solely on platforms. All these activities represent a type of work that can be categorized as *platform-mediated* and *platform-related content creation* work, as explained in the categorization of platform work in the previous chapter. Influencers are not employed by platforms; they are contracted by the companies that hire them for promoting services or products on platforms. Yet, they fully depend on platforms as though they are employees, as their profession and presence are constructed on platforms and social media. They are equally dependent on the platformization of corporate marketing, and are managed by the companies and corporations that hire them. Earlier, the key elements in any claim to professional status were autonomy provided by the expertise, control over own work activities and contents, a clearly defined monopoly over an area of work, and most importantly, a knowledge base recognized belonging to an expert or a professional (Abbott and Meerabeau, 1998). This is no longer the case at platforms. Professionalizing strategies have invaded market economies, and instead of autonomy or control over work, control over the knowledge base may have become more important for the recognition of professions.

Despite the differences technology brings about to the core of one's profession, old and new professions share a few similarities, one of which is the close relationship and strong interdependency between an individual's identity and work, where work becomes an integral part of their identity, making it difficult to act against the professional code of conduct, for example. A systematic review of professional identity construction research shows that individuals merge their professional and personal roles, as well as public and private roles, in a process of constructing professional identity on social media (Kasperiuniene and Zydziunaite, 2019; Davis and Jurgenson, 2014). As professionals, influencers are not related to the state and conventional institutional ties of governance that have given classical professions a strong

DOI: 10.4324/9781351038546-6

foothold and position in society. It may be relevant to ask if building up a sustainable profession is possible outside of formal institutional structures and ties. Formal and informal networks are established and incubated, and identities are shaped in formal institutional structures, such as education. The social positions of professions are established and developed further through professional guilds. These and other ties are essential in building up, supporting, and maintaining the social closure of professional groups such as doctors, lawyers, and teachers. For professional groups that are sometimes classified as semi-professions in research, questions of autonomy and independence remain relevant. Such categories include gendered and gender-segregated occupations such as care work, social work, nursing, and librarianship, to mention a few.

Influencer is a prime example of a *new profession in technology-mediated times*, where formal education and traditional social closures in relation to the role of professions in society play very little, or no role at all in profession formation and maintenance. New professions are based on *identity* and *personality* that are respectively performed and mediated, staged, and performed online. Thus, there is no formal path of education or entry into this profession. Both mediated identity and personality relate to an influencer's ability to project audiences' attention and consumption patterns and desires, and their desire to connect. These identity-attached elements of the profession build the professional core, sustainability, and status of an influencer. Two concepts relate to the construction of a mediated platform profession: authenticity and credibility. Both are discussed in this chapter.

Social media users do not passively use platforms, but are active and engage with websites, brands, and social media authorities or influencers. Platforms are active intermediaries and shape the world through co-production with their users including businesses and consumers. Consumers, through their choices, teach algorithms their likes, selections, taste, and consumption patterns. Thus, algorithms do not fetch information neutrally from a vast, transparent sea of data, but follow users' choices. Thus, they typically offer 'more of the same'. The active role of consumers and social influencers funnels economic activities and productions in specific ways. Mediated selections are coded as governance by algorithms. This does not offer power to algorithms or platforms where algorithms work; instead. the question of algorithmic power lies in the embodiment of systems of strategies, where power is immanent to the field and situation in question. The question of power is about who has access and how in situations and spaces where algorithms are defined and written. Influencers may not necessarily have a central role in these processes, but their knowledge and co-produced understanding of realities may affect how algorithms are shaped. As technology has become a mundane part of life, it is difficult, if not impossible, to demarcate a line between algorithms and humans. In the influencer profession, the human overpowers the machine. For example, bots that are given human features such as age, name, and location are not appreciated by consumers (Arsenyan and Mirowska, 2021). People's resistance to overt behavior and attitude manipulation fall into aims of influencing activities. Although virtual agents permeate and interact on publicly visible human networks, virtual algorithmic agents are penalized for their 'almost human appearance' (Arsenyan and Mirowska, 2021, 102694; Jacobson et al., 2022).

Constructing platform professions

The platform economy produces new professions and occupations, and with them, a set of very different types of polarizations and social closures that do not necessarily follow distinctions created by human capital. Occupations are emerging through routes other than formal educational institutions and licensing practices. When membership in associations is no longer a requirement for practicing an occupation and when the code of ethics is global but follow-up is not regulated, theories based on the structural progress of occupations are weak in explaining societal change. Other mechanisms that build distinctions between occupations include differences in human capital and skills. The growth of occupational polarization in terms of earnings is a reflection of technological change (Kalleberg, 2011). The classic notion by Weber (1922/1978) on social closure has mostly been addressed in social science research as professional and occupational closure, as discussed more closely in Chapter 4.

The contemporary notion of social closure widens the field and addresses 'processes of drawing boundaries, constructing identities and building communities to monopolize resources for one's own group, thereby excluding others from using them' (Mackert, 2012, 1). Institutional arrangements play a key role in the renewal and strengthening of social closure through professions at the social level. Institutional settings lay the groundwork and foundations for differences and distinctions between occupations and professions. The constant strengthening of social closure takes place perhaps more effectively through flexible day-to-day interactions and everyday practices, in a manner similar to how professional and occupational cultures are formed and boundaries are rebuilt in daily activities and interactions (Manza, 1992, 286). Reskin (2005) described social closures as specific processes that link individuals' characteristics to workplace outcomes and redirect the attention from motives to mechanisms of economies and working lives. Task specialization differentiates between professions and occupations, and job descriptions strengthen these divisions.

New platform professions range from social media-related professions such as influencers, bloggers, and content creators, to various supporting professions for platform agencies such as social media coders and intermediators and managers. None of them are related to public and state institutions, professional guilds, and other social closure institutions; rather, they stem from and are entirely related to digital markets, market relations, and social media performances, presence, and performing activities. Platforms and platform professions do not function within national borders and do not recognize state boundaries in their activities. Digital social media works across national and language barriers. The social media influencer profession is fueled by online connections to parasocial relationships with followers and attention. The offline work of social influencers exists, and comprises gigs. These relate to online and social media presence, product promotions, and appearances at gigs, such as in the promotion of products. The novelty of the influencer profession, especially when compared to strong, established, and recognized professions such as law and medicine, stems from two features that describe social changes generally.

First, an influencer as a profession epitomizes a full uncoupling between the status of a profession and its formal state and public institutions. As described in Chapters 1 and 2, the birth of strong professions such as law and medicine took place in close alignment with state development and the molding of state institutions and public organizations. The influencer has developed and is established with a position of power entirely within and through platforms and digital markets, in close relation to global and national market platforms and social media development. The influencer profession is a new but established phenomenon that epitomizes several features of the digitized media society. The platform profession is controlled through a mediated network of followers, for example. Once the ties and parasocial relationships are established, the bonds with the followers allow influencers to be perceived as authentic.

Second, the influencer as a profession epitomizes values and features that oppose the more traditional values attached to strong professions. This separates the influencer profession from traditional professions, as the influencer lacks formal and standardized qualifications with social closures that relate to and are characteristic of traditional professions. The social media influencer exists in corporeal and imaginary worlds: performances at product launch events differ from those on social media or blog pages. The profession comprises performances of a personal online identity and its monetization. The influencer relies on how the materiality of a medium permits identity presentation and possible products (Suzor, 2019; Bollmer, 2018), the strength of visual and consumer cultures, and the aesthetics of digital media. Digital platforms, their infrastructure, and network effects shape culture and consumption for new platform occupations and professions.

How influencing becomes an accepted profession in society

One route for social recognition is a degree earned in educational systems. Earning formal credentials in the education system systematizes formal qualifications in new platform professions. Credentials comprise levels of education, experience, and/or both. Formal credentials and certificates verify that a professional level in the education system has been achieved in a subject, which is defined as having professional credentials. Certifications are earned through professional societies or continuing education units. In new professions, education is dispersed and partially achieved via platforms, not necessarily through face-to-face classroom education. This brings in global elements as part of the training and education procedure for platform professions. In their curriculum formulation and online platform education, platform professions are disconnected from state institutions. This decoupling is done through flexible, dispersed, and global provisions of credentials. Credentials are provided not only by public organizations or established private institutions but also increasingly in collaboration with businesses, nongovernmental organizations (NGOs), and online courses offered in partnership with learning platforms (OECD, 2021). New platform professions and occupations have originated at the cusp of digital markets, social media, and platforms. This implies a wide variety of skills and capabilities, along with a widespread lack of formal educational qualifications. Therefore, standardized education for new platform professions can improve their professional status and signal skills in social media. Partners identify the quality of candidates' skills more reliably. In many countries, coordinated public responses to alternative credentials have been led by NGOs.

The move between formal and informal learning and the global availability of online courses has meant that the scope of education for new platform professions has expanded considerably. This is partially related to the rising demand for upskilling and reskilling, made possible by digitalization. Businesses and other institutions are currently offering credentials that help form new platform professions and signal the competencies that those working at platforms may already have. Educational expansion institutionalizes and formalizes the establishment of platform professions as new types of professions. Systematic training courses and university degrees for influencers have been developed in universities in several countries. These courses and degrees often comprise the content of studies on social media, content production, entrepreneurship, communication, and marketing adopted in universities and applied science universities' academic curriculums, in addition to several existing online courses. These factors influence serious career choices with separate university or applied sciences degrees. Most university degrees in social media influencing are based on university-level established study modules in business, marketing, and media studies. In Finland, for example, degree-awarding studies in influencer marketing take up to 3.5 years, and the title offered is Bachelor in Business Administration. Formal, higher education, and university studies with higher education degrees help establish and stabilize credentials for new professions, and entrench their societal status as a profession.

The influencer profession is established and borne within the digital social media field, where identity and image-building are integral and intertwined with consumption and its features. Product or message promotion, placement, marketing, and digital identification and interaction with social media account followers are the most important parts of professional image-building. Strategic image-building may be connected with carefully selected, limited yet powerful consumer/follower audiences, and equally, the targeted audience can comprise other identifiable groups. In the US in the 2010s, most social media influencers as well as their platform followers were women (Duffy and Hund, 2019; Hund, 2019; Duffy, 2013). Duffy (2017) and Duffy and Pooley (2019) have shown how social media content creation tends to distribute financial returns unevenly. For many influencers, the compensation takes place in the form of gifts and products rather than money. This is particularly usual in nano and micro levels of social influence activities.

Platforms create the possibility for thick markets and play a key role in facilitating greater outreach and influence. To understand the nature of the influencer profession, we must address how influencers work with their own images, identity constructions, and the products, services, and brands they advocate and advertise on social media and offline. Influencers are independent when it comes to content creation on platforms (Bishop, 2021; Truong et al., 2022). However, independence is subject to critical scrutiny, even though influencer economies have gradually been formalized. We claim that independence in the influencer profession is restricted and relative, as earnings depend on the willingness to work. Earnings, for example, are highly contingent on the possibility of capitalizing on the knowledge- or aesthetic-based appeal and consumeristic values of followers on social media, and on the network effects of social media agency. The stability of parasocial relations with followers is uncertain and uncontrollable, and the monetized social media identity is vulnerable to 'wrong' calculations of monetization or appeal. As there is no formal globally accepted and standardized education on the field, other measures are necessary to estimate the value of an influencer. In measuring the number of followers, estimating roles and visibility in campaign success, and capitalizing on brand value, the influencer image and personality are proxy measures for professionalism and market value.

Based on social media marketing, research has developed several types of influencer indexes that have components such as engagement, reach, sentiment, and growth. Measurements aim for accuracy, and techniques like linear modeling, for example, are used to identify niche influencers and secure greater accuracy in the influencer index (Aggrawal et al., 2018). Influencer scores can be counted across the most-used social media platforms (Facebook, Twitter, Instagram, TikTok) and variations can be found between influencers on their scores on these platforms (Arora et al., 2019). The focus on quantification and social media metrics is powerful in their precision and accuracy: quantification determines which people and products have visibility and thus also power at markets (Schaefer, 2012). The qualitative measures of influencer power are important as they evaluate symbolic values attached to objects. Equally importantly qualitative measures enable the evaluation of consumers' emotional and transformative reactions to such values, among other things (Semaan et al., 2019).

Authenticity and credibility as assemblies of platform professions

Studies show that influencer communities exercise significant power over brand perceptions and consumer preferences, and that such power is growing with the growth of social media (Childers et al., 2019). Social media arising from and enabled by platforms have grown into their own fields of economy and industry, where cultural scripts, several meanings of influence, and mediated authenticities play crucial roles in building and maintaining the field. Constructed authenticities of influencers mediate the lifestyles, brands, and ideas that are wanted and admired by consumers. This power is based on social networks and highlights the influence of platforms and social media in the platform economy. Influencers amplify the message and enhance the visibility of a brand. Through several means, influencers add user experiences and narratives to brands and strengthen consumer adoption. Influencer marketing has evolved into a full-fledged marketing strategy deployed by various businesses (Ye et al., 2021).

As social media professionals, influencers are successful in creating trustworthy images on a variety of platforms such as web pages, blogs, videos, and other social media platforms, especially those with user-generated content, identifiable by consumers and social media users alike. Mediated authenticity and systematically built credibility function as assets in influencer image-building. For brands, collaborations with influencers seem to be a more effective marketing strategy than collaborating with celebrities who have built their reputations offline, such as actors, movie stars, or musicians (Schouten et al., 2019). This strengthens the importance of parasocial relationships. Not only do the number of followers, likes, or comments on social media matter, but also more closely monitored product and service consumption figures and indexes relate to influencer's activities and promotions. Every influencer campaign involves several agents, at least the influencer, the brand, and the followers (Stubb et al., 2019). As various social networking sites provide platforms for brands to interact with their consumers, customer, and influencer value are created on these platforms. While content characteristics are important and encourage customers to follow, assetization is more personal and far-reaching. Therefore, parasocial relationships are important as they build and mediate the persuasiveness and trustworthiness of the influencer, product, brand, and/or service. Influencers manage their personal social media identities to increase their followers.

What role does *authenticity* play in social media professions? In social media professions, followers' need and ability to connect and form parasocial relationships with the influencer is crucial. It fosters favorable endorsements and adds stickiness, that is, the sustainability of parasocial relationships with followers and the audience in general. This relationship is reciprocal: for influencers, the opportunity to build strong relationships with followers is the main objective of these interactions. These relationships build the future potential and existing assets of the influencer, which can be monetized in the next brand contract. Like social media velcro, each brand contract can draw potential new contracts and assetize the influencer further.

Authenticity is central to modern thought and social presence, but what does it mean and what role does it play in the formation of new professions such as platform professions? The general moral philosophy offers an answer: authenticity means being true to oneself. In social science, authenticity refers to a variety of things, relating to other conceptual categories such as sincerity, truthfulness, and originality, and ranging from ideas of staged and performed authenticity and marketable identity (Fromm, 1947; Goffman, 1974; MacCannell, 1973; Lash and Urry, 2004).

The content, roles, and importance of authenticity in professions are subtle and opaque. It relates to competence, qualifications, craftsmanship, and practice in professions, and to environments, institutions, and cultural settings where professions are actualized. Social media presence reproduces a different kind of arranged authenticity. Social media engagement is a driving force for commercialization (Hallinan et al., 2021; Gehl, 2014). This engagement is often understood as instantaneous, most visible and obvious signifiers such as likes, comments, and other visually or verbally articulated relationships. However, the power of the algorithmic media landscape cannot be undermined, as life is infused with the use of media, and increasingly 'takes place in and through the mediated landscape' (Bucher, 2018, 1). Social media encourages ordinary individuals to construct online identities, negotiate and verify identity claims, and even enact multiple identities (Kasperiuniene and Zydziunaite, 2019). This makes the straightforward governance of social media highly complex, at least from the point of view of corporations in relation to their need for influencers and other professionals.

For the social media influencer, the aspect of authenticity is important. Hallinan et al. (2021, 209) distinguished among three notions of authenticity on social media: informational, individual, and cultural. *Informational authenticity* is the idea of authenticity as *external truth* and in that the importance of validating facts is crucial part of the authenticity. *Individual authenticity* for its part refers to the desire to express the 'real self', which comes forth in parasocial relationships between influencers and followers (Abidin, 2018). The third notion is *cultural authenticity*, which according to Hallinan et al. (2021), concerns various facets of culture, modifying it to own needs.

These distinctions help locate the importance of authenticity, and its different facets in social media influencers' positions and influencers' relations to own activity fields, such as news, social media postings, promotions, etc., done online. Critics of social media have brought up the aspect of *lost authenticity* in relation to technical features that may increase attractiveness, such as the use of photo filters and 'numbers of popularity' such as public display of visibility or engagement metrics. Similarly, the prominence of sponsored content prioritizes highly idealized representations of people and their lives. Followers recognize specific aesthetic qualities and subject matters also as indicators of authenticity (Hallinan et al., 2021). In some contexts, for example, choosing not to use a photo filter can be a way of *performing authenticity*, which refers to the point that authenticity is a matter of aesthetics and affordances. In a hyper-capitalized and mediated world, authenticity is perhaps best described as a mediated and controlled emotional and social registry available for interactions and public life. Pooley (2010) called this *calculated authenticity*. Hochschild (1989) defined the phenomenon in relation to psychological factors that increase alienation, as *emotional labor*, which comprises the management of one's own and others' feelings through face-to-face or voice-to-voice interactions. It addresses the physical and emotional presence at work (such as in air hostesses' service work, for one prominent example) and is a defining feature in contemporary professional roles (Yeoman, 2021).

Online work and mediated platforms call for different forms of emotional labor in comparison to the physical environment. The mediated promotional culture pervades both physical and online work environments, and all these factors require emotional labor, despite differences among spaces for work. According to Goffman, these manifestations can be called 'benign variations' (1974, 87) that we inherently adopt and use in everyday interactions. In the Goffmanian sense, authenticity does not have a definitive meaning, but is about presenting oneself to others as a front-stage self, which is what professional influencers do systematically and entrepreneurially. If they succeed, they mediate authenticity to the extent that they can mediate their own image(s) trustworthily. The built and mediated authentic self should be a continuous source of material value that can be capitalized as a sign of trustworthiness or reliability (Whitmer, 2019).

How does authenticity relate to the social influencer work and its becoming a profession? Aside from mediated consumer culture, *prosumer capitalism* (Ritzer, 2015) underlines the consumer-based preoccupation with belonging to the right group. Authenticity requested of social media influencers represents a test to gauge one's contingent logic of consumerism more than a request for the 'real thing'. At the same time it builds the authority of social influencer as professional. The logic of consumerism rests on the self-branding of social media influencers. Self-branding may include numerous attributes such as ruggedness, sophistication, sincerity, excitement, and competence, among many others, which make the product or service or indeed an opinion shared by the influencer more relatable to those in search of the same or similar types of attributes (Khamis et al., 2017).

The promise of authenticity is based on consistency, attributes, and image, which mitigate risks for the consumer. The shifts in mediated authenticity of influencers in the digital context take place within the prevailing changes of commodification. The images of influencers need to be relatively predictable and flexible enough to accommodate any changes needed in the process of capitalizing the identity/image/body. The control of the influencer profession is thus based entirely on market logics, and various metrics support these logics as they operate as key performance indicators of influencer success. These are universally used.

Influencer endorsements, subtle or loud, are part of the professional act and reputation-building. Owing to the perceived real and authentic experience, consumers consider 'ordinary' social media influencers often more approachable than celebrity influencers, even if the difference between the two is not clear-cut. The difference in approachability seems to be important for consumers: ordinary social media influencers have achieved their social media status and raised in ranks through citizen-consumer endorsements and an increasing number of followers, in contrast to more traditional celebrity-position-based influencers and their product endorsements. Firms have realized the power of influencer marketing and user-generated content, and this gives influencers relatively strong control and power in their profession. The experience of an audience concerning the 'authenticity' of an influencer is crucial in influencer marketing effects.

Thinking of influencers with 'traditional' qualifications for professions – or even occupations – gives little support for recognizing social media influencer as a profession or occupation. Yet the operating field – internet audiences and various platforms as well many of the other signifiers of professions, are present in social media influencer position, albeit permeated and mediated through media, markets and platforms.

We argue that the core of the influencer profession is the *audience-experienced authenticity of the mediated identity*, which may seem almost industrially manufactured and has contextual dependency. The profession and its nature are manifested and visualized in the 'authenticity' experiences of followers and audiences, the identification process of the said audience, and the images the social media influencer is able to furnish for and through the influencer presence.

It is possible to create proxies to measure success, such as number of followers. Also, social media identity formation can be measured in different ways, as described earlier (e.g., with the spread of messages or indexing various activities, such as interaction with followers, profiling the followers, their social media identities, etc.). The aim of such measures is the monetizing aspects of the influencer's online personality that the influencer has been able to build and maintain. This 'authenticity image' and its management are important parts of the influencer profession. The authenticity of an influencer can be based on their sharing of daily experiences, which produces feelings of interpersonal intimacy and targets the identification experiences. The strength of these parasocial relationships serves as the underlying mechanism for influencer credibility as professional. One mechanism through which social media influencers foster relationships with their followers, is based on the followers' evaluations of the communication process with influencers, although influencer may at different platforms highlight different features that affect users' perceptions of the influencers (Yuan and Lou, 2020). These constant evaluations by followers play an indispensable role in building and maintaining influencer–follower and parasocial relationships and exploiting their importance for the influencer profession.

Platform professions and parasocial relationships

Parasocial relationships are audiences' non-face-to-face, that is, mediated, psychologically attuned relationships with social media influencers. The idea that positive parasocial relations lead to a more frequent adoption of consumer goods and services was originally based on parasocial interaction theory (Horton and Wohl, 1956), where parasocial relationships refer to the (imaginary) bond that followers develop with influencers over time. The relationship between brand, consumer, and influencer is more complex than often assumed (Giertz et al., 2022). Personal brands extend their influence over parasocial relationships and shape public opinion and consumer decision-making. Actual results may reside elsewhere than in product loyalty and consumeristic choices alone; however, social media platforms differ in terms of their purpose, functionality, and communication (Giertz et al., 2022), and thus disperse the overall role and meaning of parasocial relationships to professionalism.

The realms of influencer profession vary: the informational influence refers to processes where social media influencers give direct or indirect suggestions, which have a role in the followers' and audiences' decision-making processes (Kurtin et al., 2018). The ways in which informational influence is performed range from subtle hints to scientific evidence – types of information spread. Part of the informational influence is the building up of the image and role of the influencer as a professional.

For audiences, professional knowledge is more appealing and useful than other attributes, and higher perceived credibility makes audiences consider influencers on social media trustworthy. In research such credibility is found to motivate audiences for purchases (Su et al., 2021). Credibility refers to trustworthiness and expertise. Thus, companies increasingly turn to social media influencers, and relate the brands to their identity work. Parasocial relations strengthen the experiences of followers. When followers subscribe to an influencer's channel, they engage with and react to the activities of the influencer, for example, by leaving a comment or liking a picture (Kurtin et al., 2018). Parasocial relationships are gendered: research on celebrity endorsements shows that the endorser's gender is an important characteristic in determining celebrity endorsements' efficacy (Hudders and de Jans, 2021; Pradhan et al., 2017). These activities enhance the impression of a two-sided interaction and formation of parasocial relationships between the influencer and their followers.

Owing to their parasocial relationships, some followers, if suitable to brand, imitate the looks and experiences created or popularized by influencers (Lou, 2021), although not all influencers are about lifestyles, outlooks, or consumption of goods and services. Social media influencers include also news, media, and opinion influencers, who equally may build brands, images, and professions by spreading (mis)information, aiming to govern news and building their own profile through social media feeds, and in general aiming to influence and even govern the media and opinion climates. The analyses of authenticity among social influencers suggest a broader rule about relationships, such as how the followers attach to influencers, and their values. Accordingly, the values presented at platforms – if such exist – by social influencers may not be reducible to the commitments built into the social media infrastructures but may be more mediated and multifaceted.

Parasocial interactions are multiple and have a central role in the influencer profession. These interactions call for feelings of closeness through persuasive intimacies, which are often strengthened as objects of identification (Arsenyan and Mirowska, 2021). The governance of audiences remains a highly volatile business: there are fast-growing strains and fields of creative work, experts, and workers, but those who are favored and followed can change rapidly. Brand-building is thus subject to high insecurity, and influencer work is highly laborious, often underpaid, and mostly precarious; a permanent source of a stable income is far from guaranteed (Belanche et al., 2021; Caplan and Gillespie, 2020; Gorwa, 2019; O'Meara, 2019; Cotter, 2018). For these reasons, the governance and management of influencers and audiences are highly volatile, and is related to a new type of work shaped by platforms, namely relationship management work. Relationship management work was exercised earlier in organizations as public relations and covered much of the relationship work done by corporations. It has now become relationship labor, and is carried out in corporations and platform companies (Barley, 2020). Some form of knowledge sharing and/or consumption of products and services relates to the influencer profession, and that knowledge is used in various forms of e-commerce, viral and social media marketing, and brand management, wherein the identification of key influencers is essential. Most influencers have specific profiles and fields, such as fashion, sports, health, and/or luxury. Consequently, they are viewed by followers as experts and trustworthy sources in their fields (Schouten et al., 2019).

The image the influencer wishes to build requires monetization and planning. For brands, finding, identifying, and using the 'right' kinds of influencers is a major issue, as well as avoidance of wrongly attuned influencers in relation to brands. Social media influencers select the brands they endorse systematically, as they have to rely on their parasocial relationships with followers to obtain brand endorsements and likes. Their opinions on and recommendations for a product are based on affects and emotions. To be persuasive, influencers' followers need to feel related. Parasocial relationships build on emotive and affective reactions and identifications. Consumers are likely to align their attitudes with those of the social media influencers with whom they have parasocial relationships. Relational intimacy in parasocial relationships means that, for example, though noncelebrity micro-influencers may have less relationship-hijacking power than celebrities, they may nevertheless be perceived as trustworthy or authentic corporate brand endorsers. Professional power is no longer based on authority backed by social closure, and closed educational and institutional ranks. It takes a different shape on social media. The overall participatory culture of social media sets new requirements for the reciprocity and front-stage presence of professionals.

Digital market-based professions

In new platform work, the divisions between jobs do not follow the same logic as in established professions and occupations. The stability of content in terms of job descriptions may vary and depend on the image of an influencer, for example. The image as part of professionalism relates to the marketization of the profession within established professions such as law or medicine. However, for new platform professions, the role and position of the image are entirely different. The establishment of platform professions takes place entirely in and through markets and digital channels. There, the trustworthiness of images is crucial. The image built is the only earning capital for many platform professions. For many organizations, the utilization of social media influencers is a strategic communication practice. Several studies show that organizations seek authentic matches between their message and the endorsing influencer and that the content should align with the 'usual' style of the person in question (Borchers and Enke, 2021; Pöyry et al., 2021), thus seeking for the authenticity. Organizations' expectations in comparison with the social media influencer's image management pose a question of control that may be beyond the scope of an organization's power.

Some researchers have drawn a parallel between influencers and creative freelance workers, especially concerning the precarious and creative features of the work itself (Neff et al., 2005). They have labeled influencers 'entrepreneurial laborers'. However, there seems to be a major difference between influencers and freelancers. The volatility of gigs and instability in income may be similar, but the likeness is problematic in several ways. First, Neff, Wissinger, and Zukin claim similarity in skills and capabilities between freelancers and influencers. This similarity is assumed to exist in terms of work and its outcomes, and possibilities for work. However, most freelancers have formal education for the skills they capitalize on as freelancers. To freelance, one needs to have special skills in their freelancing field, generally acquired through training for specific 'sellable' skills, such as translation, coding, acting, or singing, for example. Influencers may have a formal education background and particular professional skills, but their influencer position, career, or profession does not have to be based on the skills acquired through education. Influencing grows from and gains momentum through influencers' personalities, outlooks, and/or identities, which become monetized assets in the business. These are not skills sold by freelancers via platforms as expertise. The argument on the similarity between freelancers and influencers assumes, problematically, that the pertinent modus operandi would be *similarity of capitalization procedures* of those in freelancing and those in social influencing businesses. However, the influencer profession is built on an entirely different logic than most freelancing work, and does not exist outside of the capitalization processes taking place within and on social media platforms (whereas freelancing work exists both within and outside it). Influencers' work is based on visibility, narrativity, and identity presence on social media.

Influencing as a profession is constructed through the logic of images of identity, personality, outlooks, and/or body all staged upfront, visualized, narrated, and mediated on social media platforms. Thus, drawing a parallel between a freelancer and influencer undermines the power of staging on platforms and the systemic nature of influencers' labor, careers, and labor-, career-, and brand-building. Many influencers construct and build their images and front-stage presented identities/personalities systematically, with potential follower-consumers in mind, and often with the help of paid experts ranging from photographers and stylists to accounting services and intermediary offices and managers. Thus, even if social media and platform influencers narrate their personal lives and manage their feelings for an unlimited number of unknown followers, it is not necessarily unplanned or spontaneous. The spontaneity may be the aimed and desired effect of a well-planned and scripted manuscript. Accordingly, the argument that claims similarities between freelancers and influencers ignores the formal qualifications typical to freelancing. Freelancers build their professionalism through specific acquired skills that are sold at and required by platform market purchasers of those specific services. If no demand for such skills appear, there is no room for capitalizing on those skills. In contrast, influencers can shape their staged identity to fit other products or market opportunities, as long as they maintain their parasocially idealized values. Intermediaries needed by influencers range from agencies offering consultation and total brand-building and maintenance services to more traditional talent agencies (e.g., Lobato, 2016), and managers who find brands and negotiate individual deals and contracts. Most 'influencer management tools' used are algorithms that form a part of the ecosystem that analyses the sales qualities of influencers. Talent agents and corporate brand liaisons evaluate platform professionals through scoring, and those with lower scores are less likely to be hired by a brand (Bishop, 2021). Influencers have to be agile, platform-ready, and contingent – or, ready and responsive to platform policies and algorithmic changes (Poell et al., 2019). Social influencers welcome the sphere of consumption. This does not take away the authenticity of such spheres.

Duffy and Pooley (2019) called social media influencers 'idols of promotion', and contended that their stories of self-made success are today's allegories for making it in a precarious employment economy. There may be similarities between the success stories of self-made entrepreneurs and social influencers' narratives, but the economies on which these successes are built are entirely different. The varieties of the ways in which influencing can turn into a profession are numerous, and the medium has a high impact, ranging from professional-level video production on YouTube to video clips on TikTok or Twitter, to mention a few. What unites influencers is a changeable and often highly unpredictable volatility of the demand at the identity/personality consumer markets, which the influencer business depends on fully.

The sustainability of new influencer professions

The professionalization of influencer activities differs dramatically from 'traditional' and established professions connected to the state and its institutions. The differences are major in at least four ways: platform professions are entirely market-borne, -based, and -dependent; the professions are entrepreneurial, most often based on self-employment; formal education qualifications are not an entry barrier; and they are entirely dependent on the development of Internet and app user logics. The latter dependency includes a constant investment in 'tools', that is, in platforms and their modifications to deal with changing algorithms and apps. It is therefore crucial to analyze the permanency and vulnerability of the platform profession. Permanency relates to the sustainability of profession.

Sustainability refers to the modes of living in economically, ecologically, and socially justifiable ways. In this analysis, sustainability is used in a different context, referring to the durability and longevity of the work and careers in the platform era. Sustainability is especially relevant in the influencer profession, in relation to its durability and the sustainability of professional qualifications in platform professions. These run parallel with the ideas of corporate sustainability (Berne-Manero and Marzo-Navarro, 2020). The estimation of profitability of influencer marketing can range from robust estimates to detailed follow-up of discounts and coupons delivered to followers.

Social media influencers and other professions borne by and supported through social media have the demands of presence, the 'visibility mandate' (Duffy and Pooley, 2019, 4984) as key elements in the profession. The demand for social media presence is inherent as career success is entirely based on and reflected in data-driven metrics such as followers, likes, and comments that establish and legitimize their influence and status. What if an influencer changes and/or their followers change, which is bound to happen at some point? What if an influencer's identity and personality no longer align with the marketing materials and content of the products, services, or ideas to be promoted? With any change, there is a fear of losing professional status, followers, and/or corporate collaborators. We lack longitudinal studies, stretching over several years, on the longevity of influencers' marketing activities and promotion campaigns. Such studies could enable a follow-up over a long period of time, and the analysis of changes and their effects can answer the questions posed earlier.

An interesting case of authenticity and sustainability comes forth in the way ethics is defined by influencers. Studies have shown that influencers use the concept of *authenticity* as their ethical guideline in producing sponsored content. The *ethics of authenticity in social media influencing* is based on two central principles: being true to oneself and to the brand, and being true to one's audience and followers (Wellman et al., 2020). The professional aim of influencers is to develop deeper bonds with their followers and thereby to nurture long-term relationships. These long-term relationships form the basis of their influence (Dhanesh and Duthler, 2019). The factors that impact promotions on influencers' credibility – from followers' perspective – are crucial for the longevity of influencer profession. For followers, it is easy to stop following an influencer, and therefore the credibility of marketing campaigns and promotions must be in line with the influencer's person and identity.

The key characteristics of the new professions at platforms are the ways the profession gets constructed at virtual platforms. The social media profession does not necessarily need to have formal institutional ties. Technical skills in order to able to manage social media accounts and channels can be obtained in many ways. Who manages new platform professions? Is it algorithmic control, measuring the number of followers, or more nuanced content? Can skills, capabilities, ethical norms, and behavioral patterns be mediated within and through algorithmic management, as proposed earlier with the emotional work concept suggested earlier by Hochschild (1989) and later by Irani (2015)? Relationship labor, as suggested by Shestakofsky and Kelkar (2020), governs some of the emotional burden on platforms. Relationship labor is referred to in passing in studies on digital labor platforms. Rahman (2019) and Gerber and Krzywdzinski (2019) noted that some freelancing platforms employ workers who work online for the corporation's online discussion boards. Such emotional labor works in favor of the corporation and can mediate the worries of co-workers who may not know of the double role of the emotional laborer.

Social media platforms and content have become increasingly professionalized (e.g., van Driel and Dumitrica, 2021; Kanai, 2019; Hou, 2018), to the extent that corporations produce professionally created content (Fuchs, 2017) to maximize different audiences. Social media influencers are a key group relied on by corporations in this process. van Driel and Dumitrica (2021) argued that even though influencers can position themselves in more authentic ways than average corporate advertisements can, they are not any less dependent on corporations. The tensions that influencers have to negotiate may result in their content becoming more and more like traditional advertising content: standardized and highly curated, both of which characteristics may eat up their credibility as an influencer, or alternatively, their resistance to such content (van Driel and Dumitrica, 2021). The new profession faces the question of how to preserve authenticity, if the presentation of oneself differs from traditional advertising content? These are major dilemmas for any profession, and more so for new platform professions.

The omnipresence of digital technology and digitized services in society have enabled social media content production to become integral parts of everyday life, ranging from services that are needed and used by citizens, to consumption patterns and lifestyles. In the new economy, product and service lifecycles, brand creation, sales, and marketing, are built and flourish online. The digital economy and traditional brick-and-mortar industries require, use, and support digital social media channels in their businesses. The mediators in these channels are influencers. Thus, influencing is not a profession with preset skills but takes many forms owing to its multifaceted characteristics.

Characteristics for new professions, such as social media influencer, are features that distinguish them from traditional professions and the accumulation of their core skills. New professions are characterized by the following features: The profession is built on and thus is entirely dependent on digital platforms and markets. Reputation-building is integral to the profession and is based on mediated presence on digital channels. It is substantiated through networks and consumer choices of following, liking, or commenting on posts. Professional identity construction and its longevity are changing concepts. Social media enjoys growing importance in the construction of professional identities for old professions and in the construction of new platform professions, such as that of social media influencer.

References

Abbott, P. and Meerabeau, L. (1998). Professionals, Professionalization and the Caring Professions. In: P. Abbott and L. Meerabeau, eds., *Sociology of Caring Professions*. London: Routledge, pp. 1–19. doi:10.4324/9781003070955.

Abidin, C. (2018). *Internet Celebrity: Understanding Fame Online*. Bingley: Emerald Publishing Limited. doi:10.1108/9781787560765 978-1-78756-076-5.

Aggrawal, N., Arora, A., Anand, A. and Irshad, M.S. (2018). View-Count Based Modeling for YouTube Videos and Weighted Criteria – Based Ranking. In: M. Ram and J.P. Davim, eds., *Advanced Mathematical Techniques in Engineering Sciences*. Boca Raton: CRC Press, pp. 149–160.

Arora, A., Bansal, S., Kandpal, C., Aswani, R. and Dwivedi, Y. (2019). Measuring Social Media Influencer Index – Insights from Facebook, Twitter and Instagram. *Journal of Retailing and Consumer Services*, 49(49), pp. 86–101. doi:10.1016/j.jretconser.2019.03.012.

Arsenyan, J. and Mirowska, A. (2021). Almost Human? A Comparative Case Study on the Social Media Presence of Virtual Influencers. *International Journal of Human-Computer Studies*, 155, pp. 1–16. doi:10.1016/j.ijhcs.2021.102694.

Barley, S.R. (2020). *Work and Technological Change*. Oxford: Oxford University Press.

Belanche, D., Casaló, L.V., Flavián, M. and Ibánez-Sánchez, S. (2021). Building Influencers' Credibility on Instagram: Effects on Followers' Attitudes and Behavioral Responses

Toward the Influencer. *Journal of Retailing and Consumer Services*, 61, p. 102585. doi: 10.1016/j.jretconser.2021.102585.

Berne-Manero, C. and Marzo-Navarro, M. (2020). Exploring How Influencer and Relationship Marketing Serve Corporate Sustainability. *Sustainability*, 12(11), p. 4392. doi:10.3390/su12114392.

Bishop, S. (2021). Influencer Management Tools: Algorithmic Cultures, Brand Safety, and Bias. *Social Media + Society*, 7(1). doi:10.1177/20563051211003066.

Bollmer, G. (2018). *Theorizing Digital Cultures*. London: Sage Publications.

Borchers, N.S. and Enke, N. (2021). Managing Strategic Influencer Communication: A Systematic Overview on Emerging Planning, Organization, and Controlling Routines. *Public Relations Review*, 47(3), p. 102041. doi:10.1016/j.pubrev.2021.102041.

Bucher, T. (2018). *If . . . Then: Algorithmic Power and Politics*. Oxford; New York: Oxford University Press.

Caplan, R. and Gillespie, T. (2020). Tiered Governance and Demonetization: The Shifting Terms of Labor and Compensation in the Platform Economy. *Social Media + Society*, 6(2). doi:10.1177/2056305120936636.

Childers, C.C., Lemon, L.L. and Hoy, M.G. (2019). # Sponsored# Ad: Agency Perspective on Influencer Marketing Campaigns. *Journal of Current Issues & Research in Advertising*, 40(3), pp. 258–274.

Cotter, K. (2018). Playing the Visibility Game: How Digital Influencers and Algorithms Negotiate Influence on Instagram. *New Media & Society*, 21(4), pp. 895–913. doi:10.1177/1461444818815684.

Davis, J.L. and Jurgenson, N. (2014). Context Collapse: Theorizing Context Collusions and Collisions. *Information, Communication & Society*, 17(4), pp. 476–485. doi:10.1080/1369118x.2014.888458.

Dhanesh, G.S. and Duthler, G. (2019). Relationship Management Through Social Media Influencers: Effects of Followers' Awareness of Paid Endorsement. *Public Relations Review*, 45(3). doi:10.1016/j.pubrev.2019.03.002.

Duffy, B.E. (2013). Manufacturing Authenticity: The Rhetoric of 'Real' in Women's Magazines. *The Communication Review*, 16(3), pp. 132–154. doi:10.1080/10714421.2013.807110.

Duffy, B.E. (2017). *(Not) Getting Paid to Do What You Love: Gender, Social Media, and Aspirational Work*. New Haven: Yale University Press.

Duffy, B.E. and Hund, E. (2019). Gendered Visibility on Social Media: Navigating Instagram's Authenticity Bind. *International Journal of Communication*, 13(20), pp. 4983–5002. doi: https://ijoc.org/index.php/ijoc.

Duffy, B.E. and Pooley, J. (2019). Idols of Promotion: The Triumph of Self-Branding in an Age of Precarity. *Journal of Communication*, 69(1), pp. 26–48. doi:10.1093/joc/jqy063.

Fromm, E. (1947/1994). *Escape from Freedom*. London: Macmillan.

Fuchs, C. (2017). From Digital Positivism and Administrative Big Data Analytics Towards Critical Digital and Social Media Research! *European Journal of Communication*, 32(1), pp. 37–49. doi:10.1177/0267323116682804.

Gehl, R.W. (2014). *Reverse Engineering Social Media: Software, Culture, and Political Economy in New Media Capitalism*. Philadelphia: Temple University Press.

Gerber, C. and Krzywdzinski, M. (2019). Brave New Digital Work? New Forms of Performance Control in Crowdwork. In: S.P. Vallas and A. Kovalainen, eds., *Work and Labor in the Digital Age*. Bingley: Emerald Publishing Ltd, pp. 121–143.

Giertz, J.N., Hollebeek, L.D., Weiger, W.H. and Hammerschmidt, M. (2022). The Invisible Leash: When Human Brands Hijack Corporate Brands' Consumer Relationships. *Journal of Service Management*, 33(3), pp. 485–495. doi:10.1108/josm-06-2021-0211.

Goffman, E. (1974/1963). *Stigma: Notes on the Management of Spoiled Identity*. New York: Simon & Schuster, Inc.

Gorwa, R. (2019). What Is Platform Governance? *Information Communications Society*, 22(6), pp. 854–871.

Hallinan, B., Scharlach, R. and Shifman, L. (2021). Beyond Neutrality: Conceptualizing Platform Values. *Communication Theory*, 32(2), pp. 201–222. doi:10.1093/ct/qtab008.

Hochschild, A.R. (1989). *The Second Shift: Working Parents and the Revolution*. New York: Avon Books.

Horton, D. and Wohl, R. (1956). Mass Communication and Parasocial Interaction: Observations on Intimacy at a Distance. *Psychiatry*, 19, pp. 215–229.

Hou, M. (2018). Social Media Celebrity and the Institutionalization of YouTube. *Convergence: the International Journal of Research into New Media Technologies*, 25(3). doi:10.1177/1354856517750368.

Hudders, L. and De Jans, S. (2021). Gender Effects in Influencer Marketing: An Experimental Study on the Efficacy of Endorsements by Same- vs. Other-Gender Social Media Influencers on Instagram. *International Journal of Advertising*, 41(1), pp. 1–22. doi :10.1080/02650487.2021.1997455.

Hund, E. (2019). *The Influencer Industry: Constructing and Commodifying Authenticity on Social Media*. [online]. Available at: https://repository.upenn.edu/dissertations/AAI27540302 [Accessed: 20 Jan. 2022]. University of Pennsylvania. AAI27540302 [Accessed: 11 Aug. 2022].

Irani, L. (2015). *Justice for 'Data Janitors'*. [online] Public Books. Available at: https://www.publicbooks.org/justice-for-data-janitors [Accessed 16 Mar. 2021].

Jacobson, J., Hodson, J. and Mittelman, R. (2022). Pup-ularity Contest: The Advertising practices of Popular Animal Influencers on Instagram. *Technological Forecasting and Social Change*, 174, p. 121226. doi:10.1016/j.techfore.2021.121226.

Kalleberg, A.L. (2011). *Good Jobs, Bad Jobs: The Rise of Polarized and Precarious Employment Systems in the United States, 1970s to 2000s*. New York: Russell Sage Foundation.

Kanai, A. (2019). *Gender and Relatability in Digital Culture: Managing Affect, Intimacy and Value*. Cham: Palgrave Macmillan.

Kasperiuniene, J. and Zydziunaite, V. (2019). A Systematic Literature Review on Professional Identity Construction in Social Media. *SAGE Open*, 9(1). doi: 10.1177/2158244019828847.

Khamis, S., Ang, L. and Welling, R. (2017). Self-Branding, 'Micro-Celebrity' and the Rise of Social Media Influencers. *Celebrity Studies*, 8(2), pp. 191–208. doi:10.1080/19392397.2016.1218292.

Kurtin, K.S., O'Brien, N., Roy, D. and Dam, L. (2018). The Development of Parasocial Interaction Relationships on YouTube. *The Journal of Social Media in Society*, 7, pp. 233–252.

Lash, S. and Urry, J. (2004). *The End of Organized Capitalism*. Cambridge: Polity Press.

Lobato, R. (2016). The Cultural Logic of Digital Intermediaries. *Convergence: The International Journal of Research into New Media Technologies*, 22(4), pp. 348–360. doi:10.1177/1354856516641628.

Lou, C. (2021). Social Media Influencers and Followers: Theorization of a Trans-Parasocial Relation and Explication of Its Implications for Influencer Advertising. *Journal of Advertising*, 51(1), pp. 1–18. doi:10.1080/00913367.2021.1880345.

MacCannell, D. (1973). Staged Authenticity: Arrangements of Social Space in Tourist Settings. *American Journal of Sociology*, 79(3), pp. 589–603. doi:10.1086/225585.

Mackert, J. (2012). *Social Closure*. Oxford: Oxford University Press.

Manza, J. (1992). Classes, Status Groups, and Social Closure: A Critique of Neo-Weberian Social Theory. *Current Perspectives in Social Theory*, 12, pp. 275–302.

Neff, G., Wissinger, E. and Zukin, S. (2005). Entrepreneurial Labor among Cultural Producers: 'Cool' Jobs in 'Hot' Industries. *Social Semiotics*, 15(3), pp. 307–334. doi:10.1080/10350330500310111.

OECD. (2021). Training in Enterprises. In: *Getting Skills Right*. Paris: OECD Publishing. doi:10.1787/7d63d210-en.

O'Meara, V. (2019). Weapons of the Chic: Instagram Influencer Engagement Pods as Practices of Resistance to Instagram Platform Labor. *Social Media + Society*, 5(4). doi:10.1177/2056305119879671.

Poell, T., Nieborg, D. and van Dijck, J. (2019). Platformisation. *Internet Policy Review*, 8(4). doi:10.14763/2019.4.1425.

Pooley, J. (2010). The Consuming Self: From Flappers to Facebook. In: M. Aronczyk and D. Powers, eds., *Blowing Up the Brand: Critical Perspectives on Promotional Culture*. New York: Peter Lang Publishing, pp. 71–92.

Pöyry, E., Pelkonen, M., Naumanen, E. and Laaksonen, S.-M. (2021). A Call for Authenticity: Audience Responses to Social Media Influencer Endorsements in Strategic Communication. In: N.S. Borchers, ed., *Social Media Influencers in Strategic Communication*. London: Routledge, pp. 331–365. doi: 10.4324/9781003181286.

Pradhan, D., Kapoor, V. and Moharana, T.R. (2017). One Step Deeper: Gender and Congruity in Celebrity Endorsement. *Marketing Intelligence & Planning*, 35(6), pp. 774–788. doi:10.1108/mip-02-2017-0034.

Rahman, H. (2019). *Invisible Cages: Algorithmic Evaluations in Online Labor Markets*. Stanford: Stanford University ProQuest Dissertations Publishing, 28113148.

Reskin, B.F. (2005). Including Mechanisms in Our Models of Ascriptive Inequality. In: L.B. Nielsen and R.L. Nelson, eds., *Handbook of Employment Discrimination Research*. Dordrecht: Springer, pp. 75–97. doi: 10.1007/1-4020-3455-5_4.

Ritzer, G. (2015). Prosumer Capitalism. *The Sociological Quarterly*, 56(3), pp. 413–445. doi:10.1111/tsq.12105.

Roth, A.E. (2016). *Who Gets What – and Why: The New Economics of Matchmaking and Market Design*. Boston: Mariner Books/Houghton Mifflin Harcourt.

Schaefer, M. (2012). *Return on Influence: The Revolutionary Power of Klout, Social Scoring, and Influence Marketing*. New York: McGraw-Hill.

Schouten, A.P., Janssen, L. and Verspaget, M. (2019). Celebrity vs. Influencer Endorsements in Advertising: The Role of Identification, Credibility, and Product-Endorser Fit. *International Journal of Advertising*, 39(2), pp. 1–24. doi:10.1080/02650487.2019.1634898.

Semaan, R.W., Ashill, N. and Williams, P. (2019). Sophisticated, Iconic and Magical: A Qualitative Analysis of Brand Charisma. *Journal of Retailing and Consumer Services*, 49, pp. 102–113. doi:10.1016/j.jretconser.2019.03.011.

Shestakofsky, B. and Kelkar, S. (2020). Making Platforms Work: Relationship Labor and the Management of Publics. *Theory and Society*, 49(5–6), pp. 863–896. doi:10.1007/s11186-020-09407-z.

Stubb, C., Nyström, A.-G. and Colliander, J. (2019). Influencer Marketing: The Impact of Disclosing Sponsorship Compensation Justification on Sponsored Content Effectiveness. *Journal of Communication Management*, 23(2), pp. 109–122. doi:10.1108/jcom-11-2018-0119.

Su, B.-C., Wu, L.-W., Chang, Y.-Y.-C. and Hong, R.-H. (2021). Influencers on Social Media as References: Understanding the Importance of Parasocial Relationships. *Sustainability*, 13(19), pp. 1–19. doi:10.3390/su131910919.

Suzor, N.P. (2019). *Lawless: The Secret Rules That Govern Our Digital Lives*. Cambridge; New York: Cambridge University Press.

Truong, H., Jesudoss, S.P. and Molesworth, M. (2022). Consumer Mischief as Playful Resistance to Marketing in Twitter Hashtag Hijacking. *Journal of Consumer Behaviour*, 21(4), pp. 828–841. doi:10.1002/cb.2040.

van Driel, L. and Dumitrica, D. (2021). Selling Brands While Staying 'Authentic': The Professionalization of Instagram Influencers. *Convergence: The International Journal of Research into New Media Technologies*, 27(1). doi:10.1177/1354856520902136.

Weber, M. (1922/1978). *Economy and Society: An Outline of Interpretive Sociology*. Berkeley: University of California Press.

Wellman, M.L., Stoldt, R., Tully, M. and Ekdale, B. (2020). Ethics of Authenticity: Social Media Influencers and the Production of Sponsored Content. *Journal of Media Ethics*, 35(2), pp. 1–15. doi:10.1080/23736992.2020.1736078.

Whitmer, J.M. (2019). You Are Your Brand: Self-Branding and the Marketization of Self. *Sociology Compass*, 13(3), p. e12662. doi:10.1111/soc4.12662.

Ye, G., Hudders, L., De Jans, S. and De Veirman, M. (2021). The Value of Influencer Marketing for Business: A Bibliometric Analysis and Managerial Implications. *Journal of Advertising*, 50(2), pp. 1–19. doi:10.1080/00913367.2020.1857888.

Yeoman, R. (2021). The Future of Meaningfulness in Work, Organizations, and Systems. In: K. Breen and J.-P. Deranty, eds., *The Politics and Ethics of Contemporary Work. Whither Work?* New York: Routledge. doi:10.4324/9780429243394.

Yuan, S. and Lou, C. (2020). How Social Media Influencers Foster Relationships with Followers: The Roles of Source Credibility and Fairness in Parasocial Relationship and Product Interest. *Journal of Interactive Advertising*, 20(2), pp. 1–42. doi:10.1080/15252019.2020.1769514.

7 Platformization of professions and expertise

Based on efficient technologies, the platform economy is without doubt creating new jobs, occupations, and professions, as evidenced in Chapter 6. It is reorganizing many work relations, and renewing the ways in which individuals can possibly earn their living income. The interactions of different digital systems in society and in the economy vary and are not always without problems, as shown in Chapter 5. Some of the changes are also slow. This chapter continues the discussion begun in earlier chapters, and addresses the questions of how digital technologies change established professions and how professions are transformed by the introduction of platforms and partially even transferred to platforms, to a sufficient extent that we can talk about platformization. Given the often rapid emergence and salience of digital technologies in most professions, it is important to find ways to systematically develop digital skills in professions. For this activity, platformization may offer new possibilities, but it also poses new problematic fields and even threats.

Technologies transforming professions

The ways in which technology is present in professions, and becoming part of all professions, are multiple, as discussed in earlier chapters. Equally numerous are the effects and predicted effects of technologies on professions, occupations, jobs, and on the future of work in general (Korinek and Juelfs, 2022). Technologies also shape organizing forms of work, as the platformization of many work activities currently shows. In the case of platforms and technology development, previous earning logics and novel income generation models enforce the effects of technology, but the effects of technology at the platform level do not stop there. Digital technology forms the core of any platform activity, and these activities in turn multiply and bud into other activities that require the presence of digital technologies. Any new work task involves or is connected to digital technology, whether as part of the job, the profession, or the occupation. In these myriad versions of technological development, which is by no means straightforward, platforms play an increasingly important role. In that role, platforms also transform societies

DOI: 10.4324/9781351038546-7

and the institutional relations of state, institutions, markets, and the private sector, as described by classics such as Weber. These arrangements emerge partially by transforming work internally.

For most people, work forms the main source of living income and use of time, and increasingly thus forms and builds self-identity and a sense of belonging. For these reasons, the importance of work should not be underestimated. Increasingly, however, prevalent arrangements for any form of expert work are epitomized by weakening employer–worker relations, for instance in the form of independent contracting and own-account working – increasingly on platforms – and possibly by social loneliness due to lack of co-workers and of team formation. Finally, the strong reliance on technologies such as algorithmic and platform-mediated management – a trend that is growing – is transforming the existing organizational forms of work arrangements.

Technologies encircle and enmesh existing and future professions and occupations and transform them. How do these transformations take place? Often through everyday practices of doing work, ways of performing profession/occupations, and, thereby, wiring-up of sectors and industries. As shown in earlier chapters, digital technologies give rise to fully new, market-based professions, and abet the rise of others. In this process, technologies also transform the ways other professions and occupations operate. Research (Autor and Dorn, 2013) has shown that with technologies' impact, many occupations and expert professions may in fact become more multifaceted, being able to develop new, more complex, and increasingly demanding tasks. The question of how to accommodate the new tasks introduced or enabled by technologies to the old tasks that most often remain part of the tasks at work is pertinent for most occupations and professions.

Many studies taking technological development as the starting point have, however, left untouched the formation of content in professional work and how technologies change the contents. The presumptive human-centered development of activities is assumed to remain unchanged with the adoption of new technologies, but, in fact, this is seldom the case. The perception of technology as linear progress and betterment often clouds the rough edges, uneven processes, and incompatibilities of adopted technologies. While the progress achieved with the help of technology may be real in the professions, in particular canonical ones such as medical or legal professions, it may not be so with many less skilled or unskilled jobs and work tasks. The machine-first, instead of human-first, work environment is in fact already a reality in many factories, warehouses, and stores, where automated technology is part of frontline workers' everyday work, according to several research reports (Mateescu and Elish, 2019).

Automated technologies may effectivize and intensify work in good ways, but they can also reconfigure work-related skills and create new shadowy responsibilities that fall on workers. One example of these shadowy new informal work tasks is the human infrastructure work required by self-checkout machines' technologies in shops. Self-service check-out depends upon the successful interaction of customers and machines, but it also demands surveillance by shop personnel, assistant, and the type of shadowy work involved in monitoring self-checkout, which lies in between that of cashier and shop detective (Andrews, 2018). Some researchers find growth in the use of self-service, reflecting stronger engagement in all type of unpaid work in society (Andrews, 2018; Hochschild, 1989).

The analyses of technologies' positions and roles in working life, and especially the current platform developments, show that currently, many major trends in working life (and in the economy) are technological by nature. What then follows is an increasing decline in human intervention and involvement. The effectiveness of the earning logic of platforms is based on apps, which in fact greatly increases the type of intermediating expert work that relates to app development and its connectivity and suitability to markets. However, technologies' immersion and adoption in professions does not necessarily mean that these jobs are displaced or that work, in general, is disappearing, but on the contrary, that new occupations, jobs, and tasks emerge while old ones are transformed and renewed internally, as the example of pathology as a transforming profession discussed in Chapter 1 shows.

Professional expertise is thus not a distinct or separate sphere where technology would enter differently than in other fields or occupations, nor is professional expertise introducing independent, different versions of technology in practice. Instead, digital technologies enter professional fields and professions through a complex interplay, competition, and mutual constituency by various actors within and between professions, organizations, and institutions. In that, both the material and the discursive practices of the constituting positions and roles of professions, as well as their relations to markets and institutions, are changing. Thus, the question of the role of technologies in professions is not a straightforward nor a time-bound one, but rather, related to job and task transformations. Much of the reskilling of experts and expert work may take place through on-the-job training and professional development programs.

Furthermore, the amount of technology transformation and adoption in professions is related to the issue of how digitized the whole industry in question is. For some industries, new technologies crucially change the core functions and logics, while for some industries the transformation is less visible and takes place gradually. According to a global survey (World Economic Forum, 2020), the majority of employers recognize the value of human capital investment, but the constant renewal of workers' skills with new technologies may still be considered as a costly investment, even though most employers are set to digitalize various working processes and expand remote work possibilities. For many professions the question of renewal of skills with technological development is a more complex matter, as it relates also to professional identity within the realm of work.

Among and compared with all industries globally, the high-tech sector, telecommunications, and financial services have short histories, with technology at the core of the contents of the industry and sectoral development, investment, and overall striving to be first adopters of digital tools at work. Hence, multiple and complex technologies are inscribed in professional work contents, work practices, and protocols in these sectors. This is especially true in sectors where technologies constitute the core of the industry; in those sectors where technology development only partially touches the core of the expert profession, the effects of technological development may be steeper, such as the research on expert recruitment procedures or algorithmic bank loan offers shows (Ajunwa and Greene, 2019; Ajunwa, 2020). The new functions of technology operate increasingly on algorithms. In most professions, however, the ability to read, code, and design algorithms are not part of the profession, nor a core feature of expertise in most occupations. Often, due to that, the underlying and reinforcing discriminatory mechanisms of algorithms that are inherently part of work done in expert positions remain largely unnoticed in the expertise of many professions.

Technology in general shapes both the ways practices are arranged as part of the work design and how practices are shaped into work processes. Thus, with the help and introduction of technology within professional practices, ranging from education and learning in professions to the practice of professions, technologies shape and align with the renewal of professions. Digitally enhanced teaching has unfurled new ways of learning and updating professional skills, and widened the learning experiences in general. ICT-based learning builds on different conceptions of learning the profession, including gaining access to information and resources. Machine learning can indeed help to identify new skills, and can do automatic grading of information needed, among other things. Integration of technologies in education transforms learning processes qualitatively – also for professional learning. In highly skilled professions, transdisciplinary skills and capabilities will in the future form the assets that help in navigating the changing work environment.

In working life contexts, the dynamics between occupations change, and the traditional divisions between professions and occupations get renegotiated anew. Technological solutions are seen – right or wrong – as answers to many societal or economic problems. Technological imperative is pressing but its implementation and practical solution-searching activity is not one single activity, but a processual and multipart activity in most workplaces. The immersion of technologies in professions takes place through many activities and processes, at different paces and longevities. The detailed studies of work practices and work processes provide a richer understanding of technology culture within professions, and of the changing roles and positions available to professions in societies.

Addressing the role of technology, one could ask whether technology does have such a foundational impact on professions as 'modernization' has allegedly had. Research has shown that the pace of technology adoption in industries and increasingly in services is expected to persist and intensify – there is no turning back (Baldwin, 2020). Technology adoption does, however, accelerate; this occurs in ways dependent on the actual product/service dimensions, but two features, cloud computing, and big data, will remain high priorities throughout economies in the near future. When the impacts of technologies are systematically analyzed, including the ways platforms shake the socioeconomic foundations, the unequivocal answer is yes, the impacts of technologies are imperative to professions, and this aspect has not been thoroughly analyzed as yet.

As shown in earlier chapters, technologies become integrated into professions in many ways. First, technology in general adheres to globalization processes, basically enabling the detachment of professions from their traditionally local and national contexts. Professions in that sense are universal, even if, for example, national education systems for professions may differ widely. National systems tie professions into national settings through culture, institutions, and institutional establishments. That also means controlling and restriction the possibilities of professions through laws, rules, and regulations. Here resides the power of platforms, as they can operate simultaneously globally and locally, transcending national boundaries and challenging national and transnational regulatory frameworks and orders for professions as well as for all types of work. This does not necessarily mean that platforms would actively support or call for a surpassing of the national or transnational regulatory or restrictive frameworks, but the prospects for such transgression exist with platforms (Aloisi and De Stefano, 2022). The legislative regulation of platforms may require national and even local responses, but is most effectively a supranational, and not only a national, question.

Second, technologies can become immersed in professions by rearranging professions' sources of knowledge, building closer linkages and interdependencies to other fields and professions, and reorganizing professional procedures and practices. In these processes, it is difficult to distinguish the exact effects of the transformational power of technologies on professions. Much of the effects of technologies in professions are visible in the practical work and outcomes of professions, in particular areas of work of professionals. The new practices involved, with new sets of technologies immersed in practices, may demand new ways and new forms of collaboration. A prime example is the medical professions, where closer, technologically driven collaborative work between different professions and occupations is required. Technological practices may also strengthen competences, add specialties, and increase competition within professions. Both of these processes, intensified collaborative elements, and competitive elements, may have an effect simultaneously, adding complexity when trying to dissect the technology effects from other effects, for example.

Platforms have introduced user-generated models of knowledge production and consumption and have also contributed toward a general shift in the decentralization of new knowledge. Partially because of that, platforms are now emerging as a dominant model for organizing and operating activities, professional activities included. The platforms access the data, and through that access, the network effects achieved are superior to other forms of organizing and operating activities.

Technologies replacing professions

When evaluating the general effects of technology – indirect effects included – at work, the discourse most often circles around the two topics: the effectivization of work as work tasks and processes, and the displacement of humans at work – both processes taking place with the help of technology. The first topic, effectivization of work, relates in simplest form to measurements of time used for work, and the outcomes of work produced as functions of time. The outcomes can be products, services, activities, any type of unit measured as a fit outcome of work activity. Most often technology investments at workplaces are justified through the effectivization of work, measured through and by these outcomes.

The latter topic, the displacement of humans at work by technology, refers to technologies that can replace, or will take the partial or full place of humans in a range of work activities, and here expert work is included. The displacement refers also to the development of human–robot cooperation models for any tasks, ranging from robot-led or robot-assisted surgery to shop-floor tasks in factories, and the use of robots in industry (Lee and Lim, 2021; Riis Andersen et al., 2017). The disappearance of work tasks due to digital technologies, software, automation, robotization, artificial intelligence (AI), and machine-learning addresses the prevailing uncertainties in the future of work. The analyses of the displacement power of technologies over human work are usually based on the identification of central tasks in each occupation and the assessment of the *automation potential* in each task within the occupation.

Partially due to the pandemic, some types of jobs and labor has risen into focus of platformization. One informal work sector in households in many countries is the domestic cleaning, where platformization has brought partially informal work into markets. The use of the services continue to exist with or without online domestic cleaning platforms, but platforms have made these services more visible, thus creating some extent formalization of the activities. If the platforms at some point share their data with governments they also make work less invisible and informal (Frenken and Schor, 2017), and tie new governance relations between platforms, labor, and government. The ways in which future job demand and technological skills among workers will develop are highly complex to predict, and predictions such as this may reflect more on the current flow of supply and demand for jobs rather than the actual future conditions.

The lay assumption often is that occupations and professions are rather stable in their contents. This stability assumption is especially true when the impact of technology on professions or occupations is evaluated. But occupations in the service sector, for instance, seldom have such stable qualities and defined task structure that they can directly be compared to manufacturing factory floor occupations and their work tasks. Typically, machine operators are taken as an example of those occupations and jobs, where routine tasks comprise the majority of the work, making these jobs prone to automation. At the other end of the 'automation threat' spectrum are professions and professionals whose work consists of nonroutine interactions and tasks and complex problem solving. Their work is claimed to be more shielded from automation threats than that of routine occupations (Riis Andersen et al., 2017). But the various dimensions of their work will undoubtedly transform with technologies, as well.

The immersion of technologies in everyday tasks of any work, and the introduction of AI and machine-learning technologies, can in some cases lead to a productivity rise that is not dependent on or due to technology but instead on other matters. The research has shown that productivity rise depends on sensible work and task arrangements and on team- and individual-level re-training for new work tasks, as shown in studies where digital robots have been adopted to work alongside humans (Vähämäki et al., 2020). Adopted digital technologies may change the characteristics of tasks through automatization and by providing new digital tools for humans. The well-planned and organized re-arrangements of work are at the core of the successful task- and team-level changes that carry new elements of automatization forward and add new content-related elements to human work.

This is in contrast to projected fears of the replacement of humans and the increasing monotony of human jobs with the growth of technology. But this effect – how technology impacts work and its contents – is entirely dependent on the context, quality, and type of work. As shown by many research reports, contrary development is also taking place, and the proliferation of bad jobs occurs. Much of the worsening of working life is in fact estimated to take place due to some technical rationale or bad technological solution adopted, or indeed, lack of training in relation to new technology (Aloisi and De Stefano, 2022; Raisch and Krakowski, 2021; Kalleberg, 2011).

Many of the recent developments in and of bad jobs are tied to the platformization of services and jobs. With digital management, platformization, and the replacement of stable employment relationships with contracting, working life deteriorates, and with that, the social dimension of the digital society weakens. Monitoring of the multiple consequences of technology and its development and positioning in working life requires a recalibration of how we understand and explain the role of technology in the development of contemporary professions and in society at large.

Platforms reinforcing old and creating new types of inequalities

New platform professions and the overall platformization of 'old' professions do not escape from the stubborn reproduction of inequalities of different kinds – also within professions. These inequalities have different social markers. Within professions, inequalities of different kinds get strengthened and find new digital channels. The concept of the digital divide refers to those who have access, training, and ability to make use of digital media versus those who do not. Since its original launch, the content of the concept has widened from its original meaning to refer to many existing divisions in relation to the adoption of information and communication technology, such as the ability to learn, use, and take advantage of digital tools and media. Many researchers ask the question of whether the digital divide is really a new divide or whether it results from existing inequalities and reinforces them (Van Dijk, 2020; Tsatsou, 2011).

The platforms may strengthen the effect of persistent societal inequalities, especially when resources for skill updating or renewal for individuals are scarce. Professions have a societal position as experts that both innovate and bring about new knowledge, but also maintain and withhold access to resources (e.g., employment) (Romani et al., 2020; Rodriguez et al., 2016). Recent studies on successfully completed projects on platforms show that skills or performance as measures for completed projects are associated with the quality of work carried out at the platform by the sampled workers, and that for its part is related to the variation in pay and employment in the online labor market (Martindale and Lehdonvirta, 2021). For those who do not have adequate skills to otherwise participate, platforms have connective capabilities to offer, despite persistent inequalities of different kinds. Still, digital and traditional inequalities overlap and may prevent access to the material benefits of social platforms (Marler, 2022). On platforms, the legal identity of on-demand platform workers has become a center point of disputes in the US and also in Europe, addressing the questions of definitions – is it a new regulatory category or not – and compensation (Dubal, 2021). In these disputes, several inequality aspects become prevalent, such as the reproduction of racial subjugation.

In addition to internal changes within professions, technologies produce shifts in the status basis of professions in societies, as research on professions such as legal, teaching, and medical professions shows (Torres and Weiner, 2018; Susskind and Susskind, 2017; Sommerlad, 1995, 2016). Legal professions are an example of a professional group where societal development has shaped and also transformed the context of profession – parallel with the marketization of society – from a profession based on traditional status categories, to one where various mechanisms function simultaneously. New mechanisms in effect are based on meritocratic practices (Schinkel and Noordegraaf, 2011; Sommerlad, 2016; Abel, 2003), and increasingly are market-derived and entangled with demands based on bounded rationalities. Market interests and needs are brought forward and articulated through institutions, such as educational institutions, stakeholders, or professional interest groups. None of these mechanisms, be it meritocracy or market-derived mechanisms, automatically safeguards professions from discriminatory elements and practices; on the contrary, these two mechanisms can amplify them within profession.

Research results show that meritocratic beliefs among those educating new professionals reproduce the existing mechanisms of inequality in professions, especially in relation to gender. Meritocratic beliefs build on the problematic idea of success achieved through working vigorously toward goals (Razack et al., 2020). Meritocracy may have economic rationality as a goal, but simultaneously it contains hidden dynamics that result in an inequitable valuation of workers. Gender disparity in many professions entangle with other unequal categories and processes and with discriminatory elements built into working life, showing that neither professions nor working life are neutral (Romani et al., 2020).

This 'modernization' of professions through diversity development, for example, does not mean that the hegemonic status of profession would diminish. Diversity may mean, for example, the number of women in professions increases, as has happened in medicine or in legal studies in several countries (Sommerlad, 2016). Diversity may also increase new inequalities within professions, as has happened for those selling their work as online platform work (Bergvall-Kåreborn and Howcroft, 2014). Through these types of changes, the position of professions evolves with society. For the profession here taken as an example, the legal profession, this evolvement will mean that coherence with the law's discursive construction as value-free and neutral is no longer valid; instead, the legal profession is forced to correct its own self-imagery as a 'disembodied' profession and reveal itself to itself as a classed, gendered, and racialized profession (Collier, 2003; McNay, 2008, 1999). It is exactly these sociocultural aspects that for their part strive to change legislation and to change and widen the basis of the profession.

There is a well-established body of research literature highlighting the importance of generic skills; less well-understood is the importance of skills needed to master new technological changes within professions. The dynamic nature of contemporary job requirements, need for adaptive experts, and emphasis on on-the-job learning diminish the need to prepare the workforce only during formal education. Instead, in addition to expertise-specific knowledge, there is an increasing need for continuous updating of skills. The difference to earlier periods of automatization is that the current generation of technology is automating nonroutine tasks, as shown earlier in Chapters 1 and 2, in professions such as medicine, for example, in diagnosing diseases. This has direct impacts on the profession per se and on professional education. The transformation of occupations and professions is an ongoing process throughout economies.

Technologies and hybrid professions

The platformization of society unfolds across society. In our everyday lives, the platformization of society manifests to citizen-consumers in many ways. Despite these singular-type manifestations, platformization should not be understood as a singular or isolated action or activity on social networking sites, but as an ongoing process change with many levels. Platformization of society ranges from systematically purpose-built digital structures and platform-integrated infrastructure in cities to decentralized social networks.

Website traffic increasingly comes from social media platforms, which function as initializers for a series of platform-based interactions (Gerlitz and Helmond, 2013; Helmond 2015; Helmond et al., 2019). The platformization of institutional functions and services ranges from taxation to healthcare and from education to judicial systems. Both the education system and judiciary are examples of how technology entrenches itself into institutions and established arrangements assumed to be fixed and unchanging. In platformization, not only do established platforms offer sites where work and economic activities take place, but they also set patterns for arranging economic and social activities.

Some researchers claim that new technologies will lead not to amalgamation of old and new but rather to *hybrid professions*, and refer to these professionals as *third space professionals*, in an emergent territory between academic and professional domains, colonized primarily by less *bounded* forms of profession (Whitchurch, 2013). The term relates, however, to undefined new roles emerging between professions (Cox, 2022), and not to new professions as such.

Some studies show that the effects of technology immersion may increase similarity and not diversity within professions (Annabi and Lebovitz, 2018). One of the major obstacles in thinking about how professions change with technology is the technology itself. When technology adoption at work and in organizations ranges from human-centric AI systems to deep machine learning, or alternatively, when algorithms play a prominent role in curating the information that people receive, it is plausible that the range of technologies will change professions. But the shared understanding of what technology does to professions is in fact void, as a shared basis for comparison is missing.

Currently, blockchain technology and data analytics are disrupting the organizations and content of some professions in a major way. Auditing is one example of this. The auditing profession is transforming into a technologically driven and data-driven profession where the role of individually acquired knowledge of the field is replaced by technology. Blockchain technology is a *distributed ledger* technology; a distributed ledger is a kind of digital record – a chain of verification, where every visit and activity leaves a trace and thus creates in principle a transparent document. It is shared and distributed among those who have agreed and connected to it. The blockchain creates an online ledger that allows the verification of online transactions. With such features, blockchain has in principle in the future the potential to change the audit profession entirely.

The transformative effects of blockchain have been widely discussed within the profession, such as enabling secure, timely documented transactions (Foti and Vavalis, 2021; Frenken and Fuenfschilling, 2021; ten Have, 2022). These transactions would be valid for many professions, from medicine to legal professions. Some researchers argue that blockchain will replace bookkeeping, as all transactions are recorded and verified by blockchain technology. Besides blockchains, the use of software to perform routine and repetitive tasks such as invoice processing and collection of accounting data, has changed work processes, enabling growth in efficiency due to the minimization of costs (Cooper et al., 2021; Jackson and Michelson, 2022). Experts and auditors interviewed in recent studies expect the audit profession to be more technological and more data-driven in upcoming years, as AI and technologies such as cloud-based software and blockchain will significantly impact these professionals' daily responsibilities and expertise in general (Bakarich and O'Brien, 2021; Sastry et al., 2021). Employers are expecting business schools and higher education institutions to provide them with 'work-ready graduates with solid skills and knowledge' (Daff, 2021, 519; Chen et al., 2021) for key business activities such as auditing, accounting, and finance-related work tasks.

Auditing and accounting are not the only professions in business sectors being transformed by blockchain technologies. For many sectors, the ability to produce traceable proof – a chain of evidence of the origins of a product, or of the chain of logistics – is a major advantage. In a similar fashion, the whole financial technology sector has faced major technological changes with increasing automated processes and decreasing human labor. So do have other professions and semi-professions, such as nursing. It is assumed that AI technologies will take over some tasks performed by nurses (Dunn and Hazzard, 2019); on the other hand, with technology, several new tasks in nursing will appear, such as managing and interpreting complex data. The next generation of remote patient monitoring will use such technology, which will bring in new tasks and will require health literacy skills. Second-generation remote monitoring includes the detection of environmental and individual factors such as breathing and abnormal heart rhythm, including fibrillation. Managing and interpreting this type of complex, unique, individualized digital health data requires a completely new set of skills for data interpretation.

The ways technology affects actual work are numerous. They range from the time used in various work tasks, to new independence in task arrangements. For all work, technologies have transformative power. Many detailed technology effect examples in extant research come from work done in manufacturing and industrial sectors (Bailey and Leonardi, 2015; Gerber and Krzywdzinski, 2019). However, the effects of technologies on work content and tasks extend also to services, including expert work in healthcare (as mentioned earlier) and also in business-to-business services such as consulting. Technology changes the ways nurses use their working time in patient care or delivering medication, for example. In nursing professionals may possibly become information integrators, health coaches, and deliverers of human care, supported by AI technologies, not replaced by them (Robert, 2019).

Occupations such as science technicians and medical technicians are exemplars of scientific, medical, and technical occupations, the kind of support work without which professions would not be able to function. The work in these occupations is often highly technical, requires a complex knowledge base (Barley, 2020), and is situated along the invisible boundaries between professions and occupations. In these expert jobs, technology is used to monitor for example the time used in performing work tasks. The more complex tasks the work consists of, the less value mere time monitoring adds to overall surveillance and evaluation data of the output.

Technologies transforming the education of professions

With platformization, the organizing principles of institutions training people in professions are transformed. The institutions become open markets, where digital platforms operate and offer courses more efficiently and widely than earlier. Prior platformization technology companies did create globally expanding markets in higher education, and data has become a commodity on the education market, even in professional education (Komljenovic and Robertson, 2016). Professional education programs – in most educational institutions – compete for the best students, and amid that process, platforms open up new space for university brand-building. In many countries, for example, in Europe, the privatization of public services that many traditional professions – such as medical doctors, nurses, and dentists – provide, and the rise of new organizational forms in relation to them – such as platforms and entrepreneurship – change how professions can be trained, reskilled, and managed within organizations.

Digital platforms are not only a new means of organizing professional work but also a means of training and retraining professionals. Those with higher education and even established careers who shift to platform work may often lose or give up salaried jobs and positions, with the accompanying benefits such as pensions and health insurance. Such professionals sometimes turn to entrepreneurship or, more often, become own-account or self-employed workers, which involves increased independence and very different kinds of challenges, commitments, control mechanisms, and dependencies compared to waged or salaried positions.

Technologies of different kinds currently foster and accelerate global economies, and improve both public sector and private sector performances. Technologies and their different forms are, and will continue to be, fundamental drivers in societies. In relation to work, technologies are often brought up in public discussion as displacing humans at work. As discussed earlier, technologies also accelerate the speed at which new types of injustices or problems appear in societies. Many of the skills usually described as shielded from technical automation, such as creativity and social intelligence, relate to the substance field of how people are educated more than to the length of that education. The creation of educational platforms exemplifies the multifaceted nature of speed, complexity of efficiency, and problems that relate to platforms and technology adoption at work. The essential question is how platforms take over the educational processes of a profession. Supposedly the difference between professions and occupations in this regard is not huge, but rather similar, as the platforms and data industry function similarly across all education.

Within education as a system, and in educational institutions, *platformization* as a new form of organizing learning, education, and training activities, has gained momentum in various ways, ranging from single or national to global programs and gamified learning, to mention a few examples (Perrotta, 2020; Decuypere, 2018). Apart from the growing dependency that is a typical feature of platformization, all different approaches have in common that the development of digital infrastructures relies heavily on standardization, effectivizing and unifying the educational processes, and with that, practices are gradually changing form as well. Indeed, technology shapes both the forms and contents of education, as argued by Williamson et al. (2022) who note that global technology companies are acting as governance organizations in education through platform technologies, often on behalf of, but not necessarily controlled by the state, when building platform infrastructure within education (also, Decuypere et al., 2021). While this is still very much an unexplored field, it nevertheless raises the question of how to govern the contents of education and training if not by educational institutions and professions.

Relatively little is known of the role digital platforms play in constituting, selecting, and offering data for education (Pangrazio et al., 2022). The platforms are part of the knowledge building in educational institutions already, and therefore, attention to datafication processes and economic value creation processes of education is important. The economic value created through and with the help of education platforms consists not only of the value for the current students but also increasingly for the educated future professionals who will become users of the platforms – and provide further data for platform companies. The future professionals will work in organizations that most probably function as complementors for connective platforms (van Dijck et al., 2018).

The complexity of concrete reskilling at workplaces, the arrangements for training and education, and the renewal of skills at work are visible in the vast diversity of replies to reskilling practices from organizations. Organizations – both business and public sector – were asked how to organize training at work, in order to maintain and upgrade the digital skills of employees and the overall digitalization of work. However, the proliferation of online learning and education platforms is on the rise and increasingly used by organizations that seek reskilling of their employees. Besides the flexibility of learning and time use, online reskilling frees the employer from time and costs of training during work hours. The possibilities to use online courses have grown during the restrictions of the Covid-19 pandemic in the 2020s, and this may become one pattern for reskilling.

Essentially as a part of all this, as technologies also redefine the necessary workforce skills, new educational qualifications are required. Mastering both the generic and the profession-specific technologies is crucial to building a professional career, irrespective of the sector in the economy and society. In general, such technologies range from very specific, for example, profession and task-related techniques (the use and assistance of robots in robot-surgery; data mining as part of librarianship) to AI-related generic activities (building a monitoring or surveillance system). It is therefore important to think about technologies including very generic and very specific categories in all contexts where they are used. Periods of transformative change driven by technology in working life are not novel, and therefore, their context in education is important: What are the specific fields where technologies are implemented? The key generic areas in AI development, for example, include natural language processing, text analytics, speech recognition, virtual agents, computer vision, robotics, autonomous vehicles, and machine learning based on algorithms.

While the educational system may maintain its structure, the views on learning are emphasizing informal and workplace learning (Roll and Wylie, 2016). The learning is assumed to take place at work and over the life course. The skills such as data mining, digital literacy, and coding have grown in importance both in the formal expert education system and in workplace learning systems. Several research reports emphasize the growth in the need for skills such as data mining, programming, statistics, and big data. This is visible both at the micro and macro levels. For example, with the intensifying automation and digitalization of the financial sector, the number of persons working as bank tellers, dealing with manual, routine-type tasks of deposits and withdrawals decreased rapidly in the end of the 1990s and early 2000s. Respectively, the number of persons working as bank advisors, where work includes nonroutine cognitive tasks, grew in many countries. The emphasis on several nonroutine cognitive skills, such as communication skills has risen in many expert fields and professions (Verma et al., 2021; Andersson Schwarz, 2017).

The constant challenge for the educational process in the growing technology orientation, are the ways education can keep up with developing technologies such as machine learning and AI, which have become an integral part of any profession. Machine learning refers to computers' ability to learn, without explicitly being programmed by humans. Upskilling experts and professionals to leverage technological trends needs to be situated within a broader strategy of embracing technology as part of the profession.

Deep learning, which is a subset of machine learning, is in use, for example, in the triage system at the emergency department, a nursing diagnosis system, and prenatal nursing interventions (Jeong, 2020). Research predicts that with the gradual introduction of AI to nursing and care practices, it will transform the entire healthcare system, especially nursing across all domains of nursing practices. It has been suggested that the educational curriculum in all healthcare professions should indeed include courses on big data and coding as standard curricula (Buchanan et al., 2021).

As technologies change the educational curriculum, they also change education institutions and professions. The integration of education into a global digital infrastructure challenges the institutional pedagogical autonomy of schools and universities alike (Saks and Muzio, 2020; Kerssens and van Dijck, 2022; Nichols and Garcia, 2022). Massive open online courses (MOOCs) have created and made widely available materials and conditions for participatory learning, and platforms offer the possibility to participate in the courses. MOOCs are internet-provided courses, open to anyone and to an extent free of charge with no penalties for nonparticipation. The phenomenon of massive open online courses has changed the landscape also in terms of virtual and global accessibility to education, and in terms of the student population. The access is widening the possibilities, but simultaneously the online education possibility is changing the institutions that offer education, and often into a more competitive direction.

Technologies such as AI and its widening use in education have further changed the idea of learning toward a technologically driven and developing system. If earlier learning used to be defined in relation to the structure such as educational institutions, and the length of the educational process in order to achieve degree, it is now being defined in relation to lifelong learning. This change in perspective has given space to the growing movement of MOOCs (Rathore and Dangi, 2021; Napier and Orrick, 2022; Bjursell et al., 2021). MOOCs take place in a space of digital learning culture, irrespective of basic knowledge, curriculum, or location (Young, 2021; Sigahi and Saltorato, 2019). For professional education such as medicine, MOOCs have offered possibilities to specialize and save time and for institutions to create greater flexibility for their students (Harder, 2013). Within clinical practice in medical professions, or updating skills in legal professions, for example, online courses undoubtedly help in reskilling and deepening knowledge (Grealy et al., 2019). In general, platforms as multisided markets link their users and their data to social, technical, and political-economic ecosystems, and as a result of that process, education process no longer consists of definitions given to content by standalone institutions and their professions. Increasingly, with connections to education platforms, both materials and their users are brought to connections with markets of various kinds.

In studies on higher education, learned and internalized skills as part of occupational and professional training are often measured as outcomes, posts, and job positions and successes (Couldry and Mejias, 2019) addressing basic tasks needed in profession. The general skills needed in any profession are often provided as skills lists, even itemizing a specific number of individualized skill sets ranging from creativity to flexibility (Di Gregorio et al., 2019). Whether such individualized and itemized skillsets and lists can function as a general instruction for the future of professions is rather problematic. However, they can give indications of what kinds of new technology-related skills are needed in the near future. Technology-related skills merge content and technicalities into a new holistic approach needed in professions. These are not dependent on platformization, but rather on basic soft skills such as the nontechnical skills acquired in education.

For institutions, the platformization of education means that they can offer relevant courses and programs for professionals more easily than earlier, using online platforms and courses to reach the masses in need of reskilling or updating of knowledge and skills. For professional associations, online education means in practical terms a question of recognition of skills that are acquired online and of their relation to professional education more generally.

Currently, datafication is changing the operations of educational units and institutions, along with much of the practice of teaching and learning. These changes have implications for how individuals learn their profession in educational institutions, surrounded by the logics of data in information-gathering, knowledge of the field, and tools of the trade, but not in these alone. As Couldry and Mejias (2019), among others, argue, the links between contemporary data practices and uses in teaching and learning are related to wider global inequalities (Kwet, 2019) and therefore need specific attention, especially vis-à-vis new teaching technologies.

Education platforms, global and national, offer an implicit promise to democratize education, training, and reskilling by widening the possibilities and largely obliterating access and location problems. Leaning on effective online courses and contents, they also tend to universalize some dominant voices in the curriculum, while others, not being so marketable, may be left out. In this process, some of the knowledge may disappear from the digital layers of knowledge, or indeed, may even never enter the online course level. In addition, as argued by several researchers within education sciences (Langseth et al., 2019; Swinney and Elder, 2012), there is in general a clear trend toward short, free courses that persuade learners later to pay for more courses behind paywalls and earn online certificates. There is, however, no assurance of recognition of the online certificates in working life even if employers support MOOCs as a reskilling tool (Banks and Meinert, 2016; Johnson, 2019).

Analyses have shown convincingly the intermediating roles and entangled connections between the educational technology industry, digital platforms, and data use and ownership (e.g., Mirrlees and Alvi, 2020; Williamson, 2019). However, with many education-related assets, the entrepreneurial modes of introducing and using technology in education and educational institutions may only partially be replaced by new forms of economic activities, such as rentiership (Komljenovic, 2021; Birch and Munieza, 2020).

Digitalization and technology are entangled with all-encompassing and even rapid changes in working life and society at large, and the repercussions will extend far beyond the experiences of automation and rationalization of the last decades (McAfee and Brynjolfsson, 2017). Partially due to their all-encompassing nature, algorithms have become an invisible part of everyday life and its activities, with their power ranging from mundane consumption to working life and the economy at large, and also to educational and work career choices. The use of digital tools at work and in social life, the monitoring power of algorithms, and algorithmic management are currently all transforming the ways we work as well as the contents and processes of work on digital labor platforms and in 'traditional' companies and public sector institutions (Poutanen and Kovalainen, 2022). Digitality is thus no longer a separate sphere in professions or education for professions, but rather woven throughout activities and actions. It can be argued, as several researchers do, that as we live in a postdigital world (Decuypere et al., 2021; Macgilchrist, 2021; Knox, 2019), where the term 'postdigital' perhaps describes more accurately than mere 'digital' the attempt to surmount a binary that dominates discussions of education and technology. In general, there are few cases where it is possible to distinguish before-and-after situations in technology adoption and implementation in occupations and professions.

References

Abel, R.L. (2003). *English Lawyers between Market and State: The Politics of Professionalism*. Oxford; New York: Oxford University Press.

Ajunwa, I. (2020). The Black Box at Work. *Data & Society*, 2. doi:10.2139/ssrn.3665772.

Ajunwa, I. and Greene, D. (2019). Platforms at Work: Automated Hiring Platforms and Other New Intermediaries in the Organization of the Workplace. In: S.P. Vallas and A. Kovalainen, eds., *Work and Labor in the Digital Age: Research in the Sociology of Work*. Bingley: Emerald Publishing, pp. 61–91.

Aloisi, A. and De Stefano, V. (2022). *Your Boss Is an Algorithm: Artificial Intelligence, Platform Work and Labour*. Oxford; London; New York; New Delhi; Sydney: Hart Publishing.

Andersson Schwarz, J. (2017). Platform Logic: An Interdisciplinary Approach to the Platform-Based Economy. *Policy & Internet*, 9(4), pp. 374–394. doi:10.1002/poi3.159.

Andrews, C. (2018). The End of Work or Overworked? Self-Service, Prosumer Capitalism, and 'Irrational Work'. *Sociological Inquiry*, 88(4), pp. 649–672. doi:10.1111/soin.12223.

Annabi, H. and Lebovitz, S. (2018). Improving the Retention of Women in the IT Workforce: An Investigation of Gender Diversity Interventions in the USA. *Information Systems Journal*, 28(6), pp. 1049–1081. doi:10.1111/isj.12182.

Autor, D.H. and Dorn, D. (2013). The Growth of Low-Skill Service Jobs and the Polarization of the US Labor Market. *American Economic Review*, 103(5), pp. 1553–1597. doi:10.1257/aer.103.5.1553.

Bailey, D.E. and Leonardi, P.M. (2015). *Technology Choices: Why Occupations Differ in Their Embrace of New Technology*. Cambridge: The MIT Press.

Bakarich, K.M. and O'Brien, P.E. (2021). The Robots Are Coming . . . But Aren't Here Yet: The Use of Artificial Intelligence Technologies in the Public Accounting Profession. *Journal of Emerging Technologies in Accounting*, 18(1), pp. 27–43.

Baldwin, R. (2020). *The Globotics Upheaval: Globalisation, Robotics and the Future of Work*. London: Orion Publishing Group.

Banks, C. and Meinert, E. (2016). The Acceptability of MOOC Certificates in the Workplace. In: *International Conference e-Learning. International Conference on E-Learning*, pp. 215–218. https://files.eric.ed.gov/fulltext/ED571496.pdf.

Barley, S.R. (2020). *Work and Technological Change*. Oxford: Oxford University Press.

Bergvall-Kåreborn, B. and Howcroft, D. (2014). Amazon Mechanical Turk and the Commodification of Labour. *New Technology, Work and Employment*, 29(3), pp. 213–223. doi:10.1111/ntwe.12038.

Birch, K. and Munieza, F., eds. (2020). *Assetization: Turning Things into Assets in Technoscientific Capitalism*. Cambridge: The MIT Press.

Bjursell, C., Bergmo-Prvulovic, I. and Hedegaard, J. (2021). Telework and Lifelong Learning. *Frontiers in Sociology*, 6. doi:10.3389/fsoc.2021.642277.

Buchanan, C., Howitt, M.L., Wilson, R., Booth, R.G., Risling, T. and Bamford, M. (2021). Predicted Influences of Artificial Intelligence on Nursing Education: Scoping Review. *JMIR Nursing*, 4(1), p. e23933. doi:10.2196/23933.

Chen, C.C., Garven, S.A., Jones, K.T. and Scarlata, A.N. (2021). Is Career Guidance Sending the Right Message About Accounting Work? Comparing Accounting with Competing Professions. *Accounting Education*, 30(4), pp. 355–384. doi:10.1080/09639284.2021.1913615.

Collier, R. (2003). Reflections on the Relationship between Law and Masculinities: Rethinking the 'Man Question' in Legal Studies. *Current Legal Problems*, 56(1), pp. 345–402. doi:10.1093/clp/56.1.345.

Cooper, L.A., Holderness, D.K., Sorensen, T.L. and Wood, D.A. (2021). Perceptions of Robotic Process Automation in Big 4 Public Accounting Firms: Do Firm Leaders and Lower-Level Employees Agree? *Journal of Emerging Technologies in Accounting*, 19(1), pp. 33–51. doi:10.2308/jeta-2020-085.

Couldry, N. and Mejias, U.A. (2019). *The Costs of Connection: How Data Is Colonizing Human Life and Appropriating It for Capitalism*. Stanford: Stanford University Press.

Cox, A. (2022). How Artificial Intelligence Might Change Academic Library Work: Applying the Competencies Literature and the Theory of the Professions. *Journal of the Association for Information Science and Technology*. [online], pp. 1–14. doi:10.1002/asi.24635.

Daff, L. (2021). Employers' Perspectives of Accounting Graduates and Their World of Work: Software Use and ICT Competencies. *Accounting Education*, 30(5), pp. 495–524. doi:10.1080/09639284.2021.1935282.

Decuypere, M. (2018). Open Education Platforms: Theoretical Ideas, Digital Operations and the Figure of the Open Learner. *European Educational Research Journal*, 18(4), pp. 439–460. doi:10.1177/1474904118814141.

Decuypere, M., Grimaldi, E. and Landri, P. (2021). Introduction: Critical Studies of Digital Education Platforms. *Critical Studies in Education*, 62(1), pp. 1–16. doi:10.1080/17508487.2020.1866050.

Di Gregorio, A., Maggioni, I., Mauri, C. and Mazzucchelli, A. (2019). Employability Skills for Future Marketing Professionals. *European Management Journal*, 37(3), pp. 251–258. doi:10.1016/j.emj.2019.03.004.

Dubal, V. (2021). The New Racial Wage Code. *SSRN Electronic Journal*. doi:10.2139/ssrn.3855094. Available at: https://ssrn.com/abstract=3855094http://dx.doi.org/10.2139/ssrn.3855094 [Accessed: 9 Jan. 2022].

Dunn, P. and Hazzard, E. (2019). Technology Approaches to Digital Health Literacy. *International Journal of Cardiology*, 293, pp. 294–296. doi:10.1016/j.ijcard.2019.06.039.

Foti, M. and Vavalis, M. (2021). What Blockchain Can Do for Power Grids? *Blockchain: Research And Applications*, 2(1), p. 100008.

Frenken, K. and Fuenfschilling, L. (2021). The Rise of Online Platforms and the Triumph of the Corporation. *Sociologica*, 14(3), pp. 101–113.

Frenken, K. and Schor, J. (2017). Putting the Sharing Economy into Perspective. *Environmental Innovation and Societal Transitions*, 23(1), pp. 3–10.

Gerber, C. and Krzywdzinski, M. (2019). Brave New Digital Work? New Forms of Performance Control in Crowdwork. In: S.P. Vallas and A. Kovalainen, eds., *Work and Labor in the Digital Age*. Bingley: Emerald Publishing Ltd.

Gerlitz, C. and Helmond, A. (2013). The Like Economy: Social Buttons and the Data-Intensive Web. *New Media & Society*, 15(8), pp. 1348–1365. doi:10.1177/1461444812472322.

Grealy, F., Collender, S., Lunney, J. and O'Boyle, R. (2019). Education, Empowerment and Access to All – Public Legal Education and Massive Open Online Courses at the Law Society of Ireland. *International Journal of Public Legal Education*, 3(1), p. 3. doi:10.19164/ijple.v3i1.832.

Harder, B. (2013). Are MOOCs the Future of Medical Education? *BMJ*, 346, p. f2666. doi:10.1136/bmj.f2666.

Helmond, A. (2015). The Platformization of the Web: Making Web Data Platform Ready. *Social Media + Society*, 1(2). doi:10.1177/2056305115603080.

Helmond, A., Nieborg, D.B. and van der Vlist, F.N. (2019). Facebook's Evolution: Development of a Platform-as-Infrastructure. *Internet Histories*, 3(2), pp. 123–146. doi:10.1080/24701475.2019.1593667.

Hochschild, A.R. (1989). *The Second Shift: Working Parents and the Revolution*. New York: Avon Books.

Jackson, D., Michelson, G. and Munir, R. (2022). Developing Accountants for the Future: New Technology, Skills, and the Role of Stakeholders. *Accounting Education*, pp. 1–28. doi:10.1080/09639284.2022.2057195.

Jeong, G.H. (2020). Artificial Intelligence, Machine Learning, and Deep Learning in Women's Health Nursing. *Korean Journal of Women Health Nursing*, 26(1), pp. 5–9. doi:10.4069/kjwhn.2020.03.11.

Johnson, N. (2019). Tracking Online Education in Canadian Universities and Colleges, pp. 1–63. *Canadian Digital Learning Research Association/Association canadienne de recherche sur la formation en ligne*. Available at: https://eduq.info/xmlui/bitstream/handle/11515/37850/johnson-tracking-online-eduation-canadian-universities-colleges-cdlra-2019.pdf;sequence=5 [Accessed: 15 Mar. 2022].

Kalleberg, A.L. (2011). *Good Jobs, Bad Jobs: The Rise of Polarized and Precarious Employment Systems in the United States, 1970s to 2000s*. New York: Russell Sage Foundation.

Kerssens, N. and van Dijck, J. (2022). Governed by Edtech? Valuing Pedagogical Autonomy in a Platform Society. *Harvard Educational Review*, 92(2), pp. 284–303. doi:10.17763/1943-5045-92.2.284.

Knox, J. (2019). What Does the 'Postdigital' Mean for Education? Three Critical Perspectives on the Digital, with Implications for Educational Research and Practice. *Postdigital Science And Education*, 1(2), pp. 357–370. doi:10.1007/s42438-019-00045-y.

Komljenovic, J. (2021). The Rise of Education Rentiers: Digital Platforms, Digital Data and Rents. *Learning, Media And Technology*, 46(3), pp. 1–13. doi:10.1080/17439884.2021.1891422.

Komljenovic, J. and Robertson, S.L. (2016). The Dynamics of 'Market-Making' in Higher Education. *Journal of Education Policy*, 31(5), pp. 622–636. doi:10.1080/02680939.2016.1157732.

Korinek, A. and Juelfs, M. (2022). Preparing for the (Non-Existent?) Future of Work. Brookings Center on Regulation and Markets Working Paper #3. *Brookings*. [online]. Available at: www.brookings.edu/series/center-on-regulation-and-markets-working-papers/ [Accessed: 23 Aug. 2022].

Kwet, M. (2019). Digital Colonialism: US Empire and the New Imperialism in the Global South. *Race & Class*, 60(4), pp. 3–26. doi:10.1177/0306396818823172.

Langseth, L., Lysne, D.A., Nykvist, S. and Haugsbakken, H. (2019). MOOC Platforms: A Nordic Approach to Research-Informed Education in Higher Education. In: *Proceedings of EMOOCs 2019: Work in Progress Papers of the Research, Experience, and Business Track* (CEUR Workshop Proceedings). Aachen: Sun SITE Central Europe, pp. 157–162.

Lee, C. and Lim, C. (2021). From Technological Development to Social Advance: A Review of Industry 4.0 Through Machine Learning. *Technological Forecasting and Social Change*, 167, p. 120653. doi:10.1016/j.techfore.2021.120653.

Macgilchrist, F. (2021). Theories of Postdigital Heterogeneity: Implications for Research on Education and Datafication. *Postdigital Science and Education*, 3(3), pp. 660–667. doi:10.1007/s42438-021-00232-w.

Marler, W. (2022). 'You Can Connect with Like, the World!': Social Platforms, Survival Support, and Digital Inequalities for People Experiencing Homelessness. *Journal of Computer-Mediated Communication*, 27(1). doi:10.1093/jcmc/zmab020.

Martindale, N. and Lehdonvirta, V. (2021). Can Labour Market Digitalization Increase Social Mobility? Evidence from a European Survey of Online Platform Workers. University of Oxford Working Paper, 8 May. Available at: https://ssrn.com/abstract=3862635http://dx.doi.org/10.2139/ssrn.3862635 [Accessed: 16 Feb. 2022].

Mateescu, A. and Elish, M.C. (2019). AI in Context: The Labor of Integrating New Technologies. *Data & Society*, pp. 1–54. Available at: https://apo.org.au/node/217456.

McAfee, A. and Brynjolfsson, E. (2017). *Machine, Platform, Crowd: Harnessing Our Digital Revolution*. New York; London: W.W. Norton.

McNay, L. (1999). Gender, Habitus and the Field. *Theory, Culture & Society*, 16(1), pp. 95–117. doi:10.1177/026327699016001007.

McNay, L. (2008). *Against Recognition*. Cambridge: Polity Press.

Mirrlees, T. and Alvi, S. (2020). *EdTech Inc.: Selling, Automating and Globalizing Higher Education in the Digital Age*. New York: Routledge.

Napier, A. and Orrick, A. (2022). The Economic, Social, and Political Dimensions of Platform Studies in Education. *Harvard Educational Review*, 92(2), pp. 206–208. doi:10.17763/1943-5045-92.2.206.

Nichols, T.P. and Garcia, A. (2022). Platform Studies in Education. *Harvard Educational Review*, 92(2), pp. 209–230. doi:10.17763/1943-5045-92.2.209.

Pangrazio, L., Stornaiuolo, A., Nichols, T.P., Garcia, A. and Philip, T.M. (2022). Datafication Meets Platformization: Materializing Data Processes in Teaching and Learning. *Harvard Educational Review*, 92(2), pp. 257–283. doi:10.17763/1943-5045-92.2.257.

Perrotta, C. (2020). Programming the Platform University: Learning Analytics and Predictive Infrastructures in Higher Education. *Research In Education*, 109. doi:10.1177/0034523720965623.

Poutanen, S. and Kovalainen, A. (2022). Intersections of Platforms, Algorithms and Modern Work in the Nordic Welfare State. In: *Nordic Sociological Association Conference 2022*. Reykjavik: Reykjavik University.

Raisch, S. and Krakowski, S. (2021). Artificial Intelligence and Management: The Automation – Augmentation Paradox. *Academy of Management Review*, 46(1), pp. 192–210. doi:10.5465/amr.2018.0072.

Rathore, N.P. and Dangi, M. (2021). Embedding Artificial Intelligence into Education: The New Normal. In: A. Hamdan, A.E. Hassanien, R. Khamis, B. Alareeni, A. Razzaque and B. Awwad, eds., *Applications of Artificial Intelligence in Business, Education and Healthcare. Studies in Computational Intelligence*. Cham: Springer, pp. 255–270. doi:10.1007/978-3-030-72080-3_15.

Razack, S., Risør, T., Hodges, B. and Steinert, Y. (2020). Beyond the Cultural Myth of Medical Meritocracy. *Medical Education*, 54(1), pp. 46–53. doi:10.1111/medu.13871.

Riis Andersen, J., Corydon, B., Staun, J., Bughin, J., Lüneborg, J. and Schröder, P. (2017). *The Future That Works. The Impact of Automation in Denmark*. Copenhagen: Tuborg Research Centre for Globalisation and Firms, Århus University, and McKinsey & Company.

Robert, N. (2019). How Artificial Intelligence Is Changing Nursing. *Nursing Management (Springhouse)*, 50(9), pp. 30–39. doi:10.1097/01.numa.0000578988.56622.21.

Rodriguez, J.K., Holvino, E., Fletcher, J.K. and Nkomo, S.M. (2016). The Theory and Praxis of Intersectionality in Work and Organisations: Where Do We Go from Here? *Gender, Work & Organization*, 23(3), pp. 201–222. doi:10.1111/gwao.12131.

Roll, I. and Wylie, R. (2016). Evolution and Revolution in Artificial Intelligence in Education. *International Journal of Artificial Intelligence in Education*, 26(2), pp. 582–599. doi:10.1007/s40593-016-0110-3.

Romani, L., Zanoni, P. and Holck, L. (2020). Radicalizing Diversity (Research): Time to Resume Talking About Class. *Gender, Work & Organization*, 28(1), pp. 8–23. doi:10.1111/gwao.12593.

Saks, M. and Muzio, D. (2020). *Professions and Professional Service Firms: Private and Public Sector Enterprises in the Global Economy*. London: Routledge.

Sastry, S., Lee, T.H. and Teoh, M.T.T. (2021). The Use of Blockchain Technology and Data Analytics in the Audit Profession. *Quantum Journal of Social Sciences and Humanities*, 2(4), pp. 67–86. doi:10.55197/qjssh.v2i4.89.

Schinkel, W. and Noordegraaf, M. (2011). Professionalism as Symbolic Capital: Materials for a Bourdieusian Theory of Professionalism. *Comparative Sociology*, 10(1), pp. 67–96. doi:10.1163/156913310x514083.

Sigahi, T.F.A.C. and Saltorato, P. (2019). Academic Capitalism: Distinguishing without Disjoining Through Classification Schemes. *Higher Education*, 80(1), pp. 95–117. doi:10.1007/s10734-019-00467-4.

Sommerlad, H. (1995). Managerialism and the Legal Profession: A New Professional Paradigm. *International Journal of the Legal Profession*, 2(2), pp. 159–185. doi:10.1080/09695958.1995.9960401.

Sommerlad, H. (2016). 'A Pit to Put Women in': Professionalism, Work Intensification, Sexualisation and Work – Life Balance in the Legal Profession in England and Wales. *International Journal of the Legal Profession*, 23(1), pp. 61–82. doi:10.1080/09695958.2016.1140945.

Susskind, R.E. and Susskind, D. (2017). *The Future of the Professions: How Technology Will Transform the Work of Human Experts*. Oxford; New York: Oxford University Press.

Swinney, L. and Elder, B. (2012). Promoting Professionalism: Lessons from the Medical and Legal Professions. In: C. Jeffrey, ed., *Research on Professional Responsibility and Ethics in Accounting* (Research on Professional Responsibility and Ethics in Accounting). Bingley: Emerald Publishing Ltd.

ten Have, H. (2022). A Global Platform for Ethics Education. *International Journal of Ethics Education*, 7(2), pp. 213–216. doi:10.1007/s40889-022-00153-7.

Torres, A.C. and Weiner, J. (2018). The New Professionalism? Charter Teachers' Experiences and Qualities of the Teaching Profession. *Education Policy Analysis Archives*, 26(19), pp. 1–29. doi:10.14507/epaa.26.3049.

Tsatsou, P. (2011). Digital Divides Revisited: What Is New About Divides and Their Research? *Media, Culture & Society*, 33(2), pp. 317–331. doi:10.1177/0163443710393865.

Vähämäki, M., Kuusi, T., Laiho, M. and Kulvik, M. (2020). The Road to Productivity with Automation: Dialogue Between the Experienced and Measured. In: S. Poutanen, A. Kovalainen and P. Rouvinen, eds., *Digital Work and the Platform Economy*. New York: Routledge, pp. 116–142.

Van Dijk, J. (2020). *Digital Divide*. Bristol: Polity Press.

Van Dijck, J., Poell, T. and De Waal, M. (2018). *The Platform Society: Public Values in a Connective World*. Kettering: Oxford University Press.

Verma, A., Lamsal, K. and Verma, P. (2021). An Investigation of Skill Requirements in Artificial Intelligence and Machine Learning Job Advertisements. *Industry and Higher Education*, 36(1), pp. 63–67. doi:10.1177/0950422221990990.

Whitchurch, C. (2013). *Reconstructing Identities in Higher Education: the Rise of 'Third Space' Professionals*. London: Routledge.

Williamson, B. (2019). Policy Networks, Performance Metrics and Platform Markets: Charting the Expanding Data Infrastructure of Higher Education. British *Journal of Educational Technology*, 50(6), pp. 2794–2809. doi:10.1111/bjet.12849.

Williamson, B., Gulson, K.N., Perrotta, C. and Witzenberger, K. (2022). Amazon and the New Global Connective Architectures of Education Governance. *Harvard Educational Review*, 92(2), pp. 231–256. doi:10.17763/1943-5045-92.2.231.

World Economic Forum. (2020). *Jobs of Tomorrow: Mapping Opportunity in the New Economy*. [online]. Available at: www.weforum.org/reports/jobs-of-tomorrow-mapping-opportunity-in-the-new-economy [Accessed: 12 Apr. 2022].

Young, P.A. (2021). The Ever Evolving MOOC. *Educational Technology Research and Development*, 69(1), pp. 363–364. doi:10.1007/s11423-021-09959-6.

8 Towards platformization as a new social order

Platformization and digitalization are increasing the number of self-employed. The statistics, using traditional classifications, have difficulties capturing the amount and nature of new platform work in its various aspects, especially in relation to professions and their development. The future of professions will be defined not only by technology, corporation strategies, and consumer behavior but also by national and supranational decision making. The growth of new professions is thus bound up closely with the power of digitalization and platforms.

Evolving professions and technologies

In his now classic research on professions, Abbott noted that professionalism is the main way of institutionalizing expertise in industrialized societies (Abbott, 1988). Throughout this book, we have widened this classic idea both theoretically and empirically in relation to professions and professional expertise in postdigital societies. The debate of whether professions still have a strong foothold in contemporary societies and in their economic make-up, and whether the categorization and ideal types of professions need to be refurbished (Adams et al., 2020), is ongoing and raises several important issues regarding the role and future of professions. However, as we have indicated throughout the book, professions evolve constantly, and hence several factors give less support to steadfast and unchanging ideal types of professions and rather underline the variety across and within professions.

We have argued that alongside technologies that infiltrate, reshape, and change professions from within, structural widening of the category of professions is also taking place. Technologies have enabled the development of new professions, entirely based on markets. Technologies also currently shape established professions, through introduction of new means of production. Part of the technology also changes the state-dependent institutional structures. The adoption of various market mechanisms into state functions may stabilize institutions. However, rather than stating that institutions automatically engage in or elicit similar actions in a similar fashion everywhere, a growing body of literature suggests that institutions and their

DOI: 10.4324/9781351038546-8

actions require analysis and interpretation, which may over time lead to changes in how institutional activity is practiced (Carstensen and Röper, 2022). The domestication of a new organizational model in the public sector is highly dependent on the forms and varieties of institutions in question. Therefore, platforms are not taking one but several forms with the development of technologies. The platformization of services can become an organizing model for public services, to the extent that service provision adopts the model of autonomous (AI) systems, at least partially.

We have introduced the rise of entirely new professions that are completely market based and that derive from the professions' power position in markets. Social influencers are an example of a new profession that is entirely market-based and socially mediated, where the parasocial relationship with customers is at the core of the professional identity, and earnings relate to the mediated authenticity, image, and ability to convey messages – whether they concern consumption or (mis)information or other types of influencing – to the targeted or intended audiences. Work as influencer requires marketable skills and professionalism, and ability to work for the contractor without appearing as a salesperson of the contractor.

Research on professions has stated that while the relationship between professionals and clients is important, the influence of these interactions on professionals' identity construction 'remains poorly understood' (Adams et al., 2020, 225). The discussion we provided in the previous chapter shows how even permanent client relations can be built or based on and located in online relationships, with actions such as likes, comments, and product or service purchases being mediated and spread through social media. These types of relationships are based on parasocial connections and relationships, which are at the core of social media professions such as that of social influencer. Our argument is that influencer is a new profession with networks and relations and power built and based entirely on markets, and most often heavily dependent on parasocial relationships with followers, that is, the potential clients. The influencer as a profession shows how a consumeristic clientele can be enduring even if built entirely online. The longevity of the relationship is based on the credibility of the professional social influencer and the authentic experiences of the client.

The new professions are based on their ability to build an entire professional identity by emphasizing the crucial role of technology in shaping societies – expertise included. Technologies are indeed irreversibly altering the question of where specifically the expertise resides in societies. Some literature suggests that increasingly, machine learning and AI will displace much of the work of human professionals (e.g., Susskind and Susskind, 2017). We have suggested the importance of grappling with new technology as assembled and amalgamated actual work processes and practices, educational qualifications, and seeped into occupations and professions. This line of thinking is a more fruitful way to see technology as fused into the workings of individuals and organizations, as compared to thinking of it as a separate entity or black box type of activity that makes humans act in specific ways, often contrasted with earlier activities and actions.

Technologies cannot easily be detached from labor and its capabilities, nor can they be analytically distinguished from expertise. Technologies in general will both reshape and drive many of the changes in societal and economic institutions. In any type of work tasks, professions and expertise included, chosen technologies become part of the work activities themselves, as they are copied and implemented, adopted and immersed into practices of work and work cultures. This does not mean that the reshaping activities of technologies at work and work cultures need to be managed in any particular way; rather, technologies do also develop within organizations and in their decision-making processes, which may take place without any human intervention, such as in HR activities. The domestication of various technologies taking place in organizational contexts becomes insurmountable and part of all activities. The ongoing transformation and re-institutionalization of technology as an integrated part of the processes and mechanisms of functioning society also underline the enfolding nature of technology, not only as a part of occupations and professions, but more importantly, as a part of modern society.

The omnipotent platformization

Research on platforms and platform work (Poutanen et al., 2020; van Doorn et al., 2021) shows that digital platforms bring novelty in societies in several major ways, which can analytically be addressed through work models and different forms of work arrangements, or through the analyses of new urban consumption patterns and behaviors. The analyses focusing on work and on consumption patterns offer meticulous and detailed evidence of the new patterns emerging in society. The unexplored void in most studies addressing platforms and their invasion and presence in working life, or business life for that matter, is a systematic analysis of the increasing omnipotence of platforms as an efficient technological solution. As a technological solution, the usability of platforms extends beyond consumer-based market services. The spreading out of digital platforms into social and economic life has taken place at an overwhelming speed when compared to any previous organizing and business logics, which tells both of their efficiency and their omnipotence.

Platforms have proven to be omnipotent as an organizing model or principle for many activities, social and personal life included. In this capacity – as an organizing principle in the economy and in social life – platforms are widening their potential and applicability from an online gig business to wider gig economy encompassing professions and education. Platform is thus not a single business model, nor solely an effective algorithmic device, but its applicability spans several fields and activities. When technologies such as platformization are understood through their operations within organization, as shown earlier, that is in their material situations of use such as flexible arrangements (e.g., Evans et al., 2006), the understanding of how platforms function and spread becomes more tangible.

Despite the overwhelming majority of research on platforms focusing on the exploitation of labor at online labor platforms, for example, platforms were not specifically designed for the exploitation of labor, even if this indeed is one intended or unintended outcome of the global platforms and their functioning. Those receiving work tasks at global platforms are most often from low-wage countries, and most often hired by those located in high-wage countries (Graham et al., 2017; Inglese, 2019).

Taking platforms and their functioning in society more generally, it is important to distinguish platforms as corporations (such as online platforms) and platforms as generic solutions available to institutions and organizations alike. Platforms have proven to be efficient way of organizing markets of many types, including labor supply and demand, many business activities and their logistics, and increasingly importantly, various societal and economic activities originally owned and run by the state. The so-called regime competition (van Slageren et al., 2022), which takes place globally and regionally as a competition of gigs and of work, is another manifestation of the fluency of platforms: the call-out for offers does not recognize national boundaries. Platformization also covers other fields than online work and transportation/delivery, such as healthcare and education, both industries with strong professions. These platformized activities are currently expanding, and range from education to healthcare. Platforms are increasingly used for nonmarket-based exchange and organizing of activities in the private and public sectors. The question of how to understand platformization within healthcare draws attention to online gig work and professional services and work provided through platforms. Such networks and platforms already function across national borders and mediate work tasks and gigs and workers (or partners) to perform work and gigs.

The omnipotence of platforms and platformization is the key rationale for why we draw attention to platformization as a major societal and economic organizing form, a new social order. We do this, especially in relation to professionalism, expertise, and knowledge creation, and more generally in relation to the societal organizing power of platforms that extends beyond the aforementioned realms. With their technological superiority, functionality, and efficiency, platforms have spread from single-site technology business activities into amalgamated meta-platforms that have become one of the reigning models of arrangements within the bureaucracy. At the same time, platforms as a new fluid organizational form show the omnipotence of technology in the arrangement of various societal functions. Platforms enable new forms of expertise and professions to arise, and assemble them with new types of tools. Often these tools are platform specific, and they may thus increase dependency on the platform and its functions.

We argue that platformization has risen to the fore as a general organizing principle, and indeed to such an extent that it has become a new social order in societies, extending from individual personal online ties and connections, consumption patterns, and ways of working to industrial production modes and service models. Platformization both as a market structure and an organizing mechanism is efficient in how it governs markets, with a tendency toward monopoly. Platformization as a market structure and mechanism is also fluid in its forms of actualization. The use of platforms concerns equally governments and their public sector activities as well as NGOs. While the global spread of platforms started as market-based arrangements and tech firms' organizational model, the technical efficiency of platforms makes them superior organizing form and thus suitable for institutions, where digital forms such as digital services are at the focus. Platformization does not necessarily lessen the role of state governments, nor of constitutional legislation. The differing features that enable the platformization of governance depend on the national maturity of digitalized services and their technological implementation, for example. The governance of institutions is a crucial matter for professions and professionalism in several ways, not least due to the consequences of growth in platformization. Determining the appropriate levels and types of governance, partially as a response to domestic interdependencies among state and nonstate actors, is one of the rather permanent state governance questions (Boyer and Hollingsworth, 1998; Schmitter, 1998).

It has been stated that institutions shape the ways markets and services are evolving (Boyer and Hollingsworth, 1998; Kovalainen, 1995). This puts the organizing form of institutions such as platformization on podium. Markets allow for greater flexibility, and platformization has provided even greater efficiency in harnessing algorithmic decision making into the core of market mechanisms. Governance in relation to the spread of platformization of services and production does bring in new challenges to governance, as shown by Frenken and Fuenfschilling (2021) and Frenken et al. (2019). The tension between national labor regulations and digital labor markets prevails, partially because the gig economy is overall not strongly influenced nor regulated by national legislations and regulations (e.g., Berg and de Stefano, 2018).

Further research results specify that gig work platforms build up their own institutional infrastructures, with their own rules and regulations, which all require compliance from those using the platform (van Slageren et al., 2022). This compliance with overall rules and regulations that trump national regulations shows that platforms tend to act as 'private regulators' (van Slageren et al., 2022, 18) that build up their own institutional environment within the national institutional environment. In a similar manner, Nitzberg and Zysman (2022) argue that governance in the digital era is not about the rules of specific tools, but instead the overall challenges represented by fully new toolboxes, which include, among other things, big data, algorithms, and software. For states and their multilevel governance, this may represent challenges, as shown in a comparative study on the European Union data from 22 countries. Across the EU, there is a considerable variation in how governments approach the governance of AI (Dabrowski and Suska, 2022; Djeffal et al., 2022; Schwabe, 2022), despite the aims for supranational regulation such as European law on AI (the AI Act). In solving the governance issues, the professions are highly likely to be in key roles with acquired digital and technological skills.

Digital dimensions at work are reorganizing the contents of work in major ways in several economic sectors. Professions as occupational categories, as well as occupations alongside many work tasks, are being reshaped and inscribed anew with technology. Together with the growth of platforms and the overall platformization of services and expert work, this calls for new digital forms of governance. The governance of platformization requires skilled expertise, as platformization takes new forms when spreading across different types of institutions. Governance concerns thus not only technical and digital governance of platforms but also more multifaceted and multileveled activity, including legislative measures. We argue that despite the platform model being a new business model enabled by rapid and scalable digital technologies, platformization is much more than an organizing form of digital business. As a new governance structure, platformization needs further analysis, especially in terms of the relations between state structures, national governance, and global platforms, as well as the relations between professions and platformization.

The future of work and professions

For any profession, the key to maintenance of professional skills in the future is both what resources are drawn upon and how these resources are put into practical use. In addition to updating skills, the fields in which the professions function in general become increasingly amalgamated with various technologies. Hence, the future of professions is by no means one-directional. The dynamics within professional groups may mean that some of the resources related to technologies that currently are seen as 'additional', despite the social processes outside of professions that emphasize the same resources as 'core' skills, will become accepted, but with a time-lapse. This time-lapse may be due to the complex interplay between members of the professional ecosystem, including professionals but also providers of technologies and skills, employers, and even citizens. For example, in many fields of surgery, where automation requires upskilling of professional knowledge, citizens have become an important group with influence over the treatments developed (Fosch-Villaronga et al., 2022).

The two discussions within the research on work and labor have only a few shared analyses of how two trends, on the one hand, automation and the adoption of digital technologies, and on the other hand, the platformization of economies and societies, transform the social order in general. Known facts are that automation and adoption of digital technologies transform all work and work tasks, skills included, and that their effects cover areas from assembly line manufacturing to highly skilled work tasks, dispersed differently across countries and continents and between cities and sparsely populated areas. The extent to which customers are prepared to increase demand, despite rising costs, largely dictates the number of jobs available. As one consequence of this elasticity, or rather, lack of it, several types of inequalities may increase, as discussed earlier in the book in Chapters 1 and 2 in regard to the likely macroeconomic effects of automation and its potential to shrink specific types of jobs. The complicating matter for straightforward prediction of the effects of automation and technology is the gains achieved with regard to consumers and consumption. If consumers increase their consumption in labor-intensive industries, overall employment may rise, even if the number of workers in machine-intensive industries may fall. Thus, the gains from digitalization and automatization may have effects on service industries that otherwise are entirely untouched by the new technologies (Roberts et al., 2017). Added to that, the advent of platforms and their effects on the increase of service industries, with other new technology, complicates the picture even more.

Platforms are changing globally the digital business models and their governance (Evans and Schmalensee, 2010; Cutolo et al., 2019; Kenney and Zysman, 2016), as well as their effects – intended or unintended – that extend further than business logics. Digital platforms have become incorporated in a very similar manner to business value chains and to labor markets, seeking the best possible return for value. Whether this 'return for value' is the logic underlying why the public sector activities are increasingly using platforms remains debatable. The adoption of platforms in the public sector reformulates several of the public mechanisms that have direct effects on citizens, such as housing support decisions made by AI used by social services in the public sector. When the public sector adopts platforms as an operating mechanism, the distinctions between public and private activities in practical terms may blur. Similarly, the boundary resources, which usually have been understood as technical tools for third parties to join the platform ecosystems, are blurring. It is argued that social boundary resources have in fact become more technical than earlier (Kenney et al., 2019). The new professions emerging with social media enmesh the social and technical boundary resources, and one would not exist without the other.

Indeed, the new professions, such as social influencers and intermediaries who manage relationships between influencers and brands, both launched by social media, are prime examples of the power of plaformization and of boundary-blurring between social and technical boundary resources. The social boundary resources of platforms are technically mediated, as they are in new professions where no real-life connections are established or needed between service provision (e.g., information provision by influencer, promotion, or advertising activities) and consumption (purchase of product or service by consumer-citizens). As digitalization makes market entry easier, it also makes it easier for professional experts to enter digital markets, platforms included. Such data-driven market entry results in the expansion of the scope of digital platform firms (Gawer, 2022; Uzunca and Kas, 2022; Westermeier, 2020) and also expansion of new professions and the knowledge of established professions.

The blurring of boundaries takes place also in contemporary labor market positions. Members of strong professions, such as medical doctors and lawyers, often function as self-employed but with less volatility of work and position than other self-employed. Currently, many countries are seeing growth of self-employed professionals with highly qualified and specialized skills that respond to contemporary demands. In many countries, self-employment has grown as a response to rising unemployment rates and to national policy instruments such as institutional incentives to support new self-employment (Borghi et al., 2018). However, the paths to self-employment differ according to expertise, profession, and professional qualifications, and continue to differentiate even more over the course of economic activity on the basis of professional status. The upsurge of professional self-employment globally ranges among the population of employed from the OECD average of 16% to 29% in Italy among self-employed men with tertiary education, the corresponding shares being OECD average of 10% to 19% in Italy among self-employed women with tertiary education (OECD, 2022).

The rise in the number of self-employed professionals globally is not without tensions or even contradictions. On the one hand, the strong professions have traditionally been part of the self-employed professional and expert echelons in societies, where the state and markets usually define one's labor market status. This has meant that they have been able to define and maintain their income levels rather stably. On the other hand, the recent growth among the highly educated self-employed has also created highly diversified and specialized professions with unequal contract relations and income levels. Their individualized contract relations also entail individual bargaining of one's own working conditions. As a result of such bargaining, the legal status of self-employed does not necessarily result from individual choices alone, but can also reflect forced entry to self-employment, due to a lack of other options. The self-employment position can be imposed, and it can even lead to economic dependency and be associated with precariousness, as shown in numerous studies (Semenza and Pichault, 2019). For strong professions, the dependency may relate more to technology and less to precarity as such.

Based on statistics, self-employment is becoming a more typical work pattern for the digital economy than previously. Authors analyzing the fourth industrial revolution relate this to the growth of capitalism without capital, that is, growth in the intangible economy of knowledge-based assets

(O'Reilly et al., 2018, 7). The demand for these assets is the most vulnerable part of the growth in this type of capitalism. The possible volatility of earnings, the lack of organizational support for skills upgrading, and constant learning are some of the major paradoxes in the growth of professionalism and professional self-employment with new technology and platforms. In global labor markets, high levels of education and professional specialization are no longer a secure guarantee of high levels of income and social status in society. Individualization and specialization are seen as growing even in skilled labor markets, and this may increase in the future the need for new types of collective agreements, as opposed to entrepreneurial risks.

Platformization as new social order?

With the growth of platformization and its spread from a private online economy to services on a wider scale, and with the overall growth of the consumer society, risk in the production of services has also shifted from firms to partners. Digital platforms match client demand with a supply of partners and their skills to complete tasks. When a partner, who can be any skilled worker or professional, completes the task, the risk of the task is on that partner, and not on the platform company. Despite different types of contracts prevailing between platform firms and skilled partners, the overall risk has shifted from the firm (capital) to the worker-partner (labor). The worker-partners provide their skilled labor and resources to complete the contract, instead of being able to rely on the firm's capabilities to support them in the task.

The new platforms inevitably lead to questions concerning the ways, for example, organizations arrange professional work, and how entrepreneurship and, for example, independent gig work require new models of organization. Do algorithms require new types of professions, and if so, is this development visible already? One of the most noteworthy global aspects in current societies is the intensifying presence of technology, to the extent that we can talk about the omnipotence of technologies, a kind of technological imperative. Technologies become immersed into everyday working practices also by governments and public institutions, and complex dependencies between private platform corporations and public sector may appear. This new omnipotence, a new type of technological imperative emerges in the working life of practicing professionals from medical doctors to lawyers and from teachers to preachers. However, predicting what happens with work when technologies grow in presence is particularly difficult.

New ways of organizing professions increasingly emerge through and with the help of digital platforms. The 'easiness' of starting up a business and the 'toughness' of building up the reputation into trustworthy professional do raise new questions concerning the organization of professions (Kovalainen and Poutanen, 2018). Do large and/or trustworthy organizations 'skim the cream', or do they loosen up their corporate culture into more fluid forms of organizing? The platforms inevitably lead to new questions on the ways organizations arrange professional work and how entrepreneurship and independent gig work require novel models for organizing professional work. At the same time, new forms of Taylorism enter the professional work through platforms, perhaps freeing professions from corporate iron gage but simultaneously putting them into self-employment and entrepreneurial modes of earning logics.

The ways in which the power relations between consumers and service providers have shifted with the growth of digitalization are complex, and more complexity is added by the platformization of economies. Technology companies and platform firms have increased both their economic and political power throughout societies through possession of the means to create and capture value through data harvesting, practically without ownership of means of production or employees working for them. Social media and the digital economy have both transformed the power of consumers and augmented their role in economic value formation. Consumers' ability to use apps to fulfill needs has in fact transformed many work tasks into a variety of short-term gigs and many services to require the constant digital presence of service providers, or at least constant availability of services for consumers. With the growth of new technologies – besides displacement of jobs – there will also emerge new occupations and upgrades of existing occupations and professions, which are much more than earlier dependent on consumerism and its development.

The power of consumers has undoubtedly grown, but in their vast scope to use the app economy and social media for their personal consumption, these digital consumers have also become servants of the platform companies. They secure the growth of platformization by providing their own data, ranging from consumption pattern data, time use data, and so on, to their social media user data, to be capitalized by these companies. The consumers' customer relationship to the platforms goes beyond mere 'consumer loyalty', for example, as the consumption of app services and use of social media, both provided by platform companies, become interwoven in the tapestry of their everyday lives. The constant digital availability of professions is required, and consumer services require reputation-building in an entirely different manner than earlier. The credentials of professionals need to be displayed publicly, through professional platforms or their own webpages, otherwise the professional in competition with other professionals loses the visibility competition for the consumers' attention.

In societies, platformization constructs new digital user subjectivities, and these subjectivities are emerging at many levels, ranging from individual consumption to digital citizenship, from education to healthcare, and from workplaces to industries. As researchers note, the digital era establishes not only new possibilities for markets and for any type of information spread, but it also delivers new devices and apps for the constitution of social relations, information, and shared values, all across the markets and in publicity (O'Reilly et al., 2018). The new digital user subjectivities on platforms thus have consequences in many ways for material lives. The digital user subjectivities also diversify citizens into new categories as consumers, workers, experts, and professionals, for example.

The growth of new professions, alongside the transformation of the established professions and semi-professions, is more dependent on changes in consumer culture than ever before. The platforms make use of professions, but also create possibilities for professions. By shifting production outside of the firm or organization, platforms shift the expertise outside as well. The former employees become partners. This means rapid scalability for any firm or organization, if that is the aim of the activity. Platformization as an intermediating function is effective in its unilaterally imposed rules and conditions of operations. Digital technology and platformization currently redesign whole industries, as discussed earlier in relation to educational institutions and professions. For professions, both of the aforementioned processes may mean loose connection to organizations, growth in demand for skills and services, but also the volatility of income over time. Platformization as a market structure and mechanism is efficient in how it governs markets, with a tendency among platform firms towards monopolies, while as a market structure it seems to weaken the position of labor – highly qualified professions included.

We argue that the future of the platform economy will be defined not only by technology development, new corporation strategies, and digitally attuned consumer behavior, but also by national and supranational political decision making. The gravity of platformization as a new social order is thus based on its several fluid abilities to function as a podium for organizing platformization as a constructor of new digital user subjectivities, with consequences in material lives, and the creation of new social order rooted in new societal and economic arrangements of power and possibilities. Platform companies pose a challenge for many types of existing and 'traditional' forms of regulations, especially on issues of markets, labor, and monopoly power. Digital platforms globally shape economies such that no nation can expect to maintain its 'national order' intact; instead, new collaborative actions among established and new professions may also be needed. New political forms of governance at the national level are still to some extent missing in relation to platformization and its regulatory framework.

References

Abbott, A. (1988). *The System of Professions: An Essay on the Division of Expert Labor.* Chicago: University of Chicago Press.

Adams, T.L., Clegg, S., Eyal, G., Reed, M. and Saks, M. (2020). Connective Professionalism: Towards (Yet Another) Ideal Type. *Journal of Professions and Organization*, 7(2), pp. 224–233. doi:10.1093/jpo/joaa013.

Berg, J. and De Stefano, V. (2018). Employment and Regulation for Clickwork. In: M. Neufeind, J. O'Reilly and F. Ranft, eds., *Work in the Digital Age: Challenges of the Fourth Industrial Revolution. Identifying the Challenges for Work in the Digital Age.* London; New York: Rowman & Littlefield, pp. 175–184.

Borghi, P., Mori, A. and Semenza, R. (2018). Self-Employed Professionals in the European Labour Market. A Comparison between Italy, Germany and the UK. *Transfer: European Review of Labour and Research*, 24(4), pp. 405–419. doi:10.1177/1024258918761564.

Boyer, R. and Hollingsworth, J.R. (1998). From National Embeddedness to Spatial and Institutional Nestedness. In: J.R. Hollingsworth and R. Boyer, eds., *Contemporary Capitalism. The Embeddedness of Institutions*. Cambridge: Cambridge University Press.

Carstensen, M.B. and Röper, N. (2022). The Other Side of Agency: Bricolage and Institutional Continuity. *Journal of European Public Policy*, 29(8), pp. 1288–1308. doi:10.1080/13501763.2021.1936128.

Cutolo, D., Kenney, M. and Zysman, J. (2019). Platform-Dependent Entrepreneurs as Private Regulators in the Platform Economy. *SSRN Electronic Journal*. [online], 5 p. doi:10.2139/ssrn.3431467.

Dabrowski, L.D. and Suska, M. (2022). *The European Union Digital Single Market: Europe's Digital Transformation*. Abingdon; New York: Routledge.

Djeffal, C., Siewert, M.B. and Wurster, S. (2022). Role of the State and Responsibility in Governing Artificial Intelligence: A Comparative Analysis of AI Strategies. *Journal of European Public Policy*, 29(11), pp. 1799–1821. doi:10.1080/13501763.2022.2094987.

Evans, D.S., Hagiu, A. and Schmalensee, R. (2006). *Invisible Engines: How Software Platforms Drive Innovation and Transform Industries*. Cambridge: MIT Press.

Evans, D.S. and Schmalensee, R. (2010). Failure to Launch: Critical Mass in Platform Businesses. *Review of Network Economics*, 9(4), pp. 1–26. doi:10.2202/1446-9022.1256.

Fosch-Villaronga, E., Khanna, P., Drukarch, H. and Custers, B. (2022). The Role of Humans in Surgery Automation. *International Journal of Social Robotics*. [online], 2022-04-10. doi:10.1007/s12369-022-00875-0.

Frenken, K. and Fuenfschilling, L. (2021). The Rise of Online Platforms and the Triumph of the Corporation. *Sociologica*, 14(3), pp. 101–113.

Frenken, K., Waes, A., Pelzer, P., Smink, M. and Est, R. (2019). Safeguarding Public Interests in the Platform Economy. *Policy & Internet*, 12(3), pp. 400–425. doi:10.1002/poi3.217.

Gawer, A. (2022). Digital Platforms and Ecosystems: Remarks on the Dominant Organizational Form of the Digital Age. *Innovation*, 24(1), pp. 110–124. doi:10.1080/14479338.2021.1965888.

Graham, M., Hjorth, I. and Lehdonvirta, V. (2017). Digital Labour and Development: Impacts of Global Digital Labour Platforms and the Gig Economy on Worker Livelihoods. *Transfer: European Review of Labour and Research*, 23(2), pp. 135–162. doi:10.1177/1024258916687250.

Inglese, M. (2019). *Regulating the Collaborative Economy in the European Union Digital Single Market*. Cham: Springer.

Kenney, M., Rouvinen, P., Seppälä, T. and Zysman, J. (2019). Platforms and Industrial Change. *Industry and Innovation*, 26(8), pp. 871–879. doi:10.1080/13662716.2019.1602514.

Kenney, M. and Zysman, J. (2016). The Rise of the Platform Economy. *Issues in Science and Technology*, 32(3), pp. 61–69.

Kovalainen, A. (1995). *At the Margins of the Economy*. Aldershot: Avebury Ashgate.

Kovalainen, A. and Poutanen, S. (2018). Theories of Professionalism and Theories of Entrepreneurship – Alignments and Differences in Contemporary Capitalism. In: *International Sociological Association Conference 2018 Proceedings*. Toronto: ISA.

Nitzberg, M. and Zysman, J. (2022). Algorithms, Data, and Platforms: The Diverse Challenges of Governing AI. *Journal of European Public Policy*, 29(11), pp. 1753–1778. doi:10.1080/13501763.2022.2096668.

OECD. (2022). Self-Employed with Tertiary Education. *www.oecd-ilibrary.org*. [online]. Available at: https://doi.org/10.1787/2d36fdbe-en [Accessed: 18 Oct. 2022].

O'Reilly, J., Ranft, F. and Neufeind, M. (2018). Identifying the Challenges for Work in the Digital Age. In: M. Neufeind, J. O'Reilly and F. Ranft, eds., *Work in the Digital Age: Challenges of the Fourth Industrial Revolution Identifying the Challenges for Work in the Digital Age*. London; New York: Rowman & Littlefield.

Poutanen, S., Kovalainen, A. and Rouvinen, P. (2020). Digital Work in the Platform Economy. In: S. Poutanen, A. Kovalainen and P. Rouvinen, eds., *Digital Work and the Platform Economy: Understanding Tasks, Skills and Capabilities in the New Era*. New York: Routledge, pp. 3–12.

Roberts, C., Lawrence, M. and King, L. (2017). *Managing Automation: Employment, Inequality and Ethics in the Digital Age*. London: IPPR Reports. Available at: www.ippr.org/publications/managing-automation [Accessed: 25 Jan. 2022].

Schmitter, P.C. (1998). Levels of Spatial Coordination and the Embeddedness of Institutions. In: J.R. Hollingsworth and R. Boyer, eds., *Contemporary Capitalism: The Embeddedness of Institutions*. Cambridge: Cambridge University Press, pp. 311–319.

Schwabe, M. (2022). The Impact of Digital Transformation on the European Union's Labour Market. In: M. Suska, ed., *The European Union Digital Single Market: Europe's Digital Transformation*. Abingdon; New York: Routledge, pp. 135–149.

Semenza, R. and Pichault, F. (2019). *The Challenges of Self-Employment in Europe: Status, Social Protection and Collective Representation*. Cheltenham: Edward Elgar.

Susskind, R.E. and Susskind, D. (2017). *The Future of the Professions: How Technology Will Transform the Work of Human Experts*. Oxford; New York: Oxford University Press.

Uzunca, B. and Kas, J. (2022). Automated Governance Mechanisms in Digital Labour Platforms: How Uber Nudges and Sludges Its Drivers. *Industry and Innovation*. [online], 2022-06-14, pp. 1–30. doi:10.1080/13662716.2022.2086150.

van Doorn, N., Mos, E. and Bosma, J. (2021). Actually Existing Platformization. *South Atlantic Quarterly*, 120(4), pp. 715–731. doi:10.1215/00382876-9443280.

van Slageren, J., Herrmann, A.M. and Frenken, K. (2022). Is the Online Gig Economy Beyond National Reach? A European Analysis. *Socio-Economic Review*. [online], mwac038. doi:10.1093/ser/mwac038.

Westermeier, C. (2020). Money Is Data – The Platformization of Financial Transactions. *Information, Communication & Society*, 23(14), pp. 2047–2063. doi:10.1080/1369118x.2020.1770833.

Index